AUSTRALIA'S NATURAL WONDERS

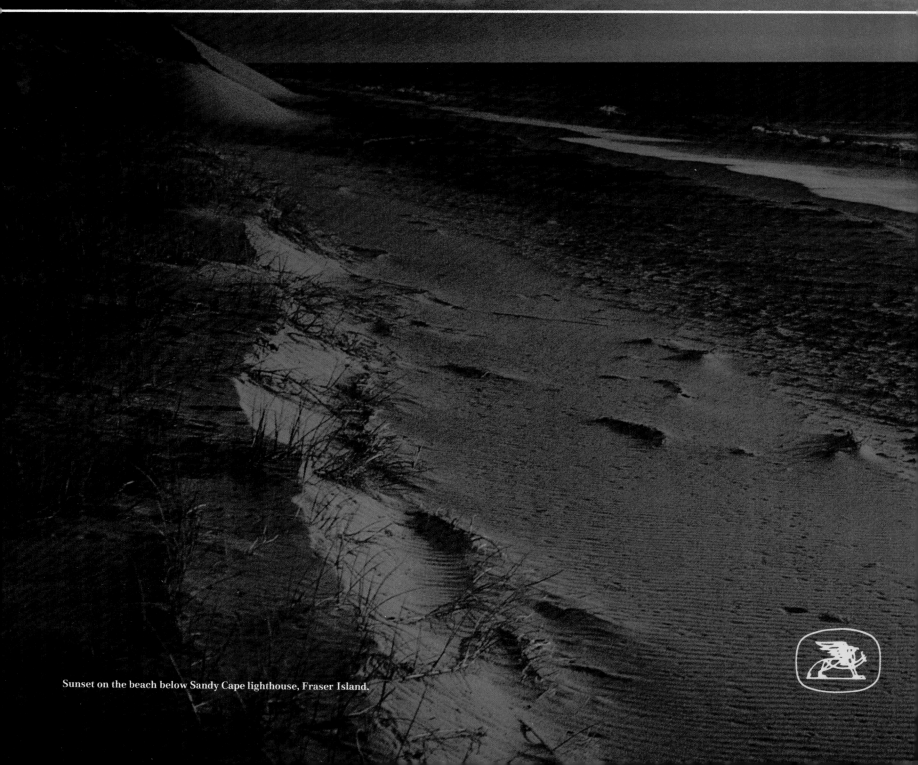

AUSTRALIA'S

Sunset on the beach below Sandy Cape lighthouse, Fraser Island.

NATURAL WONDERS

Text by MICHAEL RICHARDSON
Principal Photographer ROBBI NEWMAN

Published by Golden Press Pty. Ltd. Sydney and Auckland

Introduction

THE description of Australia as the oldest continent on earth has been used so often it has almost become a cliché. Yet in 1983 startling evidence to reinforce the claim was unearthed at remote Mount Narryer in Western Australia: scientists discovered minerals estimated to be 4.1–4.2 billion years old, truly dating from the 'dawn of time'. Although the landscape we see today is not, of course, composed solely of rocks 4 billion years old the existence of these minerals, small zircons, highlights the epochs that have been at nature's disposal, to sculpt the landforms around us. Time, with its companions, wind and water, and in the comparative absence of recent major earth movements, has created the flat, weathered vista that predominates over Australia.

Yet, to dismiss Australia as primarily an ancient landscape of semi-arid plains, plateaux and deserts broken only by the occasional low hill or minimal mountain range is to fail completely to understand its nature. Australia is a country, a continent, which one cannot easily comprehend. The Aborigines have had more than 40 000 years to form their bond with the land, such a deep and abiding bond that, after less than 200 years, we Europeans barely begin to feel something of the same empathy. It is a feeling which words are totally inadequate to express. You will know you have found it when you enter a place—a gorge, a gully, a grove of trees, a headland—so much in accord with your soul that just to be there is akin to a religious experience.

The Aborigines' sense of oneness with their land is naturally much greater than this: by taking as totems the spirit ancestors of the Dreamtime, who created the landscape, they become part of the land. From their earliest years children were taught the basic skills needed for survival in an often hazardous environment. As a result, the Aboriginal people managed to live in the most hostile parts of Australia, in places where a white man, similarly equipped, would last at most a few days. The life of the nomadic hunter-gatherers was often harsh but in the good seasons there was time to stop and think, to paint and carve on rock and bark what they saw around them and the legends of the Dreamtime.

The Aborigines took little more from the land than the animals they hunted, although they may have altered it in one fundamental way: their practice of burning the bush may have eliminated certain species and made some plants fire-dependent. Nevertheless, their impact on the country has been minimal, particularly when compared with the massive changes Europeans have wrought since 1788. Modern man's complement of technological devices (which he uses to fight, rather than to harmonise with, nature) has done nothing to improve his empathy with the land.

Recent critics of Australia's development policies have suggested that there are very few true wildernesses left, places as virgin as they were before the arrival of the First Fleet. Certainly our forebears, who faced the challenge of what they saw as an often cruel and alien land, were far too ready to tame it with axe and gun. We are paying the price for their practices today, through species extinction, soil erosion, and the salting up of our inland rivers. Yet the speed with which the bush regenerated after the breaking of the 1982–83 drought suggests that this land may be more resilient than we know. There are still huge tracts of Australia where man has but lightly placed his clumsy hand, and public support for important recent conservation issues such as the damming of the Franklin River and sand mining on Fraser Island indicates that many of these will be preserved for the future.

Australia is, for all her weathered visage, her droughts, her dust, her shimmering mirages, as varied as any country on earth. This is a continent, and as such it boasts all of a continent's diversity, from pristine snowfields to 200 metre high sand dunes; from leech-infested swamps to billabongs teeming with birdlife; from rugged mountain gorges to extinct volcanic craters. Because of her isolation, Australia is also unique in many ways. Her flora is dominated by eucalypts, but they assume a fantastic array of forms and sizes: 30 storey high mountain ashes and karris; straggly box gums bordering seasonal inland streams; multi-stemmed mallees, their roots as tough as sun-hardened railway sleepers. And Australia's wildlife, pouched marsupials, reptiles, exotic parrots, is as extraordinary as any on earth, an open-range zoo with which only the great veldt of southern Africa and the rainforests of the Amazon can compare.

Yet too many Australians would rather visit Bali than Kakadu, or Fiji than the Great Barrier Reef. Many people who speak of the 'Red Centre' in reverent terms have only ever seen it, ribbed and streaky like a butchered side of beef, from 10 000 metres up.

In this book Robbi Newman and I have attempted to show how excitingly different and varied Australia is. We do not pretend that our list of natural wonders is an exhaustive one—there are other rainforests apart from Lamington, for example; more mesas than Mount Conner; limestone caves with individual formations as beautiful as those in Jenolan Caves. But the book does include, we think, the best examples of the most spectacular and unusual natural features of Australia, interpreted, we trust, in such a way as to make you feel you have been there, too. It is our hope that it will inspire you to visit, or to revisit, some of these places.

To my father, Len Richardson, who never did see The Centre

The wilderness of the northern Simpson Desert (Michael Richardson)

The Making of a Continent

AUSTRALIA is one of the most ancient land masses in the world. It is also the most stable land mass, an island-continent that for the past 80–90 million years has been free of the major mountain-building events that elsewhere have given rise to great mountain ranges. As a result, this land is relatively flat and lacks great rivers. The average annual runoff for the whole of Australia is less than half that of the Ganges, and less than one-twentieth that of the Amazon. Only one significant mountain range exists—the Great Divide along the eastern seaboard—and its highest point, Mount Kosciusko, has never greatly exceeded its present elevation of 2230 metres.

Australia has also been isolated from the rest of the world for longer than any other continent except Antarctica, and the evolution of her flora and fauna has therefore been largely independent of outside influences. This has conferred on both animals and plants a uniqueness that at first seemed strange, even abhorrent, to European eyes. On no other continent does a single plant genus dominate in the way the eucalyptus genus does in Australia: more than 70 per cent of the country's trees are eucalypts or 'gums'. Nowhere else have the primitive pouched marsupials occupied virtually every conceivable niche in the animal kingdom. In fact, biological oddities like the ubiquitous kangaroo, which jumped on its hind legs rather than walking on all fours, were so alien to white minds that the early settlers soon introduced more familiar species, a number of which have since had a deleterious effect on the environment. Australia's is a fragile ecology; her soils are skeletal and often infertile; her water resources are poor and frequently unreliable. Unsympathetic land use, both through irrigation and over-grazing of stock, has led to the degradation of both soil and streams: to safeguard their future, Australians must carefully husband these resources.

Nevertheless, the 'real' Australia still exists, largely untouched by man: wild, inviolate, splendid. Why are the landforms as they are? What cataclysmic forces shaped them?

Much of the following brief outline of the earliest forces which shaped the Australian continent is of necessity conjecture, because it was not until the Cambrian period that positively identifiable fossils began to appear, giving a much clearer picture of when and how the rocks containing them were formed.

The oldest rocks in Australia are found in the Western Shield of south-western Australia, literally the cornerstone of the continent. This is the ancient land of Yilgarnia, which dates from the earlier part of the Archaeozoic era. The bulk of the shield is composed of gneisses, schists and granites which intruded into the base rock 2700 million years ago, but small zircons found there date from 4.1–4.2 billion years ago, when the earth was still condensing from the primordial cloud.

Yilgarnia was once much larger: its western and southern edges have sunk beneath the sea, and to the north it is overlain by subsequent formations. What remains is a roughly rectangular land mass, 650 kilometres wide and 1100 kilometres long, bordered to the west by the Darling Range (actually the escarpment of the shield) and to the east by the empty expanse of the Nullarbor Plain.

To its north lie the slightly younger rocks of the Pilbara Shield, deposited 1800–2300 million years ago beneath a sea which once lapped the shores of Yilgarnia. North-east, beyond the Canning Desert basin, rise the Kimberleys, again composed of Proterozoic rocks, even more ancient than those of the Pilbara. To the east, in the Northern Territory, is the metamorphic uranium-bearing Rum Jungle formation which, with other similar formations between Bonaparte Gulf and west Arnhem Land, was created during a great period of upheaval in the earth's crust, 2500 million years ago. This area, like much of the western half of the continent, was repeatedly submerged beneath and uplifted above the sea before it stabilised to become the basis of today's Top End.

Between 2500 and 2200 million years ago, the sea flooded across north-western Australia into the centre and inundated much of South Australia. Thick beds of marine shale and sandstones were deposited which, chemically altered by leaching and re-deposition, were ultimately to become the great iron ore deposits of the Hamersley Range and the Eyre Peninsula.

A massive orogeny 1500–1400 million years ago, which raised mountains from Cape York through Mount Isa to Broken Hill, the Musgrave Ranges, the Eyre Peninsula and west along the southern flanks of Yilgarnia, left the north-west of Australia untouched. But a subsequent orogeny, the Madiganian, 1200–1100 million years ago, affected the south and south-west of the Pilbara Shield and created a pronounced subsidence in the south, now known as the Adelaide geosyncline. A seaway existed here through the latter part of the Proterozoic era and for much of the ensuing Cambrian period, beneath which sediments up to 15 000 metres thick were laid down. A great Ice Age at the beginning of the Upper Proterozoic covered much of southern Australia with slow-moving glaciers which gouged great chunks out of the land.

Tasmania first appeared as dry land in the late Proterozoic era, 900–800 million years ago. Its emergence was probably part of a general uplift of the south-eastern ocean floor which raised many large islands above the sea, although no Pre-Cambrian formations are known in Victoria, which is the youngest state in geological terms.

As the Pre-Cambrian era drew to a close, about 600 million years ago, there appeared two large land masses of subcontinental size and separated by a shallow north–south marine strait stretching from Arnhem Land to Spencer Gulf. The eastern subcontinent was still to undergo considerable change, but by the early Cambrian period, after vast streams of lava had poured out over the Kimberley and Victoria River areas, the consolidation of the western sector was almost complete.

The central and eastern parts of the region were in fact unstable, and in the Middle Cambrian the sea invaded most of eastern Australia and the Northern Territory, leaving above sea level only a strip of land stretching from Broken Hill through Mount Isa to Carpentaria. During this time great quantities of sediments accumulated along what is now the eastern coast and in a basin reaching from the Joseph Bonaparte Gulf (between the Kimberleys and the Northern Territory) to the Queensland border. This latter region became stable at the close of the Cambrian period, 500 million years ago, and has experienced no further upheavals. It is therefore among the oldest land surfaces in the world.

Western Tasmania, on the other hand, was convulsed by strong orogenic (mountain-building) movements at the end of the Cambrian and the beginning of the next great geological period, the Ordovician. This period lasted about 70 million years and during it the sea covered much of Victoria and eastern Tasmania, resulting in the deposition of slate, shale and sandstones. Nearly all the goldfields of Victoria have been discovered in Ordovician rocks, which extend as far north as Cobar and Dubbo in New South Wales and surface again in the Einasleigh district of north Queensland.

The Delamerian Orogeny, a mountain-building event that took place in the second half of the Ordovician period, uplifted the sediments laid down in the Adelaide geosyncline in the south of South Australia, forming a chain of mountains to rival the Alps or Andes: erosion over the next 400 million years reduced these peaks to a fraction of their former might. At this time the sea covered the Canning Desert basin in north-western Australia, but considerable earth movements occurred in western New South Wales, central Queensland, parts of Victoria and central Australia.

We now enter the Silurian period (430–395 million years ago), which lasted only half as long as the Ordovician but was equally significant because of the accelerated rate of deposition beneath the seas covering the eastern half of Victoria, most of Tasmania, much of southern and central New South Wales, and north Queensland. The water was also warm and clear, ideal for the growth of coral reefs which ultimately became the beds of limestone in which Jenolan, Wellington, Wombeyan and other well-known cave systems formed.

A massive coral barrier reef surrounded the Kimberley region, thousands of kilometres to the north-west, during the succeeding period, the Devonian. Erosion of the Kimberley ranges also led to the deposition of beds of sandstone and pebble conglomerate beneath the waters of Joseph Bonaparte Gulf, creating the raw material from which the Bungle-Bungle plateau and other parts of the eastern Kimberley were formed.

At the beginning of the Devonian, much of Tasmania was still under water, but towards the end of the middle of this period a strong mountain-building event known as the Tabberabberan Orogeny lifted Tasmania, other parts of south-eastern Australia and much of New Zealand out of the water. Another mountain-building event, the Alice Springs Orogeny, took place near the end of the Devonian, 350 million years ago, creating the great folded ridges of the MacDonnell Ranges in central Australia.

The next great geological period, the Carboniferous, is so called because it was then that most of the coal and oil deposits of the northern hemisphere were formed from huge forests which flourished around extensive swamps. (Australian coal and oil basins date from the later Permian, Triassic and Jurassic periods.) Around 310 million years ago the Kanimblan Orogeny raised mountains through much of central and south-eastern Queensland and south into the New England region. Glaciers reached icy fingers down these mountains, scouring them and depositing thick beds of tillite (coarse boulder beds) at their bases. At the same time, granites which have since been exposed by erosion intruded into the New England plateau.

Glaciation increased during the Lower Permian period, when the second of the world's great Ice Ages gripped the earth. Glaciers initially covered almost all of Tasmania, except for a few isolated high peaks, and extended as far north as the Kimberleys. In the mid-Permian Artinskian epoch, 275-260 million years ago, more than half the continent (including Tasmania) was inundated by the sea; silt and a general elevation of the sea beds subsequently converted the seaways into freshwater lakes and swamps which supported great forests of primitive plants, which ultimately became vast seams of coal. In Queensland bursts of volcanic activity shattered the calm of the forests, presaging the last major Australian mountain-building event, the Hunter–Bowen Orogeny, which occurred 225 million years ago and raised mountains along the eastern coast from the vicinity of Newcastle to Bowen. Subsequent earth movements were to be of an epeirogenetic character, more of a gentle 'breathing' of the earth, rather than the cataclysmic thrusting and squeezing of an orogeny. Nevertheless, many less dramatic, but still important, geological events took place before Australia finally emerged in its current form.

During the next major period, the Triassic, enormous lakes, including 800 000 square kilometre Lake Walloon, covered much of eastern Australia, while the sea intruded extensively into Western Australia. The Leigh Creek coal measures in South Australia and the South Esk deposits in Tasmania date from this time. A shallow sea, beneath which orange Hawkesbury sandstone was deposited, covered the Sydney region, inland to Yass and Bathurst and north to the Hunter Valley. Volcanic eruptions near Brisbane buried the surrounding countryside beneath up to 1000 metres of ash and scoria, destroying vast coniferous forests. More importantly for the future of Australia, porous sands and shales accumulated beneath mighty Lake Walloon, one of the largest bodies of fresh water ever to have existed, forming the basis of the aquifers of the Great Artesian Basin.

The great mountain ranges formed during the preceding Palaeozoic era provided the raw material for these sedimentary deposits. Sedimentation continued beneath the lakes and swamps during the Jurassic period, and a new geographical feature, the Gulf of Carpentaria, formed in the north. In Western Australia, the sea covered the Canning Basin again and flowed down towards the Nullarbor Plain, as well as inundating the Carnarvon Basin between Perth and Onslow. To the south, in Tasmania, massive volcanic activity 165 million years ago caused the uplifting of sandstones which had been formed underwater in the preceding Triassic period, allowing tongues of dolerite to intrude into the strata. In Western Australia, near Bunbury and north in the Fitzroy Trough, basalts were extruded in the last outburst of volcanic activity in the west.

By the end of the Jurassic period, 136 million years ago, many of the great lakes had disappeared. The landscape would in fact have been quite similar to that of today: an endless plain, broken only by low residual hills. A general elevation in the early Cretaceous period then raised the land above the sea, but this was followed by a lowering of the continent which coincided with the formation of the supercontinent of Gondwanaland.

It is believed that Gondwanaland consisted of the continents of Africa, Australia, South America and Antarctica, the subcontinent of India, and New Zealand. It had originally been part of giant Pangaea which, 200 million years ago, was the only land mass on earth. One hundred and eighty million years ago, Pangaea divided into two enormous land masses: Gondwanaland in the south and Laurasia in the north. Later, Gondwanaland started to fragment, with South America and Africa breaking away first, then India, and, 90 million years ago, New Zealand. Only Australia and Antarctica remained united. Finally, 53 million years ago, this 'Great South Land' split up, too, and since that time Australia has been isolated from the other continents.

According to the theory of plate tectonics, the earth's crust consists of a series of lithospheric 'plates' (the lithosphere is the outer, solid 100–150 kilometres thick rock layer) which float on the fluid mantle (the asthenosphere) beneath. There are ten main plates, which are moved about by convection currents within the asthenosphere, carrying the continents with them. Areas of great seismic disturbance occur where these plates meet; for example, along the Pacific Coast of the United States. Australia, however, sits at the centre of a large plate which includes India and New Zealand, and this continent is therefore relatively immune to earthquakes and volcanic activity.

Nevertheless, the Cretaceous period would have been a time of considerable trauma for the plants and animals living in Australia, and it was also the time when the first flowering plants, the angiosperms, evolved. The sea made two major incursions into the continent: the first, 135 million years ago, and the second and more widespread one, 110 million years ago. The amount of land available to flora and fauna would have been severely restricted.

When the land rose again, impelled by a minor orogeny known as the Maryburian, 90–80 million years ago, the area now occupied by the Great Artesian Basin was dotted with lakes and swamps. Impervious shales laid down over the Triassic and Jurassic sandstones sealed off the aquifer which is of such importance to the present settlement of much of inland Australia.

And so we come to the last of the great geological periods, the Tertiary, which lasted from 65 million years ago to 1.8 million years ago, when the Quaternary, in which we still live, began. During the Palaeocene epoch, the first epoch of the Tertiary period, the largest of the inland lakes (Lake Winton) dried up, but there were still many residual lakes elsewhere in the country. Most of the landscape was flat and featureless. In the south, the sea inundated the Nullarbor region, the calcareous remains of marine animals deposited on the sea bed during the next 60 million years forming limestone which, when uplifted, became the empty expanse of the Nullarbor Plain. Part of the Granite Coast of south-western Australia was also flooded, and today it is overlain by limestone. In the succeeding Eocene epoch, the sea also inundated Gulf St Vincent, the Murray Basin and Bass Strait, withdrawing around 40 million years ago.

Much of the earth's current topography was created during the next epoch, the Oligocene, when a period of mountain-building known as the Alpine Orogeny raised the soaring peaks of the Alps, the Himalayas, the Rockies and the Andes. Its effect was much less pronounced in Australia, but a chain of volcanoes did erupt in the east, from Victoria to north Queensland, and continued to pour out basaltic lava across the countryside for millions of years, well into the Miocene epoch. The Warrumbungle Mountains, Mount Warning, the Glasshouse Mountains, the Nandewar Range, and other rugged volcanic ranges were formed during this time. The eastern seaboard was also raised by 200–250 metres, accelerating erosion.

Plants flourished in freshwater lakes and swamps which covered much of south-eastern Victoria, creating the great brown-coal deposits of the La Trobe Valley. During the Miocene, the sea again invaded much of Victoria and severed Tasmania from the mainland. But it was the final epoch of the Tertiary period, the Pliocene, which shaped most of the landscape of the eastern seaboard.

During the Pliocene the Kosciusko uplift, which created the Great Dividing Range, occurred. This gradual raising of the earth's surface was accompanied by renewed volcanic activity, particularly in western Victoria, where hundreds of points of eruption poured out lava, creating a vast basalt plain. Many of the long streams which had been flowing east changed their direction and began to flow inland, and Tasmania rejoined the mainland.

Throughout most of the next epoch, the Pleistocene, and until very recent times, volcanic activity continued in north Queensland, western Victoria and in the Mount Gambier region of South Australia. An earth movement north of Adelaide threw a land barrier across the rivers which had previously flowed past the Flinders Ranges to the sea. As a result, a vast lake, known as Lake Dieri, formed behind the barrier, its shores lush and green and teeming with life.

Climatic changes then began to mould the landscape. There were four major glacial stages during the Pleistocene, during the last of which Tasmania and the high country around Mount Kosciusko were particularly affected. It was then that the mountain cirques and lakes of Tasmania were formed. New Guinea was attached to Australia at this time.

The Ice Age ended at the beginning of the Holocene epoch, about 10 000 years ago, and with it diminished the rainfall that had fed the streams which filled Lake Dieri. The lake dried up, and sand deposited on its bed by the inland rivers blew north and east to form the sand dunes of the Simpson and Strzelecki deserts. Similar events took place throughout much of central Australia as the climate became progressively more arid. The sea began to rise, cutting off the land bridge between Tasmania and the mainland, and flooding the valleys of coastal streams to form fine harbours like Port Jackson and King George Sound.

The slow rising of the water also created conditions favourable to the regrowth of the Great Barrier Reef on the remnants of more ancient reefs which had flourished for much of the Miocene and Pliocene epochs. When the sea level fell during the first of the Pleistocene Ice Ages this regrowth ceased.

Erosion of the eastern highlands over the last few million years has gouged out deep chasms and canyons in the rock, a process which continues. At the same time, a battle has been waged between the rainforest that predominated during the Cretaceous period and the xerophytic (literally, 'dry-living') species, particularly the eucalypts, that evolved at about the same time. With man's help the xerophytes seem to have gained the ascendancy: vast areas of rainforest have been cleared for agriculture or commercial exploitation of timber, and Aboriginal firing of the bush has tended to supplant rainforest species with fire-tolerant ones.

And so we come to the last great influence on the Australian landscape, the arrival of Europeans. Increased desertification and the pollution of 80 per cent of the country's watercourses are just two of the changes wrought by 200 years of white occupation. The message is clear: conservation of the natural environment is essential to our continued occupation of this capricious land.

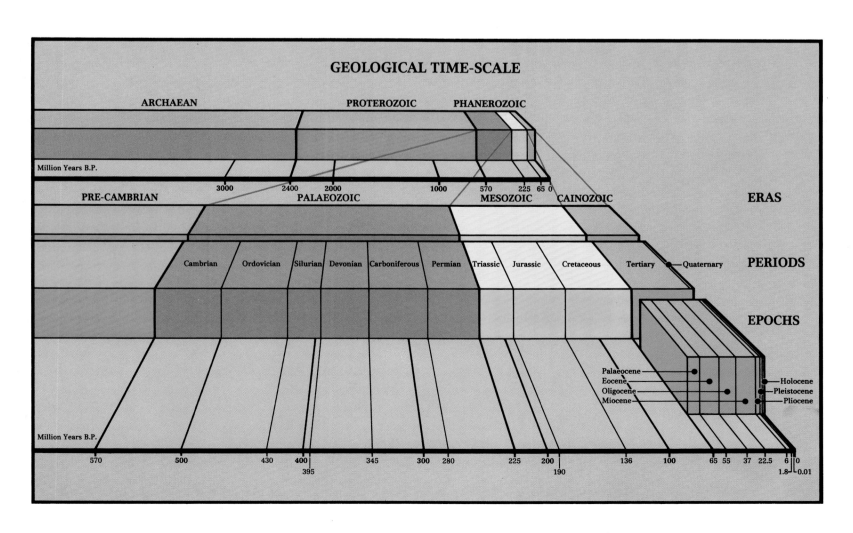

Contents

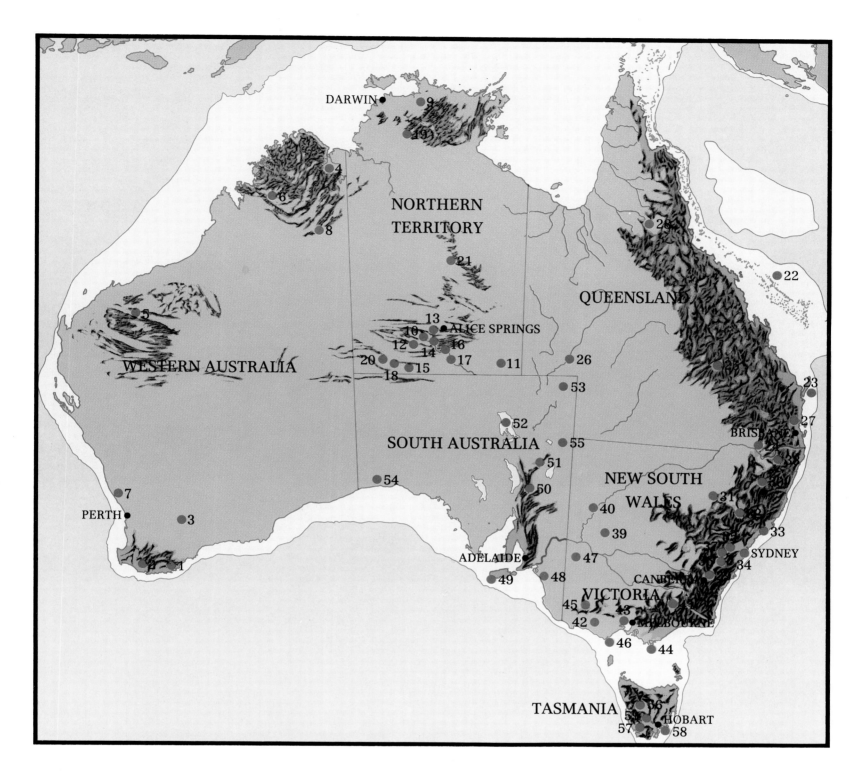

DARWIN
NORTHERN TERRITORY
QUEENSLAND
WESTERN AUSTRALIA
ALICE SPRINGS
SOUTH AUSTRALIA
NEW SOUTH WALES
PERTH
ADELAIDE
VICTORIA
CANBERRA
SYDNEY
BRISBANE
MELBOURNE
TASMANIA
HOBART

WESTERN AUSTRALIA

1 The Granite Coast
2 The forests of the south-west
3 Wave Rock
4 The Bungle-Bungles
5 The Hamersley Range
6 Tunnel Creek
7 The Pinnacles Desert
8 Wolf Creek meteorite crater

THE NORTHERN TERRITORY

9 Kakadu National Park
10 Gosse Bluff
11 The Simpson Desert
12 Kings Canyon
13 Ormiston Gorge and the
    MacDonnell Ranges
14 Palm Valley and the Finke River
15 Mount Conner
16 Rainbow Valley
17 Chambers Pillar
18 Ayers Rock
19 Katherine Gorge
20 The Olgas
21 The Devils Marbles

QUEENSLAND

22 The Great Barrier Reef
23 Fraser Island
24 Lamington National Park
25 Carnarvon Gorge
26 The Channel Country
27 The Glasshouse Mountains
28 The Undara Lava Tubes

NEW SOUTH WALES

29 Lake George
30 Wollomombi Falls
31 The Warrumbungle Mountains
32 Burning Mountain, Wingen
33 Myall Lakes
34 Sydney Harbour
35 The Three Sisters
36 Kanangra Walls
37 Jenolan Caves
38 Bald Rock
39 Lake Mungo and the Walls of
    China
40 Menindee Lakes

VICTORIA

41 The Bogong High Plains
42 Mount Elephant
43 The Organ Pipes
44 Wilsons Promontory
45 The Grampians
46 The Port Campbell coastline
47 The Pink Lakes, Underbool

SOUTH AUSTRALIA

48 The Coorong
49 Remarkable Rocks and
    Admirals Arch
50 Wilpena Pound
51 Arkaroola–Mount Painter
52 The Great Salt Lakes
53 Sturts Stony Desert
54 The cliffs of the Nullarbor
55 The Cobbler Desert

TASMANIA

56 Cradle Mountain–Lake St Clair
57 South-West Tasmania
58 The Tasman Peninsula
59 The flowering giants

Majestic ramparts of the Hamersley Range.

WESTERN AUSTRALIA

WESTERN AUSTRALIA

The Granite Coast

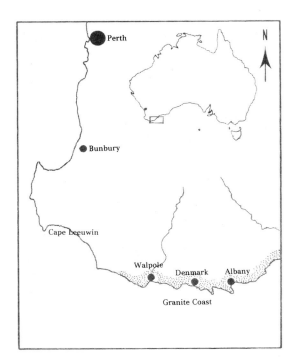

THE ancient plateau of the Western Shield meets the Southern Ocean in a coastline of astounding beauty: rugged granite and gneiss headlands crowned with grey-green mallee scrub; undercut cliffs pockmarked with caves and grottoes into which the sea rushes with a rumbling roar; shallow inlets rippling with fish; peaceful bays protected from the fury of the Antarctic swells by wave-pounded rocky islets; and dazzling white beaches upon which the surf dashes itself into oblivion. It is a coastline which does justice to this most ancient of land masses: there is a harmony here, a balance between the land and the sea, like a shaking of hands by two old adversaries wearying of a struggle neither can win.

The focal point of this diverse landscape is King George Sound, on an inlet of which the port of Albany stands, in a hollow between two granite tors. The inhabitants of Albany tend to wax lyrical about Princess Royal Harbour (described by its discoverer, Captain George Vancouver, as a 'spacious sound'), ranking it with Sydney Harbour and Rio de Janeiro as one of the world's three great harbours. This is local pride talking—nowhere is it more than 35 metres deep, and it compares more closely with Botany Bay, which Phillip abandoned in 1788 in favour of Port Jackson—but it is certainly the south-west coast's best harbour, formed by rising waters at the end of the last Ice Age.

Although the granite is of great antiquity, not all of the landscape is of similar age. The rocks of the plateau to the north and east have remained above the ocean since the

Archaean era, more than 2300 million years ago. The granites of the coast often form small hills and prominences above the plateau, and probably intruded into the base rock about 2700 million years ago. Many of these peaks, like Mount Gardner on Cape Vancouver, enclosing King George Sound to the north, are more than 400 metres high; the highest, the Dickensian-sounding Mount Manypeaks, soars 565 metres above the fretful ocean.

Yet the Granite Coast is also overlain in many places by limestone, the compacted remains of billions of sea animals which swam in the sea that covered the southern edge of the Western Shield when it sank beneath the ocean more than 60 million years ago. Since then, the granite hills have alternately formed high promontories and bleak islands cut off from the land mass by the rising sea, like the Recherche Archipelago off the coast of Esperance. Inland from Albany a great plain, green-grassed and well watered, and broken only by the looming peaks of the Porongurup and Stirling Ranges, runs northwards until it blends with the higher Shield plateau. In Miocene times this plain, too, lay beneath the sea.

Sections of the Granite Coast have been dedicated as national parks, and much of it that has not, like the massive cliffs to the west of Albany, is too remote to be threatened by 'user pressure'. The coastal landforms assume their most extravagant shapes on the straggling peninsula that enfolds Princess Royal Harbour and Frenchmans Bay, in the southern reaches of King George Sound, like a protective albatross sheltering her offspring. More than half of this peninsula is national park; part of it is also pine plantation, and a string of suburbs rings the shorelines of Princess Royal Harbour and Frenchmans Bay.

Here, at a spot on the exposed southern coastline, the granite has eroded along vertical fault lines, creating a great chasm in the cliff known as The Gap, into which the sea surges with terrifying power. Nearby, the sea has undercut another section of the cliff, leaving a thick, sloping bridge of grey granite. Deep fissures more than half a metre wide and 20 metres deep slice into the adjoining cliff top. East of Cable Beach, big seas race through other channels worn into the rock, to emerge as white plumes of spray, like miniature geysers.

Interspersed among the granite bluffs are steeply sloping promontories supporting a dense scrub of peppermint gum, hakea and Albany woollybush that lights up with colour in spring, like Munchkin Land in *The Wizard of Oz*. Above the scrub, stern granite boulders stare gloomily out across the white-beached bays towards the islands dotting the coastline. On top of Stony Hill, one of the highest points in the national park, stand the ruins of a World War II radar station.

For decades, eyes as keen as any in RAAF Coastal Command also scoured the windswept seas for the tell-tale signs of other visitors to the coast: the splash or blow that betrayed the presence of a mighty humpback, sperm or right whale. Whaling was one of the earliest industries of the fledgling colony of Western Australia and Albany was the first town settled in the west. It was founded in December 1826 by Major

Waves roar into the Gap—a sheer chasm in the cliffs eroded along a fault line.

Edmund Lockyer and a small group of convicts and soldiers, but Perth, settled three years later, subsequently became a far more important township. By the 1840s whaling was firmly established as a major contributor to the Western Australian economy, both through Australian catches and visits by foreign whalers, mainly American. The supply of whales seemed inexhaustible. Many of the animals were killed and cut up by opportunistic bay whalers, who would set up camp on an uninhabited part of the coast, then row frantically out to sea in their 9 metre boats when a whale was sighted. The life was hard and dangerous and remained so right up to the closing of the last Australian whaling station, at Frenchmans Bay on King George Sound, in 1978.

This station was operated by the Cheynes Beach Whaling Company, established in 1952 and run for most of its 26-year history on a shoe-string, using second-hand boats and equipment. In its peak years, 1974 and 1975, Cheynes Beach caught more than 1100 sperm whales, staining the waters of Frenchmans Bay bright red with blood and attracting the attention of dozens of hungry sharks. The station closed voluntarily because, its management said, the company was no longer profitable. Had this not been the case, the decision may have been made for it. For years, conservationists had been fighting to bring an end to the slaughter of the great, gentle mammals, whose oil was no longer needed to fuel household lamps and whose bones were no longer used in the making of ladies' corsets. An inquiry was already under way at Albany when the Cheynes Beach Whaling Company made its announcement.

Albany was by no means the only town in Australia to have whaling as one of its principal industries. But it was the last. As such, the conversion of the ramshackle collection of buildings and the whalechaser *Cheynes IV*, already deteriorated beyond re-use, into a whaling museum seems entirely appropriate.

BELOW Coastal granite intruded into the base rock 2700 million years ago
RIGHT Swells break against a natural breakwater enclosing a perfect swimming pool, William Bay National Park

WESTERN AUSTRALIA

The forests of the south-west

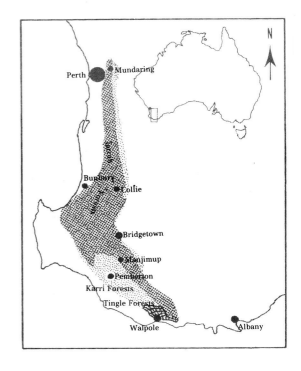

I N a state so poorly watered and with such infertile soils, perhaps the strangest thing about Western Australia's forests is that they exist at all. That they should, in fact, include some of the tallest, straightest and densest stands of trees in the world is nothing short of a miracle. Consider this: the karri regularly exceeds 60 metres in height and has been logged (in 1901) at 104 metres, the height of a 30-storey building. Many trees more than 80 metres high still stand. By comparison, the world's tallest tree (according to the *Guinness Book of Records*), the Californian coast redwood 'Howard Libby Tree', measured 111.6 metres in 1970, with others more than 90 metres tall growing near it.

The red tingle might at best grow to only half this height, but its bole may reach 20 metres or more in circumference; in fact, one famous tree in the Valley of the Giants, near Walpole, has been hollowed out by bushfires and can accommodate a car inside its trunk! The tingle may not eclipse the 50 metre girth of the massive Spanish chestnut shading the foot of Mount Etna, but it literally runs rings around the New Zealand kauri, which at best can manage only 15 metres.

Other large trees growing in the south-west include the jarrah, the most prolific forest species in Western Australia; the marri, which is widely distributed throughout both karri and jarrah forests; and the tough tuart, a tall coastal species with a range extending from Busselton to the Hill River, north of Moora. Big as they are, none of these species attain the sheer height of the karri or the colossal bulk of the tingle, which are both, like the mountain ash of Victoria and Tasmania, true giants of the plant kingdom.

The climate in which these sclerophyll forests flourish is very different from that prevailing over most of Western Australia. Rainfall in the 250 kilometre long, 40 kilometre wide karri belt, stretching from Cape Leeuwin in the west to Denmark on Wilson Inlet, averages more than 1000 millimetres a year compared with only 350 millimetres in the nearby wheat belt. Around Walpole, where the tingles shrug their formidable shoulders across the valleys, rainfall reaches 1250 millimetres a year and plentiful humus nurtures a complex understorey. The more widely distributed jarrah grows in much drier locations along the Darling Range, in laterite soils often only covering the underlying rocks by a few centimetres; not surprisingly, it takes 500 years to reach its maximum size.

Jarrah, once known as Swan River mahogany, is a beautiful red hardwood that resists termite attack and is used for everything from making telegraph poles and railway sleepers to crafting fine furniture. But this once seemingly inexhaustible resource is in danger of being destroyed for ever. More than 300 000 hectares of forest are suffering from fungus-induced dieback, for which there is no known cure, while the slowness with which the species grows means that its days as a merchantable timber are numbered. The Western Australian Forests Department tries to work on a 100-year cycle for its hardwood forests, but this must be extended to 200–250 years for jarrah, and the forests are not being replenished as quickly as they are being worked out. Finding an untouched stand of virgin jarrah, despite its widespread distribution, is at best time-consuming and at worst almost impossible.

The Forests Department has introduced quarantine procedures in an effort to contain dieback. The microscopic fungus *Phytophthora cinnamomi* is transmitted in the soil and advances only a few centimetres a year if left alone, but it will spread rapidly when picked up in the wheels and tracks of motor vehicles. For this reason large areas of jarrah forest are now off limits to everyone except those who have special permits, and vehicles are washed down before entering healthy forest. The destruction of the jarrah forests would affect more than the sawmills: over 80 per cent of Western Australia's drinking water comes from catchments located within the jarrah forest. Already, clearing of forested areas for farmland has caused some streams to turn saline. The cost to the community of contaminating Perth's water supply is incalculable.

Not all species are as susceptible to dieback as jarrah. Some, in fact, resist it well. But bull banksia, a prominent species in the jarrah understorey, does not; neither do macrozamia palms or grass trees, and the death of these species can have a devastating effect on bird and mammal populations in the forest. Karri, marri and wandoo appear resistant to the fungus, as do three exotic species of pine. Simply replanting jarrah forest with pines is not a happy solution, however: the natural habitat is gone for ever,

Forests of karri (*Eucalyptus diversicolor*) flourish in the long, narrow strip of land stretching from Cape Leeuwin to Denmark.

while the trees' roots may not thrust deep enough into the earth to prevent the discharge of salt into reservoirs.

In the great forests of karri surrounding Pemberton the problem of dieback seems remote. On a hilltop 2 kilometres east of the town towers the Gloucester Tree, the world's tallest fire look-out tree: one climbs 61 metres, up a winding series of pegs hammered into the living wood, to a small roofed platform.

These forests were opened up to exploitation comparatively recently. Captain Thomas Banister had explored the densely timbered country between Albany and Fremantle in 1830 and commented on the size of the trees, but it was not until 1861 that Edward Brockman took up land on the Warren River south of what is now Pemberton, and he was more interested in raising cattle than in logging. Milling of karri logs began at Karridale and Denmark, on the fringes of the karri belt, in the 1880s, and by 1913 the timber-cutters had nibbled into the forests as far as Pemberton.

Today, lightweight chain saws can cut down a 300-year-old tree in minutes. Destruction is alarmingly quick; the immediate effect on animal populations devastating if transitory. The Forests Department describes the eucalypt forests of south-western Australia as forming probably 'the single most important wildlife refuge in Australia'. Its strategy for conservation has been to set aside 71 areas as flora, fauna and landscape management priority areas (MPAs), in addition to the small percentage of forest, all near the coast, that is designated national park. The MPAs include Dryandra and Perup forests, virtually the sole surviving refuges of the banded anteater, or numbat, once common throughout the wandoo woodlands.

In the nineteenth century it must have seemed as if the forests would last forever. Yet after a century of logging and land clearing only remnant forests exist throughout much of the south-west. Even the marri, which contains too much gum to be suitable for sawmilling, is used to feed the voracious appetite of the woodchip industry. Most of the remaining forest bears the scars of past use. Today no tingles are being cut in state forests, for example, but the Valley of the Giants, near Walpole, is studded with the stumps of former colossi, cut off in their prime. At this famous picnic spot grow the largest tingles in the world, most of them eaten out by fire yet still thriving despite their lack of a solid core.

There are three types of tingle: red tingle, the largest and most prolific of the rough-barked gums; yellow tingle, which has a yellower timber; and Rate's tingle, a rare species not formally identified until the early 1960s, a sort of cross between the red and the yellow. So large are the tingles that each creates its own micro-environment within the forest. A mound of leaf litter, more than 1 metre high, builds up about the tree. Moss clings to the damp bark and charred walls of the 'tree-cave'. Giant knots in the timber bulge half a metre or more from the trunk. A dense understorey of wattle and other plants impedes progress through the forest.

Surrounding the tingle are karris, trunks mottled by summer moulting, the pale underside of their leaves contrasting with their deep green upper surface. The undergrowth springing from the rich humus of the forest floor includes hovea, waterbush, karri wattle and karri she-oak, intertwined with creepers. The young karris, regenerated from seed trees and hand-planted seedlings, are tall and slender; in the early stages of their growth, they shoot up almost 1 metre each year. Mature trees are an important source of honey, each bearing up to 500 000 flowers which may yield more than 250 kilograms of pure honey.

The hardwood forests of the south-west form a renewable resource that must be carefully harvested if it is to continue to yield timber. It is equally important that much of the forest remain pristine, unsullied by either chain saw or the lethal *cinnamomi* fungus, described by the Forests Department as 'the worst plant disease ever recorded'.

BELOW Young regenerated karris shoot up about a metre a year. Mature specimens may exceed 80 metres in height.
RIGHT The massive trunk of a red tingle (*E. jacksonii*). Tingles are much less widespread than karri or jarrah (*E. marginata*) and today are being logged only on private land.

WESTERN AUSTRALIA

Wave Rock

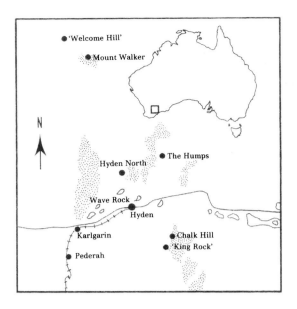

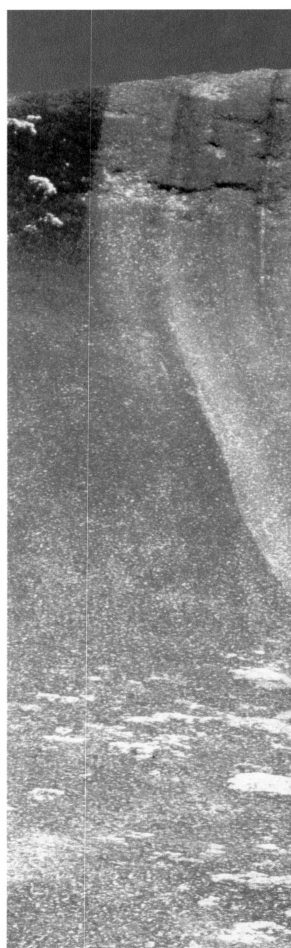

A tourist attraction only since the early 1960s, when a picture of it appeared on the front cover of *Walkabout* magazine, Wave Rock is part of a 2700-million-year-old inselberg which forms a section of the catchment area of the local water supply. A low stone wall runs along the 'crest' of the wave, channelling runoff from the high, rocky surface above into a nearby reservoir. The catchment wall does little for the appearance of the rock but, when it was built in 1929, water was of more immediate concern than preservation of the landscape.

The Hyden district was settled in 1922, by pioneers determined to convert the salmon-tree scrub to prosperous wheat farms. The town itself was named after a young sandalwood cutter called Hyde, who had camped at 'Hyde's Rock'—a mistake in the Lands Department converted the name to Hyden. No sooner had the first harvests been brought in than the Depression struck, savagely cutting the price of wheat, and a government report was released suggesting that the land in the eastern part of the district (still highly productive) was too salty to be arable. Banks refused to lend money. Many settlers left, bankrupt.

To look at the giant wheat bins now studding the district, full to overflowing even in the drought year of 1982, it is hard to understand why this study, the Teakle Report, was accepted. But there was truth in its findings. East Hyden is on the extreme fringe of the wheat belt: beyond it there is only scrub and saltpans, the gold- and nickel-mining town of Norseman, and then the flat emptiness of the Nullarbor Plain. The rainfall here is around 340 millimetres a year, ideal for wheat farming. Why, then, is agriculture so difficult? The reason is the skeletal nature of the soils, developed on the most ancient landscape in the world, the Western Shield. This is the primeval land of Yilgarnia, which has remained virtually unchanged, save for weathering and a time of uplift, probably as recently as the Tertiary period, for more than 1500 million years. Today it is only a remnant of its former size, but it is still a mighty slab of country, 650 kilometres east to west, more than 1100 kilometres north to south and 300–450 metres above sea level.

The salt lakes are such a prominent feature of this land that in the 1920s one scientist dubbed it 'Salinaland'. The lakes once formed a series of great rivers, which flowed when the climate was wetter. Since the Tertiary uplift that formed the Darling Range, their access to the Indian Ocean has been cut off and the climate has become much more arid, causing the water to collect in depressions, leaching salts from the surrounding soil.

Granite outcrops, the result of volcanic intrusion, bulge through the surrounding sedimentary rock. They are most common in the eastern section of the Old Plateau, so called for its duricrust capping which was created by prolonged weathering and is the raw material of the sand plains of the goldfields district and the primary constituent of the soils of the outer wheat belt.

Hyden Rock is just such a gneissic granite dome, as much the focal point of the town as a river or a lake might be in a more favoured locality. It is the rock which dominates the landscape, which succours the town through the adjoining reservoir, and which is the magnet for tourists from as far away as the eastern states. Wave Rock, on the north face of Hyden Rock, now features prominently in Western Australian tourist literature, even though it is relatively inaccessible. It is 350 kilometres by road from Perth and is only approachable from the east, from Norseman, via an extensive detour or a lonely, ill-defined track past the salty Johnston Lakes.

A huge, curling wave, 13 metres high and several hundred metres long, rears up from the gradual slope of Hyden Rock. Streaked with black, white and orange chemicals leached from the granite, it is almost perfectly shaped, even to the threatening lip, the 'shoulder' where a surfboard rider might tuck in, and the gentler swell over deeper water. Romantic observers have suggested that it must be the result of an earth movement frozen in time, but it is in fact the natural result of weathering, probably chemical rotting in a wetter climate, together with the horizontal release of pressure through the erosion of contiguous rock masses. The formation is not unique; there are others in the immediate district, including a lower, more overhung rock face, known locally as The Breakers, on another side of Hyden Rock, but none is as huge, as impressive, or as colourful as Wave Rock.

She-oaks grow along the base of the rock, where the cresting wave might be expected to break, and south-west, behind the dam, golfers can drive along fairways that run flush up against the granite dome. There was once an airfield here, but the runways were too close to the rock for safety, and it was moved to a nearby paddock. To the east is another natural feature, the Hippo's Yawn, a giant boulder-bubble that is perfectly named but which unfortunately has been desecrated by decades of vandals' graffiti.

Earlier, more delicately executed hand stencils adorn other eroded boulder caves near The Breakers and Bates Cave, 12 kilometres to the north. It was here, so local legend has it, that evil Mulka the Terrible lived; he was the offspring of a forbidden love and was driven from his tribe because his crossed eyes were thought to bring a curse upon those on whom he looked. Mulka was said to be a murderer and a cannibal, who eventually turned on and mortally wounded his own mother, then was hunted down and executed near Dumbleyung. According to Hyden townsfolk, most Aborigines still refuse to live in the town and those who break the taboo may meet a violent death.

More subtle, yet no less final, is the destruction being meted out to Wave Rock and its environs. Too many of the thousands of tourists who visit this famous natural wonder each year unthinkingly despoil it, goaded perhaps by the desecration of the Hippo's Yawn and the all-too-visible walls of the reservoir system, which, inevitably, will cause the rich colours of the wave to fade.

Wave Rock has become an unofficial symbol of Western Australia.

WESTERN AUSTRALIA

The Bungle-Bungles

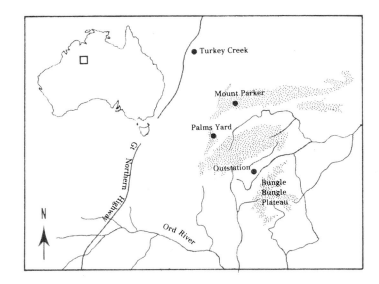

Until very recently, the only 'Bungle-Bungle' recorded on any maps of Australia was a ruined outcamp of Ord River station in the rugged eastern Kimberley, 120 kilometres north-north-east of Halls Creek. But all that is to change. Soon the name Bungle-Bungle—Aboriginal in origin, although of unknown meaning—may be as well known as that of Ayers Rock. It has been applied to a bizarre dissected plateau south-east of the remains of the outcamp, a landform so extraordinary that people are already calling it 'the eighth wonder of the world'.

There is only one way to gain a proper appreciation of the Bungle-Bungles: from the air. From a light aircraft or helicopter the incredible scale of the striated hummock formations is brought into sharp focus. Resembling some fantastic city from the Arabian Nights, the sandstone beehives fill the horizon, divided into blocks by palm-tree-lined 'avenues' that need only traffic to make the urban illusion complete.

So eroded is the plateau that access by foot is all but impossible. A number of bushwalkers have penetrated a short way into the ranges—one group walking in from the Ord River near the Great Northern Highway, a day's march—but the only white people to have trodden on the central section of the plateau have been dropped in by helicopter. Even then, the rocks are so soft and crumbling that they are difficult, at times dangerous, to climb.

It is the friability of the rocks that has given rise to this fantastic assemblage of domes and pinnacles. This is one of the largest areas of unconsolidated sandstone and pebble conglomerate in Australia. The rocks are old—laid down 350 million years ago beneath a tropical sea in which a great horseshoe-shaped coral reef formed around what was then a bulbous peninsula connected at its south-eastern corner to the Northern Territory—but they are still the youngest rocks in the Kimberleys. In fact, the last major uplift of the Kimberley region took place only 3–7 million years ago, the most recent of a series of earth movements which began in Proterozoic times, 1800–2300 million years ago, when the ancient island of Stuartiana rose above the primeval sea. Since then the land has been raised and lowered, subjected to erosion, covered with lava, partially inundated by the sea and flattened by glacial activity. Weathering has been most rapid along lines of weakness in the Kimberley plateau, which has been divided into a series of smaller plateaux and ranges separated by broad valleys and plains.

The Bungle-Bungles are not the only example of eroded hummock formation in the Kimberleys (another good example is in the Keep River National Park, 200 kilometres to the north-north-east), but they are by far the most extensive. The creeks which flow from the 30 kilometre wide, 25 kilometre deep plateau are tributaries of the Ord River, fed by an annual rainfall of nearly 700 millimetres, almost all of which falls during the four months of summer. The gorges become full of the sound of rushing water, deep channels are gouged through the surrounding plains and the land is transformed. But by June the streams have dried up, leaving only occasional pools of water glistening at the bottom of the deeper gorges.

The plateau slopes to the south, where it peters out into isolated outliers. The deepest gorges lie in the north-west, site of the plateau's highest point, 580 metres. There is no trig. station to mark this peak, though: the Bungle-Bungles have never been surveyed, even though at one point they are less than 35 kilometres from the Great Northern Highway.

Spinifex and soft grasses cling to the top of the plateau, along with many as yet undescribed species of fern and the odd stunted gum and acacia. *Livistona* palms, in places growing almost horizontally from the walls of the gorges, create the illusion of lushness, but in fact the soil is poor and there is more botanical diversity elsewhere in the Kimberleys. Euros and rock wallabies hop nimbly among the sandstone hummocks, oblivious to the danger posed by the crumbling rock. Most of the smaller mammals are nocturnal and are preyed on by keen-eyed owls like the mopoke and the shy rufous owl.

Overhangs and caves in many of the gorges are decorated with Aboriginal paintings of a more traditional nature than the strange mouthless *wandjinas* of the western Kimberley. These paintings were executed by ancestors of the Warmun community, who today live 40 kilometres to the north at the settlement of Turkey Creek. The world of the Kimberley tribes changed irrevocably in the 1880s, when pastoralists arrived to establish their empires. In 1885, Charles Hall and Jack Slattery reported they had found payable gold on a tributary of the Ord River. Western Australia's first gold rush

Eroded hummock formations of Bungle–Bungle plateau rank amongst Australia's greatest natural wonders.

began, the diggers travelling west from Charters Towers and Croydon in Queensland, across the same country that had almost beaten Forrest a few years earlier, and east from the ports of Broome and Derby, 500 kilometres away.

Wyndham was established on Cambridge Gulf, 300 kilometres north of the shanty town of Halls Creek, which by 1886 boasted a roistering population of several thousand (it dropped to 400 a year later, when the gold ran out). Today, new riches are being won from a massive kimberlite diamond pipe on Upper Snake Creek, 70 kilometres north of the Bungle-Bungles.

Yet so far it is cattle that have been the economic mainstay of the region. In the 1960s a dam was built across the Ord River where it flows through the Carr Boyd Ranges, creating Lake Argyle, Australia's largest lake; water from the 700 square kilometre reservoir was to be used for irrigation. A new town, Kununurra, was built downstream, but so far the scheme has proved to be a costly white elephant, bedevilled by insects, crop disease and high transport costs.

In 1961 the Bungle-Bungle Range, the erosion of which had been accelerated by overgrazing and by feral donkeys, was declared a rehabilitation reserve for Lake Argyle. The possibility of tourists further damaging the area has been a major consideration in deliberations over establishing a Bungle-Bungles National Park. Aboriginal land claims on the area are also pressing, and the current proposal is for joint management of the area by the Aborigines and the National Parks Authority of Western Australia. Road access would be provided to the eastern quarter, with trails leading up to the top of the plateau and back down again. Aerial sightseeing, possibly including helicopter airlifts, would be encouraged. It is a plan very different from those drawn up for other national parks in Australia—but, of course, the Bungle-Bungles are unique.

BELOW *Livistona* palms grow in sheltered canyons, creating the illusion of lushness.
RIGHT The deepest gorges are in the north-west of the plateau, where it reaches its highest point of 580 metres.

WESTERN AUSTRALIA

The Hamersley Range

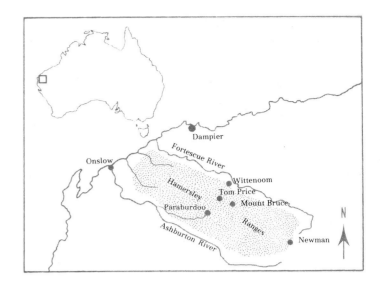

IT is hellishly hot in the Hamersleys, and the range—Western Australia's highest —seems to reflect this heat, with rocks the colour of overdone pork crackling and tufts of spinifex, dotted amongst the boulders on top of the tableland and thatching the sloping terraces of the gorges, as yellow as well-dried straw. Two hundred and twenty-five kilometres to the north-east, the erstwhile gold-mining town of Marble Bar not only revels in the title of the hottest town in Australia, but also holds the world record for the longest consecutive run of above-century (Fahrenheit scale) temperatures: 161 days in 1923–24.

The average annual rainfall in the Hamersleys is only 300 millimetres, most of which falls during the summer wet season, when cyclones tear into the coast and normally dusty roads become impassable quagmires. Yet the tributaries of the Fortescue and Ashburton, the rivers which flank the 400 kilometre long tableland to the north and south, have managed to gouge great clefts into the red sedimentary rocks: nearly two dozen major gorges and innumerable minor ones so deep that there are always green pools of water to be found at their bases.

It was, of course, wetter during Pleistocene times and much of the streams' excavation may have taken place then. We can only guess at the climate since their creation, for these are some of the most ancient rocks in the world, stable since well before the evolution of primitive life forms. The conglomerates, quartzites and shales of the ranges were deposited 1800–2400 million years ago beneath a sea which lapped the northern shores of Yilgarnia the timeless land. Uplifted, warped, then eroded into a mature plateau, the ranges have since been raised a second time, accelerating the runoff. The streams have tended to follow the joints, fault lines and depressions in the rock, the differing natures of the gorges reflecting the structure of the rocks into which they are cut.

Harder residual peaks break the flat cap of the tableland, among them Mount Meharry (1250 metres) and Mount Bruce (1227 metres), the two highest in the state. The Hamersleys form but a small part of the vast Pilbara region (444 000 square kilometres), which extends from the Tropic of Capricorn to the Kimberleys and from the Indian Ocean to the Northern Territory border.

The most spectacular gorges—Weano, Hamersley, Dales, Joffre, Red—run into the northern escarpment of the ranges, thought to be a fault line marking the southern boundary of the Fortescue rift valley and up to 300 metres high. Several, like Weano, are sheer-sided slashes in the rock, only a metre or so wide, the horizontal strata of rocks stacked like books. Four of these narrow gorges converge on a deep hole above Wittenoom Gorge. Others, like Dales Gorge, an important dry-season refuge for the Pandjima people, are broader; the pools of water are lined with reeds and the cliffs terraced like Nepalese hillsides. In Hamersley Gorge the strata are folded and banded as if with steel straps. In the cool depths of the broader gorges, river red gums and coolibahs grow; high above, native figs and white-limbed ghost gums wait and watch.

Many of the northern gorges are now contained within the 590 206 hectare Hamersley Range National Park, declared in 1969 and encompassing the highest section of the Hamersley plateau. Excluded from the park is a narrow salient of land surrounding the gorge where Hamersley mining history had its genesis: Wittenoom. The mineral they took from narrow seams 50–100 metres above the floor of the gorge was crocidolite, better known as blue asbestos and for decades a favoured insulation and building material, now reviled as the cause of asbestosis and a possible carcinogen.

Blue asbestos was discovered in the Hamersley Range in 1917, but it was not until 1934 that the reserves began to be mined, for a few years at Yampire Gorge and then from 1938 at nearby Wittenoom Gorge. One of the pioneers of this venture was local pastoralist Lang Hancock. The ore was dug from the cliff face 90 metres up, then carried by flying fox down to a primitive napping machine. Donkeys packed out the treated ore to the site of the present town of Wittenoom, built in 1947, four years after the giant company CSR had taken over the operation. But by the early 1960s the mine had become uneconomic and it was closed in 1966, the year the first shipment of a new mineral was made from the Hamersleys: iron ore.

It was Lang Hancock who persuaded the major mining companies to put forward their money for the development of the potential of the Hamersley ore deposits. And potential there certainly was: more than 20 000 million tonnes of high- and medium-

Wittenoom Gorge. Blue asbestos was mined here from 1938–66.

grade iron ore enriched by natural leaching, and billions of tonnes more of lower-grade banded iron.

Developing the choicest of these deposits became Australia's major engineering project of the 1960s. Hundreds of kilometres of railway track were laid down; air-conditioned towns sprang up at places like Tom Price and Paraburdoo; and now more than 70 million tonnes of iron ore are exported each year from an area where, in the late 1950s, it had not even been legal—because of an odd state government decree—to peg a claim.

One of the great mysteries of the north-west must be why it took so long to exploit these enormous reserves. The existence of iron in the region had been surmised since 1699, when William Dampier, charting the coast from Shark Bay to Roebuck, noted that his compass swung to the south. More than a century before the discovery of Mount Tom Price, Francis Charles Gregory, brother of the celebrated explorer Augustus and leader of the first expedition to visit the range, commented in his journal: 'Of minerals I was unable to discover any, except iron'.

Gregory had, in fact, been more interested in locating agricultural land than mineral deposits. His party of nine landed at Nickol Bay, near the present town of Karratha, in May 1861, and they spent several months exploring the country to the south and south-east. He named the Hamersley Range, after Edward Hamersley, 'one of the most liberal promoters of the expedition', as well as Mount Bruce and Mount Samson, which is only 15 kilometres north-west of Mount Tom Price. Gregory was enthusiastic about the potential of the plains south of the Hamersleys for growing sugar and cotton, but it was pastoralists who arrived in the Pilbara three years later, settling first the river flats then spreading out into the hills. So marginal is the plateau country for grazing that only a quarter of it has ever been taken up for pastoral use.

One of the pioneers of the district was Sir Edward Home Wittenoom, who bought White Peak station, just outside the present town of Dampier, in 1881, and who served discontinuously in state parliament (including a spell as Acting Premier) for more than

Spinifex clings to the ledges of Red Gorge, one of five leading into Wittenoon Gorge.

50 years. His name is perpetuated in the gorge and town of Wittenoom. The Ophthalmia Range, the eastern extremity of the Hamersleys, was given its name by explorer Ernest Giles, who was temporarily blinded by conjunctivitis there during his epic west-east crossing of the Gibson Desert in 1876.

A few Aboriginal names survive, but the local tribes were quickly initiated into white ways and much of their traditional knowledge has been lost. Convict labour was prohibited in the north-west so the pioneer pastoralists hired Aborigines as station hands. The inland tribes felt themselves to be in some way superior to the coastal people such as the Narla and Kariari, who did not practice circumcision and who were in any case largely decimated following white settlement in the 1870s. Evincing the depth of their conversion to European customs, in May 1946 Aboriginal station hands began a famous three-year strike for higher pay, the first ever by blacks.

In 1861, Francis Gregory had been intrigued by the Aborigines' method of trapping birds by strategically placing spinifex nets around their drinking holes. Today's technology, with its snorting machines and billion-dollar holes in the ground, is very different, but as yet it has impinged only marginally on this ancient landscape. Nature, too, is digging iron from the hills, washing it down the streams in every summer storm.

Water pours through the narrow chasm of upper Hamersley Gorge.

WESTERN AUSTRALIA

Tunnel Creek

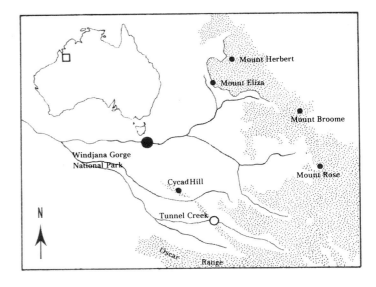

ONE of the world's best preserved and largest fossil coral reef systems embraces the Kimberley coastline between Wyndham and Broome, then swings inland for more than 300 kilometres to beyond the small town of Fitzroy Crossing. It was formed by calcareous organisms—primitive corals, algae and bryozoans—which flourished in a warm tropical sea surrounding the Kimberley (then a bulbous peninsula) in Devonian times, building limestone platforms more than 200 metres above the sea bed.

The eroded remnants of the south-western section of these reefs, now well and truly above sea level, are known as the Napier, Oscar and Geikie Ranges. Rivers and streams rising to the east of the limestone walls have forced their way through, carving deep gorges, tunnels and cave systems as yet only partially explored.

The most significant gorge is the 6 kilometre long Geikie Gorge, named in 1883 by John Forrest, then Surveyor-General of Western Australia, in honour of the prominent British geologist Sir Archibald Geikie. Here the powerful Fitzroy River has cut 30 metres into the limestone, striping it in contrasting bands of colour: the weathered cliff tops grey as slate, the bases bleached creamy-white by monsoonal floodwaters, and, in between, a layer of red rock, raw as grazed skin. Freshwater crocodiles cruise up and down the gorge in search of fish; in places, shady alluvial flats form a dry-season refuge for kangaroos and wallabies.

One hundred kilometres north-west of Geikie Gorge, a much smaller watercourse has bored through the dark and jagged ramparts of the Napier Range, following a fault line in the limestone. This is one of the Kimberley's very special places, a shady retreat from the scorching sun, where there is always water trickling from a spring in the tunnel wall into clear, still pools in which freshwater gobies and catfish swim. The roof has collapsed in the centre of the tunnel, forming a natural skylight probed by the roots of native fig trees. Fruit bats roost in the cave, feeding on the figs and breaking the silence with their noisy squabbling.

In the wet season the creek fills the cave with water and sometimes floods, jamming debris into crevices in the rock face. At other times of the year it is possible to walk through the tunnel, beneath the grey shapes of dried-up stalactites, past the faded outlines of Aboriginal paintings, to the southern side of the range, where fig and pandanus trees trail their toes in a rock-lined pool of water.

So peaceful is the setting it is hard to believe that an Aboriginal guerilla leader called Pigeon used this spot as a hideout in the 1890s, fighting a lonely gun battle with a police patrol before being shot dead. Pigeon's main base was at nearby Windjana Gorge, a deep, sandy gorge lined with eucalypts, and he alternated between the two places during his campaign against the white settlers who had taken the land of his people.

Windjana Gorge is an important gallery for paintings of *wandjinas*, the staring, mouthless heads that anthropologist A. P. Elkin called 'a visible sign and sacrament of the dreaming'. *Wandjinas* were first recorded by explorer George Grey, who in January 1839 landed at Hanover Bay, south of the Prince Regent River. His intention had been to lead his party of 13 men more than 2000 kilometres to Perth, but it was the height of the wet season and they did not manage to break out of the hilly western Kimberley.

Settlement came much later, following on the discovery in 1879 of the rich grazing lands of the Fitzroy plains by Alexander Forrest. Clay soils derived from the limestone ranges sustain an excellent cover of Mitchell grass, which Forrest enthusiastically claimed capable of supporting a million sheep—the reality is around a quarter of that number. Forrest waxed lyrical about the beauty of the local gorges, but was unable to find a way through the King Leopold Ranges to the central Kimberley region and instead struck out for the Overland Telegraph, 750 kilometres to the east. It was a nightmare journey, culminating in Forrest and one of the fitter expedition members, Arthur Hicks, leaving the other five men at a waterhole while they made a desperate 160 kilometre dash for assistance.

Forrest was the first man to recognise the homogeneity of the region, which he recommended be named the Kimberley Range after the British Colonial Secretary, Lord Kimberley. Today, the area is often referred to as 'the Kimberleys', reflecting its two-pronged development: in the west by sheep men arriving by sea from the south-west in the 1880s; in the east by cattle-droving overlanders from the eastern states.

Despite a century of development, much of the Kimberley remains as it has always been: remote, difficult of access, implacably hostile. It is a frontier land, and as such holds considerable fascination for Australians not of its soil.

A roof collapse in the centre of the tunnel forms a natural skylight.

WESTERN AUSTRALIA

The Pinnacles Desert

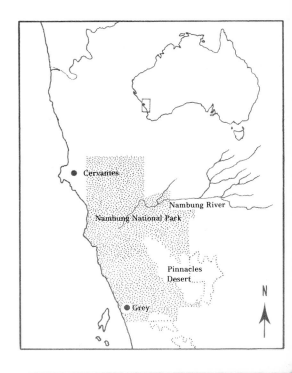

Located only 160 kilometres north of Perth, but virtually inaccessible until the 1970s, when a new road from the small fishing town of Cervantes was bulldozed in, at first sight the Pinnacles Desert challenges one's credulity. How could such an assemblage of tens of thousands of limestone pillars, some 5 metres tall, some only a few centimetres, have come into being? Were they once ant hills? the sand-blasted gravestones of a lost civilisation, perhaps? remnant tree trunks? This last suggestion approaches the truth, but it is far from being the whole answer, as we shall see.

The countryside is as bleak as any in Australia, despite a moderate rainfall of 600 millimetres a year. From the Brand Highway to the east, a giant dune system looms along the coastline, gleaming white like the roaring breakers of the nearby Indian Ocean. The soil is as poor as the presence of the dunes suggests and, except along the course of the seasonal Nambung River, the vegetation primarily consists of a low scrub of banksias, acacias and blackboys, the monotony relieved only by the springtime crackle of wildflowers.

Among this bland uniformity, the dunes, the painted deserts and silent watchers of the Pinnacles, form very distinctive landmarks. Dutch navigators, who had been sailing up the coast of Western Australia since the early 1600s, noted the Pinnacles (from sea they looked like a small city) on their charts but the treacherous reefs, which run right along the coastline and which even in modern times have claimed numerous ships, prevented them from putting ashore. The Dutch were also discouraged by the sight of those enormous dunes, some more than 60 metres high. It is these sand ridges, and others which pre-date them by tens of thousands of years and are now stabilised inland, many kilometres from the ocean beach, that are the key to the formation of the Pinnacles.

This is a young landscape, perhaps no more than 100 000 years old. During the Pleistocene epoch, when sea levels fell by up to 100 metres, the prevailing westerlies formed the great dune belts of the coastline from quartz sand and the remains of sea shells. Vegetation appeared on and stabilised the inland dunes, while other, mobile dunes formed closer to the sea. Rainwater seeping through the dunes dissolved the calcareous remains of sea shells, eventually solidifying to form limestone, which was re-deposited along the walls of underground drainage conduits. The remaining material covering these limestone pinnacles was an insoluble quartz sand which supported a plant cover of shrubs and trees. Bushfires, it is thought, killed sufficient of these plants for the dunes to become mobile again, engulfing the remaining shrubs. Rainwater percolating through the dunes calcified the tree roots and built up hard calcite on the spires buried below the surface. Wind-augmented erosion then lowered the sand level by as much as 4 metres, first exposing the pinnacles and calcified tree roots, then scouring them with its abrasive breath. The Pinnacles are 60 metres above sea level, which explains how the Dutch sailors managed to see them so clearly from their foredecks. South-westerly winds have continued to push the sand northwards, creating little deserts of coloured sands rippling through the heath and scrub.

Limestone is one of the most fantastical of nature's building blocks, able to mould itself into spires and columns, domes and cupolas, with a creativity unmatched by the masters of sculpture. This is a limestone coast, and the stalagmites and stalactites of the caves at Augusta and Margaret River, south of Perth, have their parallel in the extraordinary karst topography of Nambung National Park.

Some of the strange, eroded shapes are almost pure cones, like dunces' caps, smoothed over by millennia of sand blasting. Others are domed, like mushrooms or ice-cream cones. Many are pitted and honeycombed like coastal sandstone, or fluted like Venetian blinds. In places portholes appear, eventually enlarging to form wicked, hooked talons, while other columns are waisted like corseted women. Proud warriors of aquiline countenance glare balefully at a bevy of withered hags, across a field of grey tombstones. The gentle dune slopes are everywhere pricked like pincushions by the tiny stems of calcified tree roots, few more than 30 centimetres high, that clink like china when tapped together. The Pinnacles have all the colours of fine porcelain, too: yellows, reds, greys, browns, and a delicate rose-pink that reflects off human skin on bright cloudy days.

Into this wonderland of strange landforms stumbled a small group of weary men in April 1839. Their party, under Captain George Grey, later Governor of South Australia

and Governor and Prime Minister of New Zealand, had intended to explore the country between Shark Bay and Perth but had lost their supplies and been forced to beach their two open boats at Gantheaume Bay, near Kalbarri. Grey and his party of ten whites and one Aborigine had set out to walk to Perth, 500 kilometres distant. Their food and water supplies were limited. After three weeks they had split into two groups, with Grey leading the advance, and fitter, team. It was the second group, under Mr Walker, which crossed the Nambung Desert and located caves in the area.

Grey's name is remembered by the town site of Grey, 10 kilometres south-west of the Pinnacles. But it was Frederick Smith, who died in the desert before a rescue party could arrive, whose name is more enduringly recorded: a tributary of the Nambung (a Juat Aboriginal word meaning 'winding river') is known as the Smith River.

Within ten years pastoralists had moved into the area. Rainfall was good but the soil proved to be deficient in several important minerals: stock could be grazed there for no longer than four months each year or they would contract 'coast disease'. A stock route was surveyed from Dongara to Perth in 1869, through what is now the national park, passing by Kinchilla Pool on the Nambung River. Close to the stock route are 15 limestone caves, formed by winter runoff; two of them contain thousands of tonnes of bat guano, which was briefly exploited early this century.

Despite the area's geological significance and its closeness to Perth, it was not declared a national park until 1956 and the Pinnacles themselves were only added in 1968. Cervantes, gateway to the Pinnacles, lies 26 kilometres to the north along a rough limestone track and was laid out in 1962. The town, named after an American whaler which sank in adjacent Jurien Bay in 1844, services the crayfishing industry.

To Dutch mariners sailing off-shore, these limestone pinnacles resembled a small city.

Wolf Creek
Meteorite Crater

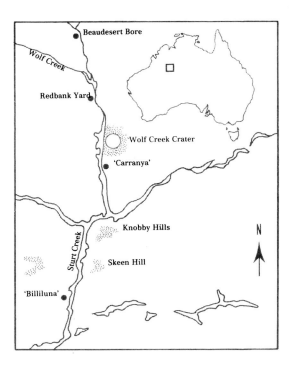

THEY flash across the night skies with all the transient surety of sub-atomic particles flickering in a linear accelerator. Their death throes usually last only a few seconds, and then they are gone, the energy they represented spent in that brief moment of contact with the earth's atmosphere. Many, like Gray's desert flower, 'blush unseen', scorching across some lonely sea or mountain range or self-destructing in the anonymity of daylight.

Scientifically, the phenomenon is known as a bolide, after the Greek word for javelin, curiously a more onomatopoeic name than the colloquial shooting, or falling, star. Man has recently created some 'bolides' himself, through expensive satellites or used booster rockets falling out of orbit; however, most bolides are meteors from interplanetary space, off-course debris perhaps from the asteroid belt between Mars and Jupiter. These inanimate intruders are travelling at unimaginably high speeds, at least 40 000 and possibly over 250 000 kilometres per hour, but the majority never reach the earth's surface. Thousands do each year, though, usually burnt up to a fraction of their former size.

The bigger the meteor, the further it falls into the atmosphere and the more spectacular its demise. The meteor may break up into fragments, showering sparks in all directions like a high-flying firework. An unearthly glow may suffuse the landscape. A few minutes after a large bolide has vanished, three sharp bangs, a rumble like thunder and a roar like a jet engine may shatter the silence as the shock waves pass, sometimes strong enough to crack glass or rattle doors. If its mass is great enough, the remnant meteor may enter a 'delay zone', usually about 12 kilometres up, at which point it loses its cosmic velocity and falls to the ground under gravity. The fragment is then known as a meteorite and the hole it makes in the ground an impact crater.

Occasionally, in the case of a huge meteor, the delay zone may be under the earth's surface, so that the meteorite strikes the earth with cosmic velocity. A mighty explosion occurs, beside which the shock waves of the bolide are no more than the breaking of boughs in a heavy wind. The meteorite is vaporised, scattering shards on the ground. A crater, at least 100 metres across, forms in the convulsing soil and bedrock.

Few meteorites have struck the earth with as much force as the lump of iron (siderite) which appeared from the north-east above the now barren and sandy plains near Wolf Creek, south of the Kimberleys, 2 million years ago. The Pre-Cambrian quartzite of the plains was smashed and tossed up like rubble. A crater formed, 914 metres across and as much as 150 metres deep (it has since been largely filled in by sand). The meteorite weighed 20 000–50 000 tonnes, but no fragment larger than 160 kilograms survived the explosion; the rest of it vanished in a breath of hot air that scalded the earth for tens of kilometres roundabout.

So remote is the area in which the impact occurred that the crater was not identified as an astrobleme until June 1947. An aircraft, piloted by Dudley Hart and carrying geologist Dr Frank Reeves and geophysicist N. B. Sauve, was undertaking routine exploration work south of Halls Creek when the trio noticed an unusual-looking formation on the otherwise featureless desert floor. Circling around, they found themselves staring down into the enormous crater of Wolf Creek.

Two months later, Reeves, Hart and assistant geologist Harry Evans visited the site, travelling partly cross-country by four-wheel drive from remote Billiluna station at the northern end of the Canning Stock Route. At first they thought they had discovered an extinct volcano but comparison with aerial photographs of the famous Canyon Diablo crater in Arizona persuaded them of its extraterrestrial origin.

The investigators spent only two hours at the crater site and were unable to find any remains of the meteorite. But a subsequent trip by Cassidy, Gross and Mertz of the South Australian Museum revealed several large shale-balls (oxidised meteoritic material) lying near the south-west outer wall of the crater, as well as many smaller nickel-iron fragments, but no complete unoxidised specimens of iron meteorite. Then, in 1965, a station hand from Caranya, 7 kilometres south of the crater, found a small piece 4 kilometres to the south-west. Scientists later went over this area with a metal detector and found many more fragments, the largest weighing 72.6 kilograms.

This should have put the origins of the crater beyond all reasonable doubt but, as late as 1983, the *Guinness Book of Records* was suggesting that it may have been due to the subsidence of a volcanic cauldron. Most scientists concur that it is the second-largest proven meteorite crater in the world, after the much more recent

Canyon Diablo (diameter, 1.6 kilometres), although there is apparently a problem in accounting for the enormous volume of rock material lost from the crater depression.

Another anomaly is the absence of 'rock flour', very fine, powdery dust resulting from the explosion. Yet perhaps it is not so surprising: over the millennia since the impact the crater has filled with sediments so that it is now only 48–55 metres deep. Outside, the rock parapet rises 18–30 metres above the spinifex- and scrub-covered red sand plains bordering the Great Sandy Desert. Both the outer slope and the twice-as-steep inner wall of the crater support a sparse cover of spinifex and occasional small trees. The crater floor is very flat and sometimes partly fills with water, which drains through sinkholes in the gypsum-encrusted centre. Some mature trees stud the crater floor amongst the ubiquitous spinifex.

Massive as Wolf Creek is, it is but a pockmark compared to some craters postulated to have been of meteoritic origin elsewhere in the world. One, in Wilkes Land, Antarctica, is 241 kilometres across and 800 metres deep. If it is an astrobleme, the meteorite which caused it would have weighed 13 000 million tonnes and been travelling at 70 000 kilometres per hour. Another possible astrobleme, on the shores of Hudson Bay in Canada, is 442.5 kilometres in diameter, the distance from Melbourne to Balranald! Others of more probable meteoric provenance include a 13 kilometre wide depression in Ghana and the 3.2 kilometre wide Canadian New Quebec and Algerian Talemzane craters.

Nevertheless, the number of mega-impacts—proven, probable and possible—in the world is very small. Fortunately for us, given the magnitude of the accompanying explosion, the chances of another Wolf Creek crater being formed in our lifetime are remote.

From the air, Wolf Creek meteorite crater assumes the unmistakable shape of an astrobleme in the flat sandridge country at the edge of the Great Sandy Desert.

Cloud shadows stroke fleeting fingers across Central
Australia's best-known landmark, Ayers Rock.

NORTHERN TERRITORY

Kakadu National Park

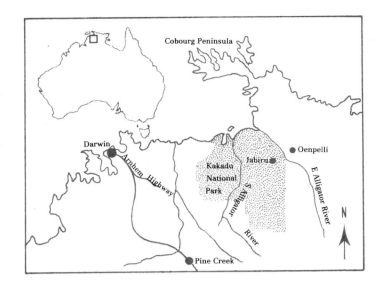

IN the dry, as Australian writer Xavier Herbert would have it, the land is a desert; in the wet, from November to May, the land is a lake. Like all of the Top End, Kakadu National Park is dominated by the seasons—by the seasons, and by the great brooding line of the Arnhem Land escarpment down which tumble the creeks that give rise to the rivers of the lowlands.

From the air, Kakadu is an impressive mosaic: blue rivers snaking through 2 metre high spear grass, open eucalypt woodlands and paperbark forests to the tidal flats, buffalo bright against the ground and flocks of birds wheeling into the trees. Biologically, it is one of the richest regions in Australia, a wilderness of diverse ecosystems.

The 6000 square kilometres that make up Kakadu* encompass most of the East and South Alligator rivers and contain the most varied rock art galleries in Australia, some of the paintings dating back an estimated 20 000 years or more, making them amongst the most ancient in the world. Little wonder that Kakadu, along with the Barrier Reef, was one of the first Australian natural wonders to be nominated for inclusion on the World Heritage list.

Only 180 kilometres east of Darwin on the all-weather Arnhem Highway, the Park is threatened less by man—despite the exploitation of vast reserves of uranium ore within its boundaries—than it is by the animals he has brought with him, the feral pigs and buffaloes that roam the flood plains. The pigs, released when Europeans abandoned the settlement of Port Essington (once described as 'the most heroic and the most hopeless enterprise in British Empire history') in 1849, churn up the soil, eat the roots of plants, the eggs and fledglings of ground-nesting birds, small mammals and reptiles, and are carriers of disease. The water buffalo, symbol of the Territory, was introduced from Indonesia between 1827 and 1849 as food for the European settlements on the Coburg Peninsula, and has caused great damage to the flood plains and woodlands, selectively grazing and trampling the vegetation. Despite a rainfall of up to 1450 millimetres a year, these ecosystems are fragile and the soils, worn over the millennia from the receding sandstone face of the escarpment, are often leached of plant nutrient.

Age characterises this land: the Pre-Cambrian sandstones, quartzite and conglo-merate of the Arnhem Plateau have stayed roughly level for more than 2000 million years; Kakadu's youngest rocks are more than 1000 million years old. Aboriginal occupation is, of course, far more recent but extends back at least 25 000 years and probably twice as long. By the seventeenth century, Macassan fishermen were regularly visiting the northern Australian coastline to harvest bêches-de-mer for sale to China. In 1623, 147 years before Cook, the first European ship to sail these waters (and return), the *Arnhem*, charted the north-east coast of Arnhem Land. Macassan praus and bulkier European sailing ships were painted on the rocks by the Aborigines: at Nangaloar, within the park boundaries, there is a fine example of a two-masted schooner, fully rigged but, oddly, at anchor.

The creeks that become raging torrents in the wet have sliced deep gorges through the plateau while in places the eroding escarpment has left behind outcrops, or outliers, of more resistant rock, like flotsam deposited by the ebbing tide. In some of the gorges relict pockets of rainforest, thought once to have been the dominant vegetation in the north, have escaped the Aborigines' firesticks and the lightning-strike fires of the monsoonal build-up.

Among the waterholes and eucalypts of the escarpment, and by the swamps and billabongs of the lowlands, the Aborigines found their richest food sources. Here, too, they left behind a priceless heritage of rock art, at favourite camp sites such as Obiri and Nourlangie Rock. There are literally hundreds of painting sites in the Kakadu region. The art encompasses such a huge span of time, dating back more than 10 000 years before recorded civilisation, that it inevitably encompasses a rich variety of styles. Polychrome paintings of great beauty may overlie simpler, one-colour art. Groups of stick-like *mimi* figures move quickly across the rock face, running, hunting, burying their dead. More recent paintings are in the graphic X-ray style, in which both the external and internal characteristics of the subject are shown, and this tradition has been maintained in contemporary bark painting. Often, at popular painting sites like Nangaloar and Little Nourlangie, where the motifs overlie each other like palm fronds on a Polynesian *fale*, nearby support rocks are worn smooth by the caress of countless generations of hands and feet. Other sandstone is dimpled and furrowed by centuries of tool-making.

Polychrome X-ray figures at Nourlangie Rock. The Aboriginal art galleries of the Kakadu region are amongst the finest in Australia.

And what a rich source of subject matter the artists had to draw upon! Not just the activities of their fellows, but the legendary heroes of the Dreamtime and the hundreds of different creatures inhabiting the flood plains and escarpment: catfish, barramundi, bream, snakes, crocodiles, turtles, goannas, wallaroos, and an enormous variety of birds. Kakadu is a living zoo that betters anything man has created from concrete and steel and expensive expeditions around the world. A boat trip along the Yellow Waters Billabong, part of the South Alligator River system, is an experience comparable to canoeing the Rio Negro in South America or hitching a ride on the *African Queen*.

This is the domain of the Australian saltwater crocodile, largest in the world. A 7 metre saltie was recently recorded inside the park, and on Yellow Waters they are frequently more than 5 metres long—longer than the average small boat! Any saltwater crocodile more than 3 metres long is considered a potential man-eater. This anachronistic carnivore was a contemporary of the dinosaurs and has changed little in the last 100 million years. It ranges widely, from northern Australia through Indonesia and the Malayan Peninsula to India and Sri Lanka; it has been found swimming many kilometres out to sea and will also live in totally freshwater swamps and lagoons, at Kakadu sharing its habitat with the fish-eating Johnston River crocodile.

Saltwater crocodiles usually nest during the wet season, building mounds of soil and vegetation on the banks of the rivers or swamps. At this time the female is territorial and aggressive towards intruders and will vigorously defend her nest. Each female lays an average of 50 eggs, only 85 millimetres long. The young hatch after about 10–12 weeks. Male crocodiles take about 16 years to mature, the noticeably smaller females, about 10 years. The hatchlings will share the shady banks and mud flats of Kakadu with a million birds, some of which will eat them for food: black-billed spoonbills, egrets, slender-necked darters, whistling ducks, walk-on-water lotus birds, yellow-masked plovers, graceful grey brolgas, cormorants, magpie geese beyond number. The jumbo of the northern skies is the pelican, gliding down for a heavy splashdown, while the more dignified jabiru assumes the posture of a Concorde after takeoff. A hawk stands defiantly astride a dead bream. A cattle egret, a recent coloniser from Africa, rides the broad back of a browsing buffalo.

To the Aboriginal people, the Gagudju, Maiuli and Djauan, this region must have been one of the most bountiful in Australia. Not for them the endless treks from waterhole to waterhole of the desert tribes, nor the fire-huddled winter nights and bleak, fog-shrouded mornings of the mountain people. The howling winds of the monsoonal cyclone would have been an infrequent unpleasantness. The mosquitoes that swarm by the billion after the storm clouds of the wet blow over would have been annoying; the crocodiles and venomous snakes must have claimed occasional victims. But, by and large, the plains and escarpment were a giant open-air supermarket, where the food was available for the taking.

I received a graphic illustration of this when an Aboriginal man in his early twenties accompanied me beyond the tidal zone of the South Alligator River. It was the end of the dry season and the river was at its lowest level for the year. He stripped off and stepped into the muddy waters, slithering around the roots of the freshwater mangroves crowding the banks. Within a minute he had located and captured a 1.5 metre long, non-venomous Javan file snake, which he handed to me to hold. Two more file snakes and a long-necked tortoise followed in quick succession. Inside ten minutes he had collected, with his bare hands, enough meat to feed an extended family.

During the dry season, the Aborigines would come down from the escarpment and fan out across the plains, impassable swamps during the five-month wet. Fire was for them a significant hunting weapon, driving the terrified animals into their waiting spears. The white settlers followed their example, burning the grasslands to improve pastures the following year. Either as a result or perhaps by coincidence, many plant species in the north, as elsewhere in Australia, now require the heat of fire to germinate.

Through all this, a large number of rare and endangered species have managed to survive . . . thus far. One striking example is Leichhardt's grasshopper, first noted by an officer of HMS *Beagle* in 1839 and subsequently collected on the edge of the escarpment in 1845 by the hapless German explorer Ludwig Leichhardt, and on the Victoria River by a member of Gregory's expedition of 1855–56. This vivid orange, black and blue grasshopper was not rediscovered until 1971; since then it has been learnt that it is more common than was at first thought.

Only a few of the Aboriginal people living in the area are Gagudju (Kakadu); the most commonly spoken languages are Maiuli and Djauan. This land still belongs to the Aborigines but they have agreed to lease it to the Australian people for management by the Australian National Parks and Wildlife Service. The first stage of the park, comprising the Woolowonga Aboriginal Reserve, most of the Alligator Waters Wildlife Sanctuary, and a large tract of vacant crown land, was proclaimed in 1979. There is a uranium mine, Ranger (Jabiru), operating within the park boundaries and two other deposits of uranium have been proven at Jabiluka and Koongarra. Conservationists believe that this uranium exploitation contravenes the spirit of a National Park. There is also a hotel, at Cooinda on Jim Jim Creek; another is located on the South Alligator River, just outside the park.

Beyond the tidal flats of the East Alligator River lies Arnhem Land Aboriginal Reserve, proclaimed in 1931 and off limits to uninvited visitors. Here, it is said, the geographic features that characterise Kakadu are repeated, only bigger and better. For most, it is unnecessary to seek permission to cross the border. Kakadu offers enough to satisfy all but the most jaded traveller.

---

* Increased to 13 000 square kilometres in 1984 with the declaration of Stage Two of the park. The new section incorporates all the land from the Wildman River estuary east to Point Farewell and south to the northern border of Stage One.

OPPOSITE, TOP LEFT **Termite mounds in the Top End may reach 6 metres in height.**
OPPOSITE, TOP RIGHT **The ant-like assassin bug (F. *Reduviidae*) sucks the body juices from its victims.**
OPPOSITE, CENTRE LEFT **Magpie geese (*Anseranas semipalmata*), search for food on the banks of the East Alligator River. (Michael Richardson)**
OPPOSITE, CENTRE RIGHT **Large saltwater crocodile glides towards the bank, Yellow Waters.**
OPPOSITE, BOTTOM **The monsoon sweeps in towards Obiri Rock. Lowland plains are an important breeding ground for many bird species.**

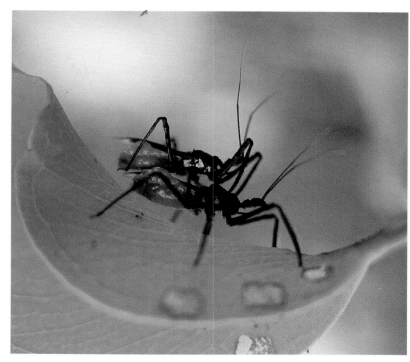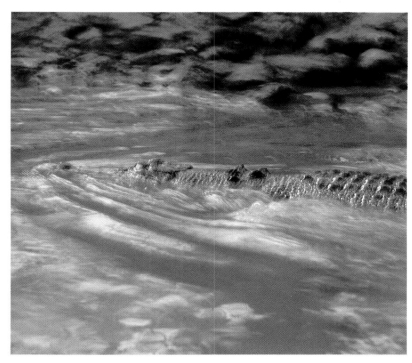

THE NORTHERN TERRITORY

Gosse Bluff

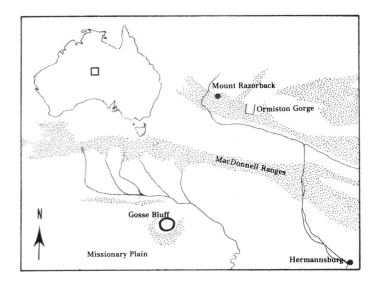

THERE seems to be no earthly reason for the existence of Gosse Bluff on the spinifex- and mulga-covered expanse of Missionary Plain, between the MacDonnell and Gardiner ranges, 160 kilometres west of Alice Springs. It is a geological anomaly which, over the years, has variously been explained as the result of igneous intrusion, cryptovolcanism, salt diapirism and mud volcano activity. The truth is, in fact, likely to be extraterrestrial: the crater-shaped bluff is in all probability an astrobleme, a 'star wound' of stupendous proportions, gouged out by chance collision with a speeding comet.

The 1980s is a decade for these wanderers of the galaxy. In May 1983 the hitherto unknown Iras-Araki-Alcock comet flashed by, a mere 4.8 million kilometres from earth, substantially closer than the recurring Halley's Comet, due back in 1985 after another 76-year orbit around the sun. Halley's Comet is said to have heralded the destruction of Jerusalem in AD70 and the death of King Harold at Hastings in 1066.

Did the Gosse Bluff comet perhaps account for some major cataclysm? The energy released would have been potentially earth shattering. The 600 metre diameter, frozen mass of gas, dust and ice, accelerated to a speed of perhaps 144 000 kilometres per hour as it entered the earth's atmosphere. The explosion was equivalent to the combined force of 24 000 1 megatonne hydrogen bombs. Earth's crust compressed, then expanded with the shock. A giant crater formed, a mountain at its centre. The earth stayed intact but global climate may have been altered for a century or more.

This event occurred 131 million years ago, long enough for the uplifted rim to have eroded away, filling the crater with sediments. The central uplift, largely composed of resistant Mereenie sandstone, remained, albeit only 50 metres above the surface. Erosion continued, sweeping away the post-impact sediments, until only the cliffs of Gosse Bluff were left, looming 200 metres high.

Why a comet and not a meteorite, as at nearby Henbury? No fragments of meteoritic material or igneous rock have been found, and the depth of impact is relatively shallow. A smaller object, such as the piece of space debris that fell in Arizona, quarrying out the world's largest proven meteorite crater, would not have formed a central uplift. Some idea of the force unleashed long ago in central Australia is given by a comparison of scale: the Arizona crater is 1200 metres across but the original Gosse Bluff crater measured 22 kilometres from rim to rim and the remaining uplift is still 2.5 kilometres in diameter!

Today a seismic track, legacy of the central Australian oil search, bisects the bluff, although the bulldozers were brought up short by the high western wall. Access to the forbidding crater is via a track winding along a creek bed, one of many to have its origins on the bluff, and through a break in the ramparts. The bluff is as sinister as any haunted castle: malevolence seems to ooze from the brooding ridge line. Despite the many attractive gum-lined creeks flowing from it, this was not a favoured camping site of the Aborigines.

From the air, the crater's colouring is in stark contrast to that of the grey-green ranges bordering Missionary Plain: it is light-brown and appears treeless. From ground level, it becomes clear this is an illusion: hardy mulga has taken root in pockets on the slopes, and spinifex covers the hillsides bordering the entrance to the floor of the plain. These are not smooth walls, rounded like those of Ayers Rock into soft, feminine curves. Rather, this is a fortress, the precipitous cliffs concealing unmentionable secrets. A small siltstone hill, appropriately named Mount Pyroclast, breaks the surface of the plain 5 kilometres to the south.

Explorer Ernest Giles passed this way in September 1872 and named the bluff, which he called a range, after Harry Gosse, a friend of his. In search of water, he followed for a short distance one of the creek beds snaking down from the ramparts, but he did not climb to their top and gaze down into that fearful circle. Nine months later, William Christie Gosse camped on Missionary Plain on his way to Ayers Rock, but his diary gives no indication that he was aware that those craggy walls, often mistakenly thought to have been named after him, were made by other than terrestrial agencies. His lack of perception was his loss: today scientists recognise Gosse Bluff as being the most outstanding example of a comet astrobleme in the world.

The Gosse Bluff crater is actually the remains of the central uplift of a much larger crater formed when a high-speed comet hit the Earth 131 million years ago. (Michael Richardson, top)

The Simpson Desert

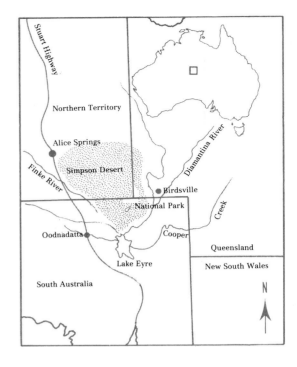

I T has a thousand valleys, this wilderness of sand, but they are far from gentle and green. Their floors and walls are studded with wart-like spinifex mounds that hinder any form of progress; the ridge tops glow orange and red in the unyielding sun. The occasional stream that flows spasmodically from the mountains to the north soon vanishes, with scarcely a puddle to mark its passing. From any valley floor the east-west horizons are limited to the next sand ridge; to the north and south the ridges come together in the middle distance like a tunnel roofed by the sky. It is the largest parallel-sand-ridge desert in the world and the most feared region of Australia—with some justification, as it was the last major unexplored part of Australia, and it still claims the lives of those who break its rules.

The common perception of the Simpson Desert as a totally barren, hostile environment, too arid even to support the nomadic Aborigines, is inaccurate, coloured perhaps by the description given by the first white man to enter it: Charles Sturt, who journeyed 55 kilometres west of Eyre Creek on the eastern boundary of the desert in September 1845. Wrote Sturt in his journal:

> The ridges extended northwards in parallel lines beyond the range of vision, and appeared as if interminable. To the eastward and westward they succeeded each other like the waves of the sea. The sand was of a deep red colour, and a bright narrow line of it marked the top of ridge, amidst the sickly pink and glaucous coloured vegetation around.

For Sturt, the Simpson (then unnamed) was the last straw, the final, insurmountable obstacle in his year-long battle to reach the centre of Australia. Imprisoned by drought at Depot Glen, near Milparinka in the far north-west of New South Wales, for six months and no doubt demoralised by the death from scurvy of his companion, James Poole, Sturt turned back from the country he had fought so bravely.

Sturt's account of the Simpson as a waterless waste, coupled with the assumption that Ludwig Leichhardt and his party of six had perished there on the eccentric German's third expedition into the outback, influenced those who followed. Burke and Wills, Stuart and Gregory all gave the Simpson a wide berth.

Yet by the 1880s a great deal was known about the region. Pastoralists settled its eastern and western fringes in the 1870s. W. O. Hodgkinson explored the eastern side of the desert in 1876, discovering the Toko Range and the Mulligan River, a tributary of Eyre Creek. In January 1878 a party of four men and 16 horses, led by H. Vere Barclay, left Alice Springs Telegraph Station to circle around the northern part of the desert, through the Harts and Jervois Ranges. Barclay recorded, somewhat fancifully: 'Nearly all the country traversed by me was very good ... much [of it] appears well suited for agricultural purposes ...'.

Barclay was to return to the desert in 1904, but 20 years before then the Northern Territory–Queensland and Queensland–South Australian borders had been surveyed and pegged out. The men who carried out this feat of endurance, frequently having to bring in posts by camel because of the lack of timber nearby, were Augustus Poeppel and his assistant Larry Wells. Interestingly, the South Australian–Northern Territory border has still not been surveyed.

In 1883 Charles Winnecke, who had already expanded on Barclay's work north of the desert, struck out north-west from Poeppel Corner, turning east at the twenty-fifth parallel and exploring both sides of the box-gum-studded Hay River, which runs into the desert from the Jervois Range and disappears near the Queensland border. At one stage the party travelled for 16 days and 445 kilometres without finding water.

A memorable expedition was made in January 1886 by David Lindsay who, with two companions, one a member of the Wongkanguru tribe, followed a chain of wells east through the southern Simpson to the Queensland border north of Poeppel's peg, and back again.

The Simpson is a unique entity, of striking uniformity. It is bounded by the Macumba and the Finke rivers to the west, Warburton Creek to the south-east; the Mulligan River to the east; and the eastern MacDonnell Ranges to the north. Its 143 000 square kilometres straddle two states and the Northern Territory. It is 480 kilometres north to south at its deepest point, and 400 kilometres wide. It is not a large desert by world standards, but it is at once the widest, fiercest and most uncompromising region in Australia: an immense corduroy of gaunt red sand dunes, largely stabilised by spinifex

Ribbed sandridges of the Simpson from 1500 metres up: running on to infinity.

and canegrass, their unyielding monotony broken only by a few low hills, the enormous claypans of South Australia and a few smaller playas associated with the Plenty River to the north. Average rainfall, so far as is known, is well below 125 millimetres a year and is unreliable; in many years no rain falls.

This is a land so hostile to life that even the rabbits have eschewed it. Whereas to the south huge rabbit warrens pockmark the straggly dunes of the Strzelecki Desert, the dunes of the Simpson—roughly 1000 of them at the desert's widest point—remain today exactly as they appeared to Sturt: unmarked save for the wheel-ruts of a handful of adventurers, the gunbarrel-straight bulldozer tracks cut by seismic crews, Poeppel's border pegs, and the bedraggled remnants of a painstakingly erected vermin-proof fence on the Queensland side, abandoned in 1931.

Surrounding the desert on all sides are sprawling cattle stations that penetrate this sandy fastness for a short way, until their stock are repelled by it like mosquitoes by the smoke of burning camphor. This desert forms a natural stock fence, shifting with the seasons. The spiky spinifex (actually *triodia* spp.) holds little nutritive value for grazing animals; it tends to grow in circular clumps, a hard-packed hump of sand retained in its centre like a bowerbird's hoard. It is the spinifex, more than the sand, which forms the main obstacle to cross-country transit.

There is a surprisingly diverse flora growing in this hostile environment: grevilleas, hakeas, cassias, mulga, and the gnarled, grotesque gidgee bordering many of the claypans. After rain, the desert is briefly carpeted with wildflowers—everlasting daisies, euphorbias, bird-like crotelarias, swainsonias, bright yellow senecios with their feathery white parachute seeds. In the beds of the creeks and rivers that run briefly after heavy rains, coolibahs and box gums grow, the only eucalypts in the desert. Sometimes the regrowth saplings are so thick it is almost impossible to force a path through them.

At North Bore, 30 kilometres north-east of old Andado station on the western fringe of the desert, and near Boulia and Birdsville on the eastern edge, grow the only waddy trees in the world. Tall, slender and drooping, they resemble casuarinas but are in fact a species of acacia, with a wood so hard that the original Andado homestead, which has a waddy framework, was wired rather than nailed together.

North Bore is one of the many tapping the Great Artesian Basin, which underlies much of the desert. In a few spots the pressure is so strong that the water bubbles naturally to the surface: one such is Dalhousie Springs on Mount Dare station, west of the desert. Water too hot to bathe in bubbles to the surface, spreading out in pools across the plain. There are rushes here, and tea tree, and once there were palms. The high mineral content of the water has raised a lip of clay and salts around the springs. Fish—catfish and spangled grunters 15 centimetres long—swim in the pool, prey for darters, herons and other waterbirds.

It is thought there may be oil associated with the basin, which is why the seismic crews have bulldozed a network of tracks across the western and southern parts of the desert. One of these, the French Track, leads across the desert from Alka Seltzer Bore almost to Poeppel Corner; it and two other tracks parallel to the South Australian–Northern Territory border are the normal routes chosen by travellers crossing the desert.

While desert crossings via these tracks are today relatively commonplace, one has only to venture off-track a few metres to rediscover the truth that Sturt learnt in 1845: this is the harshest land in Australia. An attempt to settle the desert west of the Mulligan was doomed to failure. Despite Lindsay's courageous expedition of 1886, the desert was not fully crossed until 1936, when Ted Colson of Bloods Creek station and an Aborigine named Peter set out with five camels to cross the desert to Birdsville. It had been a wet year, and Colson was gambling their lives on the belief that long-dormant seeds would sprout following rain. His theory proved correct: 16 days after leaving, the two men plodded into the single street that is Birdsville. They rested up, saddled their camels again and rode back home across the desert.

It was not until 1962 and the first years of the intensified oil search that a vehicular crossing of the desert was made. A five-vehicle team led by Geosurveys' Reg Sprigg, now owner of Arkaroola sanctuary, took ten days to cross from Andado to Birdsville. They took various routes, meeting up again on the South Australian border.

In the winter of 1973 (only fools and the foolhardy travel in summer, when the average daytime temperature is near 40°C), Charles McCubbin and Warren Bonython walked from Atula station, north of the desert, down the dunes to the Birdsville Track, towing a lightweight aluminium cart. And in May and June 1984, Adelaide adventurer Denis Bartell achieved the impossible: he walked alone and unaided across the desert from Dalhousie Springs to Birdsville, drawing water from old native wells.

One common misconception is that the Aborigines shunned the desert as 'a place of death'. In fact, as many as seven separate tribes inhabited the Simpson region. One of them, the Wonkanguru, occupied a vast tract of country stretching from Lake Eyre in the south along the Warburton and Eyre creeks as far as the present-day ruins of Annandale station in Queensland, and west into the Northern Territory as far as the longitude of Illogwa Creek. To their north lived the Wongkamala; to the east, the Lower Southern Aranda; to the north-east, the eastern Aranda; and to the west the Ngameni, Kaitanguru and Jeljendi.

Significantly, most of the Wongkanguru legends centre around water, as indeed their lives did. They camped around the chain of mickeries that Lindsay followed across the desert in 1886, and near the white sands of the Warburton. After rain, however, when water was temporarily plentiful, they would roam far and wide into the desert, hunting small mammals and reptiles, picking nardoo, yelkeri and munyeroo, falling back on the mickeries as the claypans dried out. The white man's arrival ended the proud, if difficult, history of these people. A series of infamous massacres in the 1880s by white police killed off hundreds of the desert dwellers. In 1901, during a particularly bad drought, the remnants of the Wongkanguru left the desert, splitting into three groups.

OPPOSITE, TOP LEFT Characteristic red colour of the sand is caused by iron oxide, which coats the grains as they are blown by the wind.
OPPOSITE, TOP RIGHT Descendants of wild camels, once used for Outback transport, still roam the desert. (Michael Richardson)
OPPOSITE, CENTRE RIGHT Spiky spinifex plant. Spinifex (*triodia* spp.) is the dominant vegetation in the desert, and is the main obstacle to cross-country travel. (Michael Richardson)
OPPOSITE, BOTTOM Saltwater channel threads through gypsum-encrusted dunes at the eastern edge of the desert. (Michael Richardson)

THE NORTHERN TERRITORY

Kings Canyon

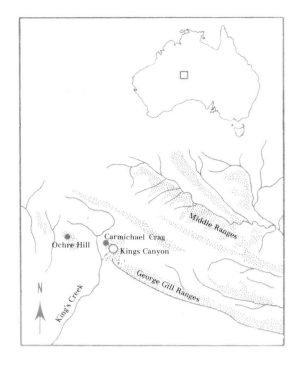

DURING Ernest Giles' first (1872) attempt to reach the west coast of Australia from the newly completed Overland Telegraph Line he bemoaned 'the facility with which other and more fortunate travellers dropped upon fine creeks and large rivers'. Subsequently, in retreat from the sterile surface of saline Lake Amadeus, he crossed a well-grassed, open valley, almost devoid of spinifex and bounded to the north by a red sandstone range of hills, and came upon 'a fine-looking creek, lined with gum-trees, [which] issued from a gorge'. Here Giles, one of the most tenacious Australian explorers, had reason to revise his opinion of his luck, for he found several pools of water in the gorge, including one 'fine little sheet of water . . . about 400 yards long and forty yards wide'. Giles called the creek Kings Creek, after Fieldon King, one of the backers of the expedition, and the high cliff to the west of it, towering over the grassy valley, Carmichaels Crag, after an expedition member. Subsequently the gorge has become known as Kings Canyon, and it has, somewhat optimistically, been compared to the Grand Canyon in the United States.

The Pitjantjatjara people, now living to the north-east at Areyonga, knew this oasis, 245 kilometres west-south-west of Alice Springs, as Watarka. It is one of a number of permanent springs and waterholes along the abrupt southern flank of the rugged, 70 kilometre long George Gill Range (misnamed 'George Giles' Range' by W. C. Gosse in his journal of his 1873 expedition). Giles discovered several of the other waterholes as well, their water pure and cool even on the hottest summer's day, their banks fertile with reeds, red gums, and clumps of wild tobacco.

Giles was lucky to find so much water in the lower canyon; his journal gives no indication that he visited the greatest treasure of all, the seemingly bottomless pools of water surrounded by fern-like cycads in the upper canyon, sheltered from the blazing heat of the sun by rock walls 30 metres high. This is the aptly named Garden of Eden, a paradise for weary travellers, reached by scrabbling up a steep, slippery path which winds up the north-western wall of the canyon entrance. At the top of the range, wind and rain have carved striking domes, shaped like the traditional beehive huts of southern Africa and up to 9 metres high, from the Mereenie sandstone. This 'Lost City' forms a maze of interconnecting pathways, shaded by ghost gums, mulga, blue mallee and cypress pines, and woe betide the traveller who strays off the marked 'roads': he may spend hours wandering the silent, kerbless streets, in fruitless search of paradise.

At several points the smooth sandstone floor breaks into telltale ripples, evidence that this area once lay underwater. The George Gill Ranges were laid down 350–400 million years ago and form an exposed part of the Mereenie sandstone formation. Their highest point is 870 metre high Carmichaels Crag. The canyon has been hewn from the rock along strong vertical joint planes, the upper canyon at a right angle to the lower and connected by an infrequently flowing waterfall.

The path down into Eden is tortuous, but the deep, limpid pools of water shaded by the primitive cycads and eucalypts provide ample reward. Along the valley floor, beyond the final pool, a rock ledge provides a natural grandstand for viewing the sheer-sided lower canyon. Short of abseiling, there is no way down: the rock pool below can only be reached by clambering up the boulder-strewn lower creek. Here there is evidence of past mighty floods, giant tree trunks tossed about like fiddlesticks, mighty boulders rolled about like marbles. Some of these rocks bear ripple marks, too, betraying their origin. River red gums and the occasional cycad grow on the canyon slopes. The cycad forms a link between true ferns and flowering plants. There are three genera: *Cycas*, *Macrozamia* and *Bowenia*; the central Australian species is *Macrozamia macdonnelli*. Most other members of the family are found in tropical and sub-tropical Australia.

After Giles and Gosse, few white men penetrated this isolated region until the early 1900s, when cattle stations were established. The stock would range out as far as Kings Canyon; beyond, they found the going as tough as had Giles. Englishman Jack Cotterill brought the first organised tour to Kings Canyon, in 1959. Two years later he founded Wallara Tourist Ranch, 100 kilometres east-south-east, and with difficulty graded a two-wheel-drive road around the edge of the George Gills, dragging lengths of railway line behind a modified Dodge weapons carrier. On a flat plain north of the ranges stands a lone oil drilling rig, Mereenie Two, a symbol of the white man's improvident society.

To the Pitjantjatjara, technology and its attendant concerns were unnecessary. They had their Dreamtime and they also had, in Watarka, one of the most beautiful oases in the outback.

OPPOSITE, TOP LEFT Deep, permanent pools of water are protected from the sun's rays by the high walls of the upper canyon.
OPPOSITE, BOTTOM LEFT Primitive cycads (*Macrozamia macdonnelli*) line the floor of the Garden of Eden.
OPPOSITE, RIGHT Sheer southern wall of the canyon follows a faultline through the George Gill range.

Ormiston Gorge and the MacDonnell Ranges

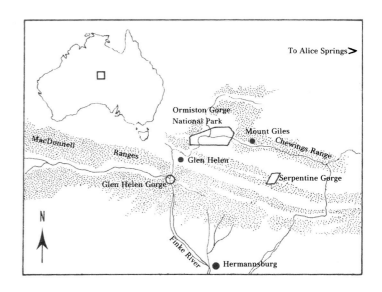

ORMISTON is possibly the most spectacular of the innumerable gorges slicing through the ancient MacDonnell Ranges in central Australia. To the local Aranda tribe it must have seemed like paradise, with its deep, pure waterholes, shady river red gums, and promise of game: euros, black-flanked rock wallabies, perenties, even fish like the spangled perch, which is able to survive periods of drought buried deep in the mud of the creek bed. The Aranda believed that Ormiston and Glen Helen gorges were home to friendly serpents, but they were reportedly less enthusiastic about the giant snakes said to inhabit the nearby Serpentine, Ellery and Redbank gorges. All these gorges have been eroded through the ranges by tributaries of the Finke River, that timeless meandering stream known to the Aranda as Larapinta. Ormiston Creek is one of two headwater tributaries of the Finke: the other, which rises on Mount Razorback, is the Davenport.

The geology of the area is shown in cross-section on the walls of the gorges. The towering, 250 metre high cliffs of Ormiston Gorge are primarily Heavitree quartzite, some grey like slate, most stained rust-red like the sands of the desert. Successive earth movements have created two distinct layers of rock, one overlying the other. Beneath these metamorphosed sandstones, laid down beneath a shallow sea in the Amadeus Basin 850 million years ago, lie the schists and gneisses of the Arunta Block, the Northern Territory's oldest known rock group, born in fire more than 2000 million years ago.

The Heavitree quartzite is the most ancient unit in the Amadeus Basin. Sediments continued to be deposited for 500 million years, to a depth of up to 9000 metres. Then, perhaps 350 million years ago, there was widespread earth movement along a 300 kilometre, east-west plane, pushing the older rocks upwards and southwards by as much as 14 kilometres. Where the folded sedimentary rocks remained uppermost, in the southern and eastern ranges, erosion has been relatively uniform and from the air the sweeping curves of the bevelled hills resemble a giant, humped caterpillar wriggling across the landscape. But where the pre-existing streams crossed the more resistant quartzite, erosion has affected only a narrow zone, in the case of Ormiston Gorge along two fault lines.

At the entrance to the gorge is a deep, permanent waterhole that refills when rain clouds gather over Ormiston Gorge, and the creek flows to its destiny with the Finke. The sand is coarse and rasps underfoot; it soon gives way to strands of quartzite, criss-crossed with lines like cubed cheese. The grey metamorphic stratum vanishes, dipping beneath the sand like a wombat burrowing. There are more pools of water, and then the gorge turns abruptly south-east as it follows the second fault line. So riven are the cliffs by horizontal and vertical fissures, so acute the angles, it seems impossible that they should remain intact. The evidence that they—and other cliffs further along the creek line—sometimes crumble is everywhere. Walking becomes a perpetual game of hopscotch, jumping from one boulder to another.

And then suddenly the gorge begins to open out. An undulating valley appears, littered with stones and spinifex, surrounded by purple mountains. This is Ormiston Pound, dominated by Mount Giles, 1285 metres high. The creek forks, east and north. If you strike out away from the creeks, to the centre of the 10 kilometre wide pound, the saucer-like emptiness can become as lonely as any gibber plain.

Ormiston Gorge follows two distinct fault lines through the ranges. It rises in Ormiston Pound, a 10-kilometre wide amphitheatre dominated by 1285 metre high Mount Giles (background).

Low scrub, including the yellow-flowered curry acacia, the crushed leaves of which have the bittersweet smell of curry, grows between the spinifex clumps. Mount Giles, named after the moustachioed explorer who passed this way in 1872, is 17 kilometres away on foot. From the surveyor's beacon on top of the mountain, the dramatic landscape of the MacDonnell Ranges spreads before the observer. To the west and north-west rise the looming masses of Mount Zeil (1510 metres) and Mount Sonder (1380 metres). One hundred and thirty kilometres to the east, beyond the noonday flicker of Standley Chasm and the Namatjira purples of Simpsons Gap, lies Alice Springs, named in 1871 by John Ross, Overland Telegraph surveyor, after the wife of the South Australian Superintendent of Telegraphs, Charles Todd. It was originally a repeater station for the 3000 kilometre line.

The Overland Telegraph was completed in late 1872, only 12 years after the doughty Scots explorer, John McDouall Stuart, first put the MacDonnell Ranges on European maps. Stuart, on the first of three expeditions he was to make in his ultimately successful bid to cross the continent from south to north, named the only major mountain range in central Australia after Governor Sir Richard MacDonnell of South Australia, 'as a token of gratitude for his kindness to me', and noted its potential as pastoral country. He entered the ranges near Brinkleys Bluff, and found the going tough, making only 8 kilometres in one day. On his final expedition it rained heavily, reinforcing Stuart's favourable impression of the country.

Only two years later Stuart died of the privations he had endured, but the trail he blazed and the telegraph line that closely followed it were to open up the inland. In 1877 Lutheran missionaries founded Hermannsburg, 34 kilometres south of Ormiston Gorge, bringing with them 3000 sheep and 17 cattle. Several other cattle properties had already been established by land-hungry settlers. The pace hotted up when gold was discovered in 1887 at Arltunga in the eastern MacDonnells, beyond the sacred spire of Corroboree Rock and the art galleries of N'Dhala Gorge. And the proud Aranda, who had owned this land, with its broad, mulga-covered plains, its red cliffs and permanent waterholes, since before recorded time, were eventually relegated to the missions and reserves, their place taken by cattlemen and tourists.

BELOW Scalloped ridges of southern MacDonnell Ranges resemble a giant, humped caterpillar wriggling across the landscape.
OPPOSITE Cracks in the quartzite of Ormiston Gorge have allowed wildflowers to gain a toehold.

Palm Valley and the Finke River

FINKE Gorge National Park qualifies for inclusion in any list of Australia's natural wonders on two counts: the Finke River flowing through it is reputed to be the world's oldest river still occupying its original bed; and in the bed of the Finke and of several tributaries within the park grow 3000 red-leafed cabbage palms, the unique species *Livistona mariae*, nearly 1000 kilometres from their nearest relatives at Mataranka. Here, in the dry heat of central Australia, the palms grow as straight-boled as those on any South Pacific island, often rubbing fronds against that stately monarch of inland Australian waterways, the red river gum. The nearby sand may be the oxide-encrusted red of the desert, but the palms look as strong and healthy as any in the well-watered tropics. Cypress pines, mulga and spinifex crowd the steep slopes above.

Ernest Giles, plodding up the bed of the Finke in the winter of 1872, was 'gratified'—and quite possibly perplexed as well—to come across his first palm tree, which he did not 'expect to meet in this latitude'. The tree was 18 metres high 'in the barrel', and there were more to come. Giles named the spot the Glen of Palms; it is 12 kilometres downstream from the present-day ranger station on Palm Creek. But Giles missed completely the greatest concentration of palms, in a narrow gorge on this creek beyond the natural feature known as the Amphitheatre. Here, as recently as 60 years ago, the local Aranda tribesmen gathered to hold their secret initiation rites, probably much to the consternation of the Lutheran missionaries at Hermannsburg mission, 20 kilometres to the north.

It was a Lutheran missionary who, it is said, riding a camel to a picnic, stumbled upon Palm Valley soon after the mission was established. That tale may be apocryphal, but the Lutherans were certainly the first Europeans to glimpse the shady gorge in the Krichauff Ranges, 130 kilometres east-south-east of Alice Springs.

The palms flourished in this low-rainfall zone because of water stored by the 350-million-year-old Pertnjara sandstones and gradually released in times of drought to quench the trees' thirst. White pockets of calcium carbonate collect where the water seeps through the rock. The palms prefer the tributaries to the broader bed of the Finke itself, however, as the ancient river, although normally dry, occasionally floods and sweeps away any seedlings in its path. It happened only a few years ago in Palm Valley, when teeming rain turned the normally tranquil pools of water into an angry torrent, tearing out by the roots 68 palms. Despite natural disasters and the extreme age of many of the palms—it takes nearly three years for a seedling to gain its first fan, and mature specimens are 250–400 years old—the palm trees are thriving, the more so because the Aborigines abandoned eating the tender inner core of young palm trees in favour of 'white man's tucker'. Botanists theorise that these trees, along with the fern-like cycads that also flourish in the valley, are relics of a wetter age when central Australia was a tropical paradise.

Safari operator Len Tuit thought the area so idyllic that he established a 'chalet' on Kunana Creek in the early 1950s. There was also an Ansett chalet on the site of the present camping area. Neither survived the creation of the 47 000 hectare Finke Gorge National Park in 1967. Palm Valley occupies only a small corner of the park and for its next meandering 40 kilometres the sandy bed of the Finke River runs within the park. It is an awesome thought that this straggling watercourse, usually no more than a necklace of waterholes, may have occupied essentially the same bed for the past 350 million years, the age of the rocks through which it flows. By comparison, the mighty Colorado River with its sledgehammer muscle is a mere tot: no more than 21 million years old. Once, when central Australia was fertile and the mountains tall, the Finke was a jostling river that may have flowed strong and deep all the way to the southern coastline.

To the Aranda tribe the Finke was Larapinta, a river bed formed by the twisting and turning of a giant serpent. Its white discoverer, John MacDouall Stuart, named it more prosaically, after William Finke, an Adelaide landholder who was one of the backers of his expeditions. Stuart's first encounter with the Finke was near Mount Humphries, more than 250 kilometres downstream from the Glen of Palms and, although the nearby countryside impressed him greatly, the creek 'with the finest gum-trees we have yet seen, all sizes and heights' apparently did not. He left it on a bearing of 329° and when its meandering path crossed his again two days later, he did not recognise it. 'At six miles we got to one of the largest gum creeks I have yet seen,' he wrote in his journal. 'It was much the same as the one we saw on the 4th . . .' Unfortunately, the water made the sandy bed very soft and Stuart's horses experienced considerable difficulty crossing it. He was also concerned that the sand indicated that the river rose in a desert, and so chose to follow a tributary, the Hugh, to the north.

The Finke rises in the MacDonnell Ranges, 45 kilometres north of Palm Creek. By the time it enters the national park it has already travelled 100 kilometres from its source. It has another 500 kilometres to go through the grey-brown James Ranges, past Henbury meteorite craters, through sand dunes, more hills and bunch-grass flats, the red gums and box gums and regrowth thick and lush, until it disappears into its sea. A strange sea, this: the waves 20 metres high, and blood-red in the noon-day sun. The Finke vanishes all right: into the implacable sands of the Simpson Desert, a lone box gum the cross on its grave. This is the Styx, the river of Hell, although to sit amongst the red gums by Boggy Hole, 31 kilometres south of Palm Creek, fishing for grunter (the fish are evidence that the river once connected with the ocean), a flight of black swans skimming the tranquil waters, is to experience yet another paradox of the centre. Only in an exceptionally wet season will the waters of the Finke reach the soft surface of Lake Eyre.

The Finke River Valley is also potentially the powerhouse of central Australia: it lies on the edge of the oil- and gas-rich Mereenie Basin. Natural gas in commercial quantities was found here in 1965, but any development that threatened that even more precious phenomenon, the 3000 palms of the desert, would of course be impossible.

Livistona mariae **palms growing in Palm Valley are nearly 1000 kilometres from their nearest relatives.**

Mount Conner

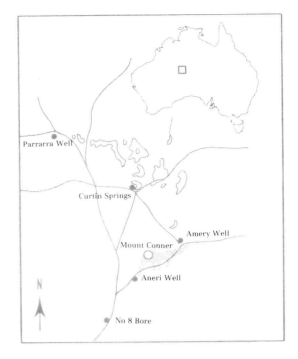

No tourist buses visit Mount Conner, the 'Cinderella' of the three great tors. They whirl by on the way to Ayers Rock, stopping only to allow passengers a few minutes to capture Mount Conner on film, at a distance.

Yet this mountain has its own mantle of uniqueness, sufficient to justify the 40 kilometre detour off the main road. It is a perfectly shaped mesa, a flat-topped, 343 metre high mountain that has remained after the surrounding countryside has been eroded away. Standing as it does, apparently alone on the vast flat sand-ridge plains of central Australia, it is immediately distinctive. Other remnants of the ancient (700 million years old) Proterozoic rocks of which it is made remain as a low, ragged cliff line, to the north-west, scarcely higher than the red desert dunes.

Although the mesa is composed of the same Amadeus Basin sediments as Ayers Rock and the Olgas, it is not part of the same structure. The soft sandstone is held together by a tough siliceous capping. As the underlying rock succumbs to the destructive forces of wind and water, the capping breaks away, crashing down onto rubble and scree slopes that surround the mountain like giant sand drifts.

To the north, Mount Conner's 100 metre high cliffs present an unbroken wall as solid and unconquerable as the great limestone cliffs of the Nullarbor. Below them lies a group of ephemeral claypans, called *puntus* by the Aborigines and beneath the surface of which, they believed, lived the *ninya*, or icemen, who brought the chill winds and white frosts of winter, creeping out while the sun-woman was wandering to the north. They knew Mount Conner as Adtilla. Here left-handed Linggi of the yellow lizard totem threw his *karlee* of light from the east. It soared into the sky like the sun that now follows its path, Linggi racing beneath it, then, feet astride, leaping into the air, thereby forming the great tor.

Mount Conner was named for South Australian parliamentarian M. L. Conner. William Christie Gosse sighted it on 18 July 1873, from near Ayers Rock, but did not approach it. The following year Ernest Giles passed close by, but thought it unclimbable. And so it is, to all but experienced rock climbers and those who skirt around its 14 kilometre perimeter to the southern face. Here several creek lines have gouged ravines in the conglomerate. In places the cliff face almost vanishes and can be scaled by agile humans, or the euros and rock wallabies that live on the mountain.

Eucalypts growing along the gorges betray the presence of water but the gullies are usually dry. There is supposed to be a permanent spring, which is notoriously difficult to locate. Mulga and grevillea crowd the tableland and although this is no lost world of Conan Doyle's imagination, replete with dinosaurs and hostile natives, in some ways the mysterious plateau of the English author's classic tale is similar to Mount Conner: deep caves tunnel into the cliffs, some of them 100 metres or more long, their floors piled with pitch-like bat dung. Outside, wedge-tailed eagles soar on the updraughts above the immense scree slopes and the spinifex and rubble-strewn plain.

Ten kilometres west of the mountain, a lonely windmill creaks amid the willy-willies spiralling off the claypans, and the crumbling walls of an abandoned homestead frame the great red mesa. This is Mount Conner homestead, once partially dug into a sand dune and established there because of the good artesian water supply. Giles described this country as a 'perfect desert', yet pioneers eked out a precarious existence from it, here in the shadow of Mount Conner, their stock nuzzling the hot sand for 'pick'. For thousands of years before them, the Luridtja people visited Adtilla, hunting the euro, harvesting the green pituri leaves from the creek gorges, and camping amongst the ironwoods and white-cypress pines.

Mount Conner is a perfectly shaped, flat topped mesa.
(Michael Richardson)

Rainbow Valley

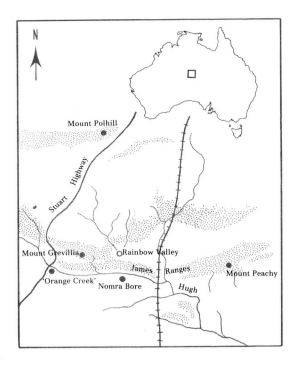

IN the late afternoon sun there is a surrealistic quality to the coloured ramparts of Rainbow Valley: it would not be altogether surprising to see a Tanguy-conceived solid black prism guarding the entrance to the valley, or a kangaroo riding a unicycle. This little-known spot, so unusual that even to the geologist its provenance is uncertain, is a composite of chalcedonic limestone, siltstone and calcareous sandstone in the James Ranges, 70 kilometres south-west of Alice Springs.

It appears that the silent, jagged cliff face could only have been carved out by explosives, or the pounding might of the sea. But man's only intrusion is the rough track in, and the only water lies a few centimetres deep in the claypan at the cliff base after drenching rain. The flat, unending spinifex- and mulga-covered plains extend to the northern horizon.

The urge to climb to the top of the weathered, 80 metre high crag is compelling. The northern face, its pink, white and red walls chisel-cut like quarry walls, is unscalable without the aid of climbing tackle but the sandy creek bed that flows into the claypan offers a possible route. The creek has cut through the range, leaving the multi-coloured rock face isolated, a saw-tooth remnant left after the hill has been hacked through with a blunt knife. Scalloped boulders, their edges rounded by millennia of erosion, litter the lower slopes at the rear of the bluff; one, pierced through by weathering, frames the path to the summit, a spinifex-encrusted ramp of drifting sand. The short, sharp climb reveals that there is a valley after all, a deceptively fertile-looking dale to the south-east. From this vantage point the joint lines in the rock face are clearly evident, the 30 metre high cliffs as vertical as the side of a house. Standing defiantly atop the battlements are three defending acacias, their weapons the giant cracks in the ramparts that threaten to crush besiegers beneath tonnes of falling rock. Sun-fired flames flicker upwards towards the battlements, intersected by spearpoints of shadow. And then, suddenly, the fire is extinguished, the attackers melt away, the colours fade into a dull brown, then grey, and Rainbow Valley slumbers until awoken again by the sun.

BELOW Multi-coloured walls of Rainbow Valley are a composite of various sedimentary rocks. (Michael Richardson)
RIGHT A featureless, sandy plain extends from Rainbow Valley to the Stuart Highway. (Michael Richardson)

Chambers Pillar

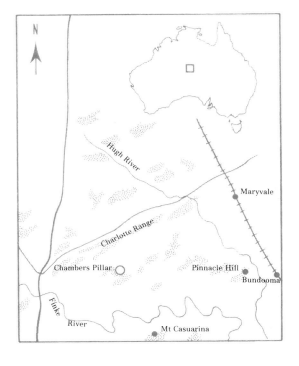

ON the flat, baked red plains of central Australia molehills become mountains as small hills and prominences float in the shimmering mirages. Small ironstone hills only 15 metres high become important landmarks in the northern Simpson Desert. Even more prominent is a sandstone butte on the edge of the desert, 125 kilometres north of the South Australian border, west of the railway line to Alice Springs. Only 45 metres high, and 3–6 metres thick, it is nevertheless sufficiently distinctive to have been used as a landmark by early explorers travelling up the Finke River to the MacDonnell Ranges.

John MacDouall Stuart was the first white man to see this remarkable monolith, on 6 April 1860. Stuart's reputation is as an explorer, not an author, but his succinct description of the pillar as 'a locomotive with its funnel' has yet to be bettered—the pillar's top is split in two and bears an uncanny resemblance to the coroneted smokestack of Stephenson's Rocket. Certainly Giles, who had some literary pretensions, did not improve on Stuart's description when, passing by in 1872, he wrote:

> . . . its outline was most imposing. Upon reaching it, I found it to be a columnar structure, standing upon a pedestal, which is perhaps eighty feet high, and composed of loose white sandstones, having vast numbers of large blocks lying about in all directions. From the centre of the pedestal rises the pillar, composed also of the same kind of rock; at its top, and for twenty to thirty feet from its summit, the colour of the stone is red. The column itself must be seventy or eighty feet above the pedestal. It is split at the top into two points.

Giles cut his name into the friable sandstone with a pocket knife, and expressed concern that he might be hit by a falling rock. Generations of visitors since have followed his example, vandalising this unique monument. Some of the graffiti are dated as early as 1853, although this is not likely to be accurate because Stuart was the first white man to find a passage to the north through the Lake Torrens 'horseshoe', in 1860.

Stuart named the pillar after James Chambers of Adelaide, one of the chief backers of his expeditions. (He also honoured his patron by naming Chambers Creek, a small stream flowing into Lake Eyre South and which proved to be the gateway to the north, but it was subsequently renamed Stuart Creek.) He commented in his journal about the other 'remarkable hills' to the north and north-east, like the pillar, breakaways from the nearby Charlotte Range which 'resemble nothing so much as a number of old castles in ruins'.

Chambers Pillar is a butte, an isolated remnant of ancient highlands, some say eaten away by a sea, others time. It is virtually the southernmost sentinel of the great folded Palaeozoic mountain ranges of the centre. The sheer-sided tower, similar in aspect to a volcanic plug, although created in an entirely different manner, is formed from a more massive sandstone than the sloping, rock-strewn pedestal on which it sits. Fifteen kilometres to the south-west, across the mulga-encrusted sandhills, stands Idracowra station, called after the Aranda name for the butte, Itirkawara. According to Professor Ted Strehlow, Itirkawara was a mythical gecko ancestor who as a young man had travelled north-east from Tjina into Queensland. During his travels he became a huge, powerfully built man of superhuman strength, with a violent temper—not a man to cross. On his way home, he cut in two several other totemic ancestors who had the misfortune to meet up with him. Pride comes before a fall, it is said, and so it was with Itirkawara. In his arrogance he broke the strict moral code of his people, having sexual relations with girls who belonged to the kinship group from which only his mother-in-law should have come, and even bringing one such girl into the camp at Tjina as his wife. His relatives banished him and the girl to the sandhills north of the river, where they turned into stone: Itirkawara into the upright pillar which bears his name, the girl into a low hill 400 metres away.

In legend the girl averted her gaze in shame from her lover, but today's visitors are far more likely to stare at him in wonderment. Chambers Pillar is part of the collage of uniqueness that makes the Dreamtime landscapes of central Australia as memorable for us as they were for their traditional owners.

Chambers Pillar was described by John Macdouall Stuart as 'a locomotive with its funnel'. A more apt metaphor has yet be be found.

THE NORTHERN TERRITORY

Ayers Rock

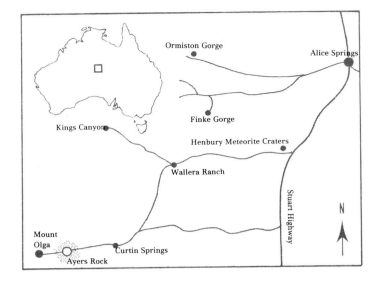

THE Rock is as magnificent as its status as Australia's third greatest tourist attraction would suggest. (The first two are Sydney and the Great Barrier Reef.) Ever since it was first sighted by William Christie Gosse in 1873, Ayers Rock has remained a source of wonder for white visitors. Gosse, on his way to nearby Mount Olga (sighted by Ernest Giles in the previous year) and, hopefully, to the west coast, was amazed to find that 'the hill east of Olga' mentioned in Giles' journal and which he first saw on 18 July was, in fact, 'one immense rock rising abruptly from the plain'. It was a good season; Gosse, with some difficulty, climbed the rock, and found water in all the rock holes on the way up; it was also 'pouring down' into the permanent spring at the rock's base, Mutidjula. 'This rock,' he wrote in his diary, 'is certainly the most wonderful natural feature I have ever seen.'

Geologically, Ayers Rock is the largest monolith in the world, but this bland statement of fact does no justice to its vastness, to its ever-changing moods, to the sheer majesty of its creation. Its oneness is a product of the lack of joint planes along which accelerated erosion can take place, and of its composition of a feldspar-rich sandstone called arkose that closely resembles granite in structure (Gosse, in fact, incorrectly described it as such).

Twelve hundred million years ago, the landscape in central Australia was a massive, folded composite of igneous and metamorphic rocks. Sediments were laid down on these hard yet eroding gneisses, granites and lavas. New upheavals during the Petermann Ranges Orogeny, 600 million years ago, twisted and folded the rocks into high mountain ranges which themselves began to erode. From high up the mountains

BELOW **The Rock changes mood with the time of day. Even at night, its presence can be felt.**
RIGHT **Maggie Springs (Mutidjula) is fed by water seeping from a rock pool in the gully above. (Michael Richardson)**
PAGE 55, **Rain pouring down the Rock gouges grooves and furrows in the gritty arkose, giving life to the trees and shrubs which ring its base.**

came the boulders and pebbles that became the Olga conglomerate, while the sandy material from further down the slopes became the more uniform arkose of the Rock, interspersed rarely with bands of conglomerate. These sediments, laid down under water, are at least 600 metres thick. Later earth movements tilted the rock, about 30 degrees at the Olgas and 75 degrees at Ayers Rock. Subsequent erosion has left the giant tors standing above a sea of red sand. In the Cretaceous period, a lake lapped the base of the Rock, gouging out bays and caves.

Yet the more the Rock changes, the more it remains unchanged. A continuous erosion process known as spalling, flakes peeling off the rock surface, creates a smooth, rounded surface. The Rock is shrinking, but at a uniform rate, so that in 50 million years from now it will still assume the same outline. The 'Kangaroo Tail', on the northern side of the Rock, is actually a huge spall that has slipped down the rock face; differential curvature has left a gap beneath.

Gosse named the Rock after the then Premier of South Australia, Sir Henry Ayers. But to the local Aborigines, the Luridtja, members of the Pitjantjatjara tribe, it was Uluru, a name now given to the 126 132 hectare national park that encompasses both Ayers Rock and the Olgas. To them, Uluru symbolised life, but the mountain itself was not secret or taboo. Within the Rock the *tjukurapa* (creation) heroes rest and wait to re-emerge.

According to the Luridtja, Uluru rose miraculously from a large flat sandhill at the close of the *tjukurapa* period. Ten different totemic mythical beings created the varied topography of the giant red monolith. Much of the southern face was created by the battle between the *kunia* (carpet snakes) and the *liru* (poisonous snakes). Mutidjula, for example, is filled with water sent flowing down the rock face by the spirit of a *kunia* man who bled to death there following a fight with the leader of the *liru*. (The water seeps down from a large rock hole above the spring.) Features on the drier northern face were created largely by the *mala* (hare-wallabies). The Luridtja, accordingly, were divided into two totemic groups: the *kunia*, whose territory extended along the southern (shady) face of the Rock; and the *mala*, who lived along the northern side.

Permanent waterholes like Mutidjula were essential to the survival of the Pitjantjatjara people; Mutidjula was also the only water supply of the first ranger, Bill Harney, when he arrived at the Rock in 1957.

Ayers Rock lies in a region of 250 millimetre average annual rainfall, with an evaporation rate 12 times as high. The rain is erratic and unpredictable. Ten other waterholes at Ayers Rock provide alternative supplies, depending on the season. But few soaks or waterholes are permanent in the vast Pitjantjatjara country, which extends from the Musgrave Ranges in South Australia north to Lake Amadeus and east to the Basedow Ranges. Most of this country is desert, dominated by parallel red sand ridges and covered with spinifex and low scrub, interspersed with drooping she-oaks.

In this flat, featureless landscape, the Rock, which rises 348 metres above the desert and is 8.9 kilometres in circumference, is awe-inspiring, a fist punching upwards, knuckles to the south. To come upon the Rock at night is perhaps the most unforgettable experience of all. The road in joins the circuit road south-west of the Rock. Through a dust-coated windscreen you sense, rather than see, the Rock's presence. Then you suddenly realise that the blackness blotting out half of the night sky is real and solid: a giant Sphinx rearing up above the darkened plain. From this time until you leave, the Rock will dominate your life; like the blue-arched sky, it is always there.

Like William Gosse, three-quarters of the visitors to the Rock climb to the summit. Thirteen people have died making the pilgrimage to the cairn at the top, five through heart attacks, eight by tumbling down the mottled red walls. The gritty arkose actually gives the surface of the Rock a rough sandpaper-like texture: Gosse blistered the soles of his bare feet so badly that afterwards he could barely stand.

The view from the top is a poor reward for effort. On a hot summer day, when you are buffeted by searing winds, the roughly painted dotted white line seems to lead on for ever, like some nightmare paper chase. The pockmarks of the weathered surface often contain water; grass, mulga and hopbush sprout from soil collecting in hollows and clefts. Spiders, insects, lizards and small mammals inhabit these miniature worlds hundreds of metres above the desert floor. Wedge-tailed eagles soar above the Rock, keen eyes searching for a telltale hop or scuttle. Remarkably, after rain, tiny crustaceans—shield shrimps—hatch from eggs laid in the mud of the drying pools.

And the rain pours down from those pools during and after heavy showers, caressing the Rock with a thousand silver streamers, channelling deep grooves and furrows, streaking the red rock with black ribbons, splashing onto the parched soil. Among the jumbled boulders that are the visible evidence of the mountain's decay, new life is generated. Small eucalypts grow among the bloodwoods and wattles. Zebra finches dart above the waterholes where the larger marsupials may come at dusk to drink.

As the myths relate, the Rock gave life to the Luridtja, as it did to thousands of other creatures. Here, in the caves at its base, they were born, cooked their food, carried out their sacred rituals, painted the walls with overlapping designs in ochre, pipeclay and charcoal, and died. Yet within 60 years of Gosse's 'discovery' most of them had left their traditional way of life, drifting away to the missions and cattle stations. Their place was taken by tourists, in far larger numbers.

Yet not even the commercialism that has swollen tourist numbers twentyfold since the national park was first proclaimed in 1958 can destroy the spell cast by the Rock. Of all Australia's natural wonders, Ayers Rock best symbolises the unchanging nature of a harsh and timeless land. If one must see Naples to die, then one must surely see Ayers Rock to live . . . in awe of the forces of creation.

THE NORTHERN TERRITORY

Katherine Gorge

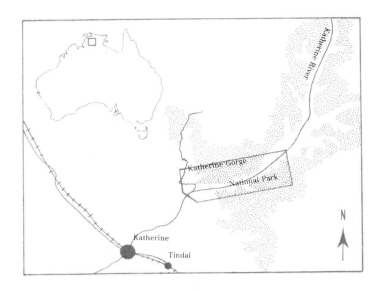

HAD Charles Darwin visited the Northern Territory during the *Beagle*'s famous round-the-world voyage he would have found for his theory of natural selection evidence as valuable as that provided by his observations of the Galapagos Islands. For it is believed that the freshwater (Johnston River) crocodiles inhabiting Katherine Gorge are pygmies, considerably smaller than their fellows who live outside the gorge. The reason? The bigger crocodiles cannot fit on the narrow banks inside the gorge, and food supplies there are only sufficient to support smaller animals. The only time big male crocodiles are seen inside the gorge is during the mating season, in August–September, and even then they do not exceed 2 metres in length. Specimens have been recorded elsewhere at over 3 metres, a significant difference.

Each of Katherine's 13 gorges has its own character. The second gorge is deep and narrow; in May, fairy martins build their nests in caves uncovered by the receding waters.

White men did not pass through the Katherine Gorge area until 1862. The explorers were led by John McDouall Stuart, travelling fast on his third attempt to cross the continent from north to south. Sixteen days after naming the Katherine River after Katherine Chambers, daughter of a backer of the expedition, Stuart achieved his goal, reaching the Timor Sea east of the Adelaide River.

The Katherine River rises in Arnhem Land and flows some 322 kilometres west to join the Timor Sea at Anson Bay; the gorge cuts deep into the edge of the Arnhem Land plateau, 180 kilometres from the river's source. This was the country of the Djauan people, who lived close to the banks of the river, where food and water were plentiful. They left their mark in Dreamtime paintings in sheltered positions on the walls of the gorge.

Since 1963 Katherine Gorge has been incorporated into a national park now encompassing 180 000 hectares of wilderness. The gorge (actually a series of 13 gorges, each with its own special character) was incised 25 million years ago into the Kombolgie sandstone of the plateau, the river zig-zagging along the fault lines in the rock. The 1800 million year old Kombolgie formation overlies igneous rocks (the Edith River volcanics) of similar age. Both rock groups have folded into a gentle syncline, the Kombolgie conglomerate at the base of the formation dipping underwater at the beginning of the gorge, to reappear some 20 kilometres upstream in conjunction with the volcanic rocks.

At the end of the 2.5 kilometre long first gorge, passage is blocked by a rock bar. Boats for use in the spectacular second, third and fourth gorges are carried across the bar at the beginning of the dry season, to be rescued again before the first of the wet season floods arrives. Here sandstone rubble litters the flats, much of it bearing ripple marks of wave and current action, indicating that the plateau was once underwater.

The 1.8 kilometre second gorge and the much less frequently visited fifth gorge are very similar: 90 metre sheer walls only 40 metres apart, the occasional narrow strip of sand, perhaps at the base of a shimmering waterfall, the sun peeping in for only a few minutes around noon. As the water level drops each May, fairy martins painstakingly build their bottle-shaped nests on the roofs of the emerging caves. Each November, the river swells and the floodwaters race inexorably through the gorge, inundating the caves and washing the nests downstream.

A rock bar at the end of the first gorge bars further progress by boat. (Michael Richardson)

The river is home to 39 species of fish, including barramundi, long toms, freshwater sharks and freshwater swordfish. They provide the staple diet of the crocodiles, which are timid and have never been known to pose a threat to man.

Immediately below the first gorge, the Katherine River is joined by a major tributary, Seventeen Mile Creek. Here, among the reeds, paperbarks and pandanus trees, is a favourite haunt of the freshwater crocodile. The Seventeen Mile valley is all composed of volcanic rock, mainly dark basalt. At the Amphitheatre, near the head of the valley, are sandstones of more recent (Cretaceous) origin, speckled with fossilised leaves. Like the Katherine River, Seventeen Mile Creek is a perennial stream. During the seven-month dry season it is fed by water draining from pockets of sand on top of the rough, weathered plateau, which soak up the 950 millimetre annual rainfall like giant sponges.

The plateau soils are stabilised by low heath over-storeyed by eucalypts, predominantly bloodwoods. Occasional palm trees appear in crevices in the sandstone; they are more plentiful on the sunnier banks of the gorge. On the sloping edges of the gorge walls, tenacious native figs and ferns thrive in the moist environment.

Some writers suggest that Katherine Gorge will one day rival Ayers Rock as the major tourist attraction in the Northern Territory. Should that day come, it will still be possible to get 'far from the madding crowd'. Katherine Gorge National Park, with its 100 kilometres of walking trails, its deep, quiet pools of water, its laughing waterfalls, and its abundant wildlife, will still be big enough for all.

BELOW, LEFT The fan palm (*Livistona inermis*) grows to a height of 10 metres on the ledges and banks of the gorges.
BELOW, RIGHT A St Andrew's Cross spider (*Argiope spp.*) weaves its distinctive web.
BOTTOM Leaves collect in a tranquil backwater of the Katherine River.
OPPOSITE A passenger launch crawls, insect-like, along the surface of the first gorge. (Michael Richardson)

THE NORTHERN TERRITORY

The Olgas

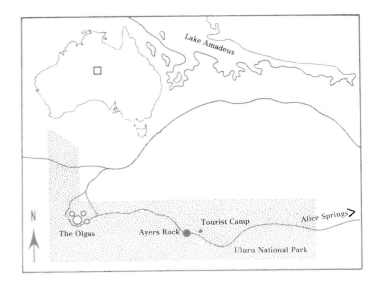

THE most remote of the three great tors was in fact the first to be recorded by white man. Ernest Giles was the explorer who named the highest peak of the group Mount Olga after an 'enlightened royal patron of science', the Queen of Spain. It was 1872, and Giles was on the first of five expeditions to the west of the recently completed Overland Telegraph Line. His journey had taken him from Charlotte Waters repeater station, now a squat ruin on the gibber flats east of Abminga Siding, north-west in a long sweep that brought him to the north of the great tors, and the island-studded Lake Amadeus. Peninsulas jutting into the briny, boggy surface offered Giles some hope of a route south but each time he came up against the lake again and was forced to retreat.

Thus it was left to William Christie Gosse, who named the two other great tors, Ayers Rock and Mount Conner, to be the first white man to reach the Olgas, in August 1873. The great, rounded domes seemed to make surprisingly little impression on Gosse, who matter-of-factly recorded in his journal that he 'walked to the top of one of the high rocks this afternoon', and that the view was 'similar to that seen from Ayers Rock'.

A month later, on his second journey, Ernest Giles finally reached the Olgas, where he found traces of Gosse's expedition. He waxed poetic about the feature he had named.

> Mount Olga . . . displayed to our astonished eyes rounded minarets, giant cupolas, and monstrous domes . . . I can only liken Mount Olga to several enormous rotund or rather elliptical shapes of rouge mange, which had been placed beside one another by some extraordinary freak or convulsion of Nature.

Later, on his 1874 expedition, Giles was to describe the Olgas from the west as being 'like the backs of several monstrous kneeling pink elephants', and 546 metre high Mount Olga as presenting 'the appearance of a gigantic pink damper'. But he was wrong when he suggested that 'Time, the old, the dim magician, has ineffectually laboured here; Mount Olga has remained as it was born . . .' We know now that those extraordinary domes and helmets are the result of weathering: vertical joint planes in a solid mountain of conglomerate, formed by the same process as the Ayers Rock arkose, have been the focal points for erosion, which has created deep, steep-sided valleys and gorges.

To the local Aborigines, the Luridtja, this was Katajuta, many heads, and it was a place of mystery and legend. A 300 metre high plinth of stone on the eastern wall of Mount Olga is known as the Malakarta, the headman of the creation period. The small hills to the south-east are the *mingarri*, or mice-women, who were deflowered by the mighty Pungalung, a hero from the west. His bones still lie as boulders in the valley that bears his name.

The heartland of the Olgas is the Valley of the Winds, beyond the sacred Bubia Valley where once only the spiritual elders of the tribe could gather. A well-defined track leads up to Bubia Creek past finches swooping on semi-permanent pools of water. Ancient eucalypts line the creek. Above a low rock ledge the gorge opens out into a narrow, apparently dead-end valley. Here the creek rises, impelled by the precipitous slopes of Ngungarra and Bubia. Suddenly an opening appears in the rock to the east; a short, sharp climb to the top of a saddle and the Valley of the Winds is revealed, spinifex and mulga whispering messages to the watchful *mingarri*.

To many it is the Olgas, not Ayers Rock, that is the more interesting formation. There is more variety in the shadowy canyons and multiple peaks, and a mystical femininity to the great, rounded shapes, glowing red and orange, cooling to blue and grey and purple. Seeming flashes of light from the hillsides are clumps of yellow spinifex catching the rays of the sun. Lichen and algae create vivid red, green, black and orange patterns on the face of Liru Mountain.

Inside Mount Olga lives Wanambi, the rainbow serpent who, when tribal indiscretions occur, vents his anger by blowing mightily through the gorges and then soaring into the sky. There are few smooth-walled caves where the legends may be recorded in ochre, but around several waterholes there are petroglyphs which the Aborigines say are the work of their spirit ancestors. So powerful are the creation myths that the Kunapippi earth-mother ritual chants which had their genesis in the sacred valley of Bubia are repeated on the northern coastline of the Territory.

BELOW The Olgas' many heads.
RIGHT Deep valleys in the rock have been eroded along fault lines. Spinifex and shrubs cling to pockets of soil on the hill tops.

THE NORTHERN TERRITORY

The Devils Marbles

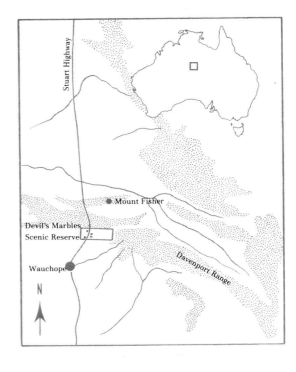

IN the spectacular MacDonnell Ranges, just west of Alice Springs, a giant, spherical boulder stands atop a cairn, a monument to the Reverend John Flynn, founder of the Royal Flying Doctor Service. Despite the almost universal love the people of the inland bear for Flynn, the monument is a controversial one: the boulder is one of the Devils Marbles, and belongs to a powerful 'Place of Dreaming' for the Warramunga people. To the Warramunga, these boulders are the eggs of the legendary Rainbow Serpent. They litter the mulga-covered peneplain on both sides of the Stuart Highway, 90 kilometres south of Tennant Creek. In the lengthening shadows of late afternoon, and in the deceptive light of the moon, a pagan spirit pervades the area, grafting thick, Australoid lips and broad, flared nostrils onto the rounded granite. Yet at other, kinder times, many of the boulders resemble nothing so much as giant muffins, oozing butter and blackberry jam.

Some boulders stand by themselves, balancing precariously on the edge of a rocky outcrop; others are neatly arranged in tiers, like Inca ruins, or piled in heaps, as though carelessly tossed aside after some elemental game. Yet it was no supernatural being who placed the granite tors—ranging in diameter from a mere 30 centimetres to 3 metres or more—on the quartz-strewn plain: it was the very natural forces of wind and water. Molten granite intruded through the earlier sedimentary rocks perhaps 1540 million years ago, solidifying in a rectangular grid of joints, like a colossal Rubik's cube. It was at the joints that the weathering process began and, of course, it was accelerated at the corners. Eventually the blocks of granite were chamfered into their characteristic ovoid and spherical shapes.

Granite often weathers quite rapidly, despite its great hardness. One aspect of the process is clearly evident at the Devils Marbles: exfoliation, in which layers of rock peel off the boulder as though it were an onion. Many of the rocks sound hollow as a result, and concave sheets of granite lie upon the ground like shields after battle. Rainfall here is light, but sufficient to hasten the weathering process and to give rise to tiny streams winding among the tors. A few slender white-limbed ghost gums cling tenuously to pockets of soil among the rocks and along the creek lines.

Granite tors occur in quite a few other parts of Australia, but nowhere quite as spectacularly as here, in the arid heartland of the Northern Territory. Perhaps the giant boulders at Tibooburra, in north-western New South Wales, compare best. Other examples may be found at Granite Downs, South Australia; on the New England Tableland; on the coast at Albany in Western Australia; on the Eyre Peninsula; and at Mount Buffalo in the Victorian Alps.

BELOW The giant boulders have been eroded from a solid mass of granite.
RIGHT To the Warramunga people, these rocks were the eggs of the rainbow serpent.

The silent beauty of Carnarvon Gorge.

QUEENSLAND

The Great Barrier Reef
Fraser Island
Lamington National Park
Carnarvon Gorge
The Channel Country
The Glasshouse Mountains
The Undara Lava Tubes

The Great Barrier Reef

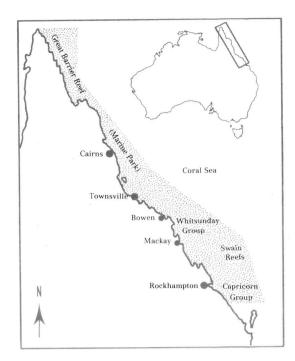

AUSTRALIA, the flattest and driest of the inhabited continents, boasts neither high, permanently snow-capped mountains nor the strong, deep rivers to which they give rise. There are no Himalayas, Rockies or Andes here, soaring monuments to evolutionary forces deep within the earth's crust. Yet if all Australia were as flat and uninteresting as the treeless Hay plains of New South Wales, this country would still be renowned throughout the world for the Great Barrier Reef, the largest system of coral reefs on earth.

It extends over 15 degrees of latitude, from Bramble Cay at 9°11′S off the coast of New Guinea, 2000 kilometres south to Lady Elliott Island at 24°07′S, near Bundaberg. The reefs form what is the most productive and most varied of all marine ecosystems, a vast area larger than Victoria and encompassing more than 1500 different coral reefs and cays.

The Great Barrier Reef protects more than 80 per cent of the Queensland coast from the giant swells of the Pacific Ocean. Inside that fantastic barrier, alongside which the Great Wall of China is a mere garden wall, the waters are often as calm as those inside Sydney Harbour, and so clear that the rich kaleidoscope of colours comprising the reefs is as vivid as any spring display of annuals in a well-stocked garden.

The reefs are of five basic types: ribbon, fringing, deltaic, dissected and platform. The most common are the platform reefs, knoll-like structures lying between the outer reefs and the Queensland mainland. Fringing reefs grow on the shores of many rocky islands and, in places, of the mainland. From latitude 11°14'S to 16°S, ribbon or linear reefs extend almost continuously along the edge of the continental shelf. To the north, the reefs are broken by meandering channels like river deltas, which eventually become so straight as virtually to dissect the reefs.

Stony corals grow in sea water with an average maximum temperature of between 22°C and 28°C. They are animals, not plants, usually living in large groups known as colonies but also occurring as solitary polyps. Each coral polyp is a sort of closed cylinder, with a mouth surrounded by tentacles at one end. It has a protective skeleton of calcium carbonate called a corallite. A lateral extension of the polyp's walls, called the coenchyme, connects the individual members of a colony. The polyp itself is quite small, with an average diameter of only 1 centimetre, but whole colonies may be vast, weighing several hundred tonnes. Each colony's lifespan may vary from a few years to centuries.

When a colony dies, its skeleton is broken up by wave action, by boring organisms and by fish seeking coralline algae. Storms and cyclones may also kill living coral communities. The calcareous remains are bound together by algae and soft coral; chemical processes then fuse them into solid rock, creating a base for new generations of coral. In favourable conditions, where the reef has grown up near the surface of the water, sand and coral shingle may accumulate, forming an island known as a cay.

Many cays are completely unvegetated; on some, grasses and succulents have established a toehold, and more mature cays, such as Green Island, support a thick forest of trees and shrubs. The primary coloniser is the drooping casuarina, which protects other plants, including pandanus and tournefortia, from wind and salt. Pisonia trees may form dense thickets and forests. Mangroves may also grow in the water bordering shingle cays, helping reclaim land from the sea. The vegetated islands are

A deep channel separates Line Reef and Hardy Reef, two platform reefs north-east of the Whitsunday Group.

nesting places for 20 species of sea birds and a number of land birds. Loggerhead and green turtles also lay eggs on some of the cays.

Most corals feed by trapping and immobilising prey with poison-spined organelles known as nematocysts and unarmed fibres discharged by other organelles called spirocysts, both associated with the tentacles. Minute food particles present in the water may also stick to mucus secreted by epidermic cells. Long threads known as mesenterial filaments may also be extended outside the animal's body to trap food. Corals which have no tentacles use a combination of these other techniques to feed.

Corals also enter into symbiosis (an association from which both organisms derive mutual benefit) with unicellular algae (zooxanthellae) living in their tissues. The algae contain chlorophyll and synthesise carbohydrates in the presence of sunlight, creating essential nutriment for the corals. Corals need sunlight to survive, and will not live in water deeper than about 50 metres (unless it is exceptionally clear). Zooxanthellae may also assist the formation of lime by the corals.

Non-solitary hard polyps may form branching (plant-like), non-branching (massive, frequently hemispherical) or plate-like colonies. Each colony is founded by a single polyp developed from a fertilised egg, but other polyps are created by an asexual process known as budding.

A coral reef is a complex ecosystem consisting of far more than stony corals and algae, however. Many other creatures are attached to the limestone reefs. As well as molluscs and barnacles, there are sea anemones, black corals, soft corals, sea pens, sea fans, stoloniferans, hydrozoans, bryozoans, ascidians, brachiopods and sponges. Many of these animals are as colourful and varied in form as the stony corals, and are often mistaken for them. Sea fans have a hard skeleton, as the name of their order, Gorgonacea (after the Gorgons of Greek legend, the women who had hair of live snakes and whose gaze turned humans to stone), suggests. Small polyps grow from the delicate side branches of the skeleton.

The bryozoans live in colonies exhibiting an enormous range of form and colour. Some, such as the so-called lace corals, look like perforated succulents; others are calcified and, like the sea fans and other calcareous organisms, contribute to reef sediments. Individual bryozoan animals are known as zooids, and are much smaller than coral polyps, there being millions in some colonies.

Equally interesting are the hydrozoans, which exist in both medusa (free-swimming, bell-shaped) and polyp forms during their life histories. The medusa form carries the reproductive organs; larvae produced from fertilised eggs create new polyps, which attach themselves to reefs, often in caves and under overhangs, and form colonies through asexual reproduction. Hydrozoan colonies vary greatly in size: some have massive or branching calcareous skeletons; others are fern-like, with a single stem and delicate side branches encrusted with polyps; some form erect colonies only a few millimetres high.

As in the rainforests of the tropics, the only other ecosystem that can match the diversity and richness of coral reefs, mobile animals exist in enormous numbers on the Great Barrier Reef. Many of these are as beautiful as the corals amongst which they swim.

The comparison with rainforests is an appropriate one, for this is no gentle Garden of Eden, but a jungle in which every fish's purpose in life is seemingly to eat or be eaten. Predators lurk behind every knoll, in every cave, amongst every coral clump on the reef. The more obvious of these are the sharks, streamlined for speed, the densely packed barracudas, the giant gropers and the savage-looking moray eels. But many other innocuous-looking fish are also fierce predators, possibly feeding on other fish so small that they tend to be overlooked by human swimmers, or invertebrates. More than three times as many reef fish are carnivores as are herbivores. Other fish, ranging from sprats and hardyheads up to the giant, but harmless, manta ray, feed on microscopic plankton floating in the water. Every conceivable ecological niche is occupied by some creature or other on the reef, all the way up the food chain to the major predators.

Familiar inhabitants of the reefs are the echinoderms: the brittle-stars, feather-stars, sea cucumbers, sea urchins and starfish. They are characteristically radially symmetrical, their principal organs arranged around a central hub. Many of these creatures' bodies regenerate rapidly after attack by predators. Brittle-stars, for example, can grow back lost arms. Some species of starfish can regenerate from a single broken-off arm, a form of asexual reproduction. Many starfish are brilliantly coloured, but for sheer beauty they are eclipsed by the delicate fronds of the feather-stars, waving languorously in the ocean currents.

The sea cucumbers are the bêches-de-mer harvested by visiting Malay fishermen from northern Australian waters for centuries before the coming of white men. The creatures were subsequently collected on the reef for export to Asia. Also valued as human food are many crustaceans and molluscs. The crustaceans range from the tiny, almost invisible, water fleas through many families of prawns and shrimps to large, edible crayfish, crabs and lobsters. They also include barnacles, which may cling to reef boulders or become parasitic, living on, for example, the shells of turtles.

The molluscs are soft-bodied creatures, many of which are protected in a hard shell. But they also include many animals without shells, such as the slugs, nudibranchs, the fancifully called sea hares, dorids and chromodorids. Many of these creatures resemble land slugs but are often vividly coloured and may carry a cluster of gills on their backs. Nudibranchs are actually gastropods, members of the class which includes limpets, periwinkles and whelks as well as the more glamorous giant helmets, cowries, tritons and murex shells.

Among the bivalve molluscs, edible families include scallops, oysters and the giant clams, some of the largest invertebrates ever to have existed. The biggest clam of all is *Tridacna gigas*, found primarily in the northern half of the Barrier Reef, which has been

An orange sea-fan (Order *Gorgonacea*). A hard skeleton characterises these colonies of animals. (Carol Carter)

recorded at a shell length of up to 1.5 metres and has no known predators, save for the Taiwanese fishermen who have removed clams in large numbers, with an unknown effect on the ecology of the reef.

Cephalopods, octopuses, cuttlefish and squid are also widely distributed on the reef, using their tentacles to seize prey which is often immobilised by toxic saliva injected by the creature's powerful beak.

The invertebrates also include worm-like animals, not all of which resemble worms at all. Some of them are scavengers, feeding on organic detritus; others are predators, eating small organisms. Some, including many of the flatworms, are parasites, living in the bodies of other animals, such as turtles, birds, crustaceans and molluscs. Other worms embed themselves in coral, leaving protruding cones of brightly coloured tentacles with which they catch food.

Not surprisingly, numerous species on the Barrier Reef have evolved elaborate camouflage to escape the attacks of predators, whilst others have developed powerful weapons which serve both to subdue prey and to deter aggressors. Many of these creatures are also dangerous to man. They include the geographer cone and tulip cone, each of which has a proboscis armed with a tiny harpoon capable of injecting sufficient venom to kill a human being. The stonefish, an incredibly ugly scorpion fish which lies amongst rocks or coral rubble and is well nigh invisible, is armed with venom glands on each of the 13 spines supporting its dorsal fin. Many unsuspecting visitors to the reef have trodden on the fish, with agonising and sometimes fatal consequences. Another member of the scorpion fish group is the butterfly cod, which is almost as dangerous as the stonefish: most of its fins are armed with barbed spines which, like those of the stonefish, can cause days of excruciating pain and partial paralysis. The box jellyfish, with its dangling, deadly tentacles, has killed many bathers in the northern waters of Queensland.

Some attached animals may also cause severe pain if one accidentally brushes up against them. They include the fire anemone, two species of stinging hydroid, and the large hydrozoan fire corals. Many other animals are poisonous if eaten, or if eaten without proper preparation. As well, there are the animals which bite: tiger sharks, bronze whalers, hammerheads, moray eels and the aggressive giant toado, which has been known to nip off the toes of waders. Many species of sea snakes, which have flat tails adapted for swimming, also live in the reef area; their venom is amongst the most potent of all snakes. Provided due care is exercised, though, it is possible to spend without injury many relaxed and uneventful weeks on the Barrier Reef. The tourist industry is served by 17 island resorts, most of them built on rocky continental islands, formerly part of the mainland.

One of the most perplexing mysteries to have taxed the brains of Australia's marine biologists over the past 20 years is the origin of the plague of crown-of-thorns starfish that has destroyed the hard-coral cover of many of the platform reefs in the central region. This unpleasant creature is the only starfish on the reef that is dangerous to man. Long spines protruding from its upper surface carry a potent toxin that causes severe pain, swelling and vomiting in those unfortunate enough to brush against them. It is indigenous to the Barrier Reef and has been identified on every reef in the region, as well as throughout the Indo-Pacific region.

The crown-of-thorns starfish, like several species of fish, some worms and a few crustaceans, eats hard coral polyps. Normally, only about six specimens are found per square kilometre of reef. But in 1961, for the first time, much larger numbers of these destructive creatures were found on reefs near Cairns. Population estimates have ranged as high as 2 million for a single reef. Green Island reef became infested in 1962 and by the mid-1970s most platform reefs from 150 kilometres north of Cooktown to Townsville had suffered the depredations of the starfish.

Recolonisation by soft corals and algae is relatively swift, but the species diversity exhibited by a coral reef system in equilibrium is missing, and the long-term effect on the Reef's ecology is unknown. Although some scientists suggest that the crown-of-thorns population explosion may be quite natural, others point to the fact that the first infestations occurred near population and tourist centres, and attribute it at least in part to the collecting by shell buffs of the giant triton, a predator of the crown-of-thorns starfish. Commercial spear-fishing, now banned like the taking of triton shells, may also have contributed.

One of the most alarming features of the crown-of-thorns plague is that the starfish, which desert a reef once most of its hard corals have been devoured, have returned in large numbers to Green Island, which had regenerated after the devastation of the sixties. More research is necessary to establish whether the increase in the starfish population is merely a periodic natural phenomenon or poses a genuine threat to the Reef.

The establishment in 1975 of the Great Barrier Reef Marine Park Authority, the Reef's inclusion on the World Heritage List, and the proclamation, between 1979 and 1983, of the eight sections of the marine park are extremely important attempts to conserve and protect Australia's most significant natural wonder.

OPPOSITE, TOP LEFT The reefs off the Queensland coast are amongst the most abundant eco-systems in the world.
OPPOSITE, TOP RIGHT A slug-like nudibranch (*Notodoris gardineri*) grazes on a sponge (*Pericharax* spp.). Many sponges exude toxic materials to which certain species of nudibranch are immune. (Michael Hill)
OPPOSITE, CENTRE LEFT A delicate feather-star floats amongst the waving tentacles of a soft coral colony of the *Alcyoniidae* family. (Carol Carter)
OPPOSITE, CENTRE RIGHT Members of the *Neptheidae* family of soft corals, like this *Dendronephthya*, form branching, tree-like colonies, with the polyps borne on the ends of the branches. (Carol Carter)
OPPOSITE, BOTTOM The blue angel-fish (*Pomacanthus semicirculatus*) is common on the reef. (Michael Hill)

Fraser Island

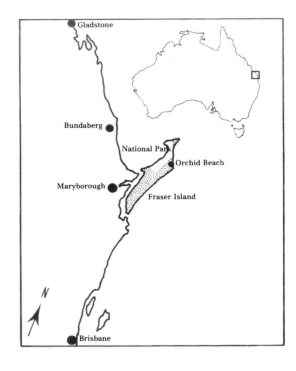

ALONG one shore the ocean currents sweep up onto two of the longest zeta-curve beaches in the world, transporting river sands that are the tiny building blocks of the island. On the other shore, mangroves reclaim land from the sluggish waters of Great Sandy Strait, which separates the island from the mainland. Fraser Island, the largest sand island in the world, should be growing bigger by the day but man, both wittingly and unwittingly, has interrupted the chain of events that created this rare jewel in the Pacific Ocean, 180 kilometres north of Brisbane. This interruption has been caused by the erection of dams across the northern New South Wales rivers that feed the currents with sand, and by mining the multi-coloured sands of the island for their mineral content.

The threat posed to Fraser Island by the sand miners has gone for the moment, vanished with the imposition in 1976 of a ban on the export of sands mined above the high-water mark. But the long-term problems relating to the supply of fresh sand will remain. They have already resulted in spectacular erosion along the skyscraper-shaded beachfront of the Gold Coast.

It has only taken a few million years for the billions of tonnes of sand to accumulate, a mere moment in geological time, yet Fraser Island is almost 125 kilometres long, with an average breadth of 14.5 kilometres and an area of 1724 square kilometres. Its sands soar to 240 metres above sea level, and plunge 600 metres below the sea to the Cretaceous sedimentary bedrock. A treacherous shoal, guarded since 1870 by a slender white lighthouse, extends for many kilometres to the north of the island. Captain James Cook, sailing by in May 1770, recorded that 'the land hereabouts, which is of a moderate height, appears more barren than any we have yet seen on this coast, and the Soil more sandy . . .'.

Cook was only partially right. The coastal dunes which he could see from his vantage position offshore concealed a central ridge of lush rainforest, the equal of anything he was to see further north. These same forests have provided timber for nearby Maryborough's mills for more than a century.

The island was named after the captain of the *Stirling Castle*, James Fraser, who, after his ship had been wrecked on Swain Reef, landed in a small boat on the north coast of the island in May 1836. The captain, along with several of the crew, was speared to death by the local Aborigines, and his wife Eliza spent nine weeks with the tribe before being rescued by a search party.

In 1842 a party led by Andrew Petrie explored portion of the island; six years later the town of Maryborough was founded on the mainland, and soon the timber-getters were seeking to exploit Fraser Island's valuable resource. When gold was discovered at Gympie in 1867, Fraser Island became a quarantine and immigration station for the port of Maryborough, and opium, venereal disease and influenza decimated the members of the Butchalla tribe. In 1897 a mission station was established at North White Cliffs, ostensibly to look after the survivors of the white man's diseases. Conditions were so appalling the mission was abandoned in 1904.

Meanwhile, the timber-getters were tapping the apparently inexhaustible forests of the island. At first they used bullock teams to haul the huge logs of kauri, hoop pine and beech out of the forests; then, in 1905, a tramline was built to take the timber from Poyungan (a Butchalla word meaning 'corroboree') and Bogimbah (meaning 'home-land') creeks to a waiting punt. By then they were cutting down the dense stands of rough-barked satinay, and blackbutt and tallow wood.

The resinous satinays, members of the turpentine family, warped too readily for most purposes, but they proved ideally suited to immersion in water and in 1925 were shipped to Egypt to prop up the walls of the Suez Canal. These trees grow more than 50 metres tall and may have a diameter of over 6 metres. The hoop pines may be half as thick. A sawmill once prospered on the island, providing work for 100 men; it closed in 1925.

The forests are carefully husbanded; replanting began as early as 1882 and even the Fraser Island Defence Organisation (FIDO), in its 1975 Plan of Management for the island, had to concede that forestry had done a good job of conservation, although it also recommended a reduction of operations. The great forests cover more than 30 000 hectares in a 67 kilometre long strip of the island. Here, amongst the giant straight-trunked trees, wreathed in vines and embellished with epiphytes, the magic of Fraser Island takes hold.

Sinuous brown thread of a creek line snakes through white sand to the sea.

Like the sands of the island, the humus which nurtures the forest collected gradually. At first there were only a few small plants, fertilised by nutrients blown ashore from the ocean. As they died, their remains created a layer of humus capable of supporting larger and more varied species. The vegetation also collected in depressions in the sand, forming a hard-packed basin impervious to water. Here rainwater (the island is deluged by more than 1.5 metres of rain each year) collects to form the largest and highest perched dune lakes in the world—more than 40 of them, up to 60 metres deep. Their waters, often stained reddish-brown by acid leached out of the lake beds, support up to nine species of fish: rainbow fish, freshwater hardyheads, carp, gudgeon, sunfish, bony bream. There are tortoises, too, and acid frogs that have adapted to this difficult environment.

Elsewhere, the sands of the island absorb up to 30 per cent of their volume in water, releasing it in springs and trickles that gouge channels from the beach sands as they return to the sea. Some of the creeks are permanent and support their own unique ecosystems, like the tropical valley of Woongoolbver Creek, with its elephant palms, exotic orchids, and *Angiopteris* ferns, atavistic remnants of an era long past.

The island is home to one of the most diverse bird populations in Australia: more than 200 different species have been sighted here, including jabirus, peregrine falcons and red-legged pairs of pied oyster catchers. Over the estuaries, beaches and mud flats soar the fish eaters, the white-breasted sea eagles, ospreys, and red-backed kites with their piercing eyes and equally sharp talons and beaks.

Reptiles and marsupials abound (there are reports of timber-cutters who, when bitten by a death adder or taipan, would suffer the instant amputation of a finger or hand rather than face a lingering death in the scrub), and a mob of about 100 brumbies roams the island. The tidal wetlands of Great Sandy Strait are one of the most important fish breeding grounds on the east coast; an artificial reef built from old car tyres and car bodies has dramatically increased the fish population. Two local delicacies are wong soup and wong rissoles, made by processing the rubbery bodies of bivalve molluscs collected from the wet sands of the ocean's edge.

A treacherous sandy shoal, glimpsed by Cook, extends for many kilometres to the north of the island.

Crumbling sandstone cliffs, stained red and orange by chemicals leached out of the humus and the ilmenite, and streaked with strands of the purest white, line the beaches on both sides of the island, carved into fantastic spires and minarets by wind and water, in places furrowed as if by a giant comb.

The cliffs are at their most brilliant in Rainbow Gorge, beyond which lie the singular miniature buttes of Enchanted Valley. Here an ancient sandstone crust has broken into small pieces, each protecting a pillar of sand around which the exposed grains have been eroded away. A similar process, but on a much larger scale, has created the 'jump-ups' of central Australia.

Not all of Fraser Island is sand. There is, two-thirds of the way along the eastern shore, just south of the holiday resort of Orchid Beach, an outcrop of volcanic rocks of Tertiary age, which probably played an important part in trapping the mobile river sands sweeping up the coast from New South Wales. The more prominent point was named Indian Head by Cook because of the Aborigines he saw gathered there. On the western side of the island, at Bun Bun Creek, is an outcrop of folded sedimentary rocks that belongs to the same formation as Big and Little Woody Islands and Picnic Island in Great Sandy Strait.

Most people who visit Fraser Island bring fishing tackle to take advantage of the great schools of fish that swim offshore: tailor, whiting, flathead, trevally, morwong and mackerel. Before World War II, an entrepreneur attempted to establish a shark factory on Wathumbra Creek, while the dugongs, or sea-cows, that swim in Great Sandy Strait were hunted for their oil.

Fraser Island was the first natural wonder to be listed on the Australian register of the National Estate. It was proposed as a national park as far back as 1873. Its beauty has inspired work by some of Australia's most gifted painters and authors, including Sir Sidney Nolan and Patrick White. Although sand mining no longer threatens the island, overuse by thoughtless visitors can still jeopardise its survival. Its conservation must be viewed as an ongoing project by and for all Australians.

The island's most beautiful perched lakes are the twin Wabby lakes, separated and threatened by a giant sand blow.

QUEENSLAND

Lamington National Park

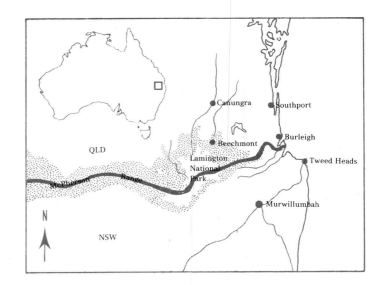

FOR more than 150 kilometres, the border between Queensland and New South Wales follows the ridge line of a range of mountains so rugged and inaccessible they have largely escaped development and where even today much of the area may never have felt the tread of a man's foot.

The mountains form the McPherson Range, named after an army friend by explorer Allan Cunningham in 1827. As mountains go, they are barely more than foothills: the highest point, Mount Barney, is only 1359 metres above sea level. But they are clothed in a magical suit of green, in brilliant contrast to the usual grey sackcloth of the Australian bush. This is sub-tropical rainforest, the largest expanse in Australia.

Rainforest was once called jungle, a term redolent of disease, mud, leeches and hostile natives. The leeches and mud are still there in profusion, but disease has not proved a problem, and the local Aborigines, the Wangerriburras—who were undeniably hostile towards the Europeans when they invaded their tribal lands—had all died out by 1931.

The white man's era began on 16 May 1770, when James Cook's ship, the *Endeavour*, nearly came to grief on the treacherous shoals off the Tweed River in northern New South Wales. Cook named a prominent peak he glimpsed inland Mount Warning, as a caution to other mariners. He mentioned other 'high and hilly country' to the north, but it seems likely the McPhersons were shrouded in mist—otherwise they could scarcely have failed to figure more prominently in Cook's journal.

Fifty-six years later, following the settlement of Moreton Bay (Brisbane), a party led by the new penal settlement's commandant, Captain Robert Logan, marched south to what he incorrectly believed was Mount Warning. Allan Cunningham, in 1827, discovered the fertile Darling Downs but was unable to reach the isolated volcanic peak. He and Logan teamed up the following year to explore the country between the Downs and Moreton Bay, climbing Mount Barney, which they named Mount Lindsay. But it was not until Queensland was proclaimed a self-governing colony independent of New South Wales, that any real attempt was made to penetrate those mysterious mountains that formed the boundary between the two colonies. The job of surveying the border was given to two men: Francis Roberts, for Queensland, and Isiah Rowland, for New South Wales. The line they drew on the map was to become in 1915 the southern boundary of the 20 000 hectare Lamington National Park and the northern boundary of its even larger New South Wales counterpart, Border Ranges National Park, created in 1979.

It seems almost inconceivable that, in the mad scramble for land that occurred in the late nineteenth century anyone, let alone the scion of a local pioneering family, should have been campaigning to have a national park set aside. Yet that is exactly what Robert Collins was doing in the 1880s. After his death in 1913, the fight was continued by sawmiller Romeo Lahey.

Meanwhile, in 1911, the O'Reilly family had taken up land on the section of the ranges known as Lamington Plateau, at what is now Green Mountains Lodge. They set out to clear farms from the wilderness, a task that would be daunting even to men equipped with today's sophisticated machinery. Their tools were axe and cross-cut saw; they risked death and serious injury a thousand times from trees that snapped unexpectedly during cutting, from hordes of wriggling tiger snakes, from the vicious barbs of the Gympie stinging tree, and they were forced to endure sodden, wretched living conditions. Yet, according to Bernard O'Reilly, they suffered no serious illness, he suggests because of the natural penicillin in the mould they ingested daily.

After the national park was declared, the O'Reillys converted their home into a guesthouse, and were followed in the 1930s by Arthur Groom and Romeo Lahey, who opened a lodge at Binna Burra on Mount Roberts, only 7 kilometres distant as the crow flies but 22 kilometres by walking track and 67 kilometres by winding mountain road. The National Parks Service maintains more than 150 kilometres of track radiating out from these two points, although the southern section of the park is virgin wilderness.

Nearby Mount Warning played a major part in the formation of the ranges. A huge volcano 20–25 million years ago, the mountain buried almost 5000 square kilometres of the surrounding countryside beneath a lava deposit up to 1000 metres deep. Other volcanoes were active near Mount Roberts, at the north-eastern edge of the Lamington Plateau. The principal crater was 32 kilometres across and it is part of its rim that now forms the high ridge of the border ranges.

OPPOSITE **Purling Brook Falls lie on the boundary of the National Park. There are more than 500 waterfalls in the Lamington area.**

Erosion has incised deep valleys into the basalt mass and worn away the softer rocks, leaving Mount Warning as an isolated volcanic plug, a mass of molten rock solidified in the throat of a dying volcano, at the centre of the almost encircled Tweed River Valley. It is the first part of the Australian mainland to catch the sun's rays at dawn. Egg Rock, a magnificent, isolated pinnacle in Nixons Gorge near Binna Burra, is another, much smaller, plug.

The twisting road that leads to O'Reillys' passes suddenly from the open, wooded slopes into the dark, closed world of the rainforest. This forest flourishes in the rich, basalt soils of the ranges, watered by an average rainfall of more than 2.5 metres each year. It is an environment quite unlike that of the eucalypt forests lower down the hillsides, a world of dripping moisture where the twin forces of growth and decay, life and death, appear to have been magnified hundredfold. The trees—more than 200 species of them, some as yet unnamed—are quite unlike the gums that dominate so much of Australia. Many have no tap roots but support their massive boles on buttresses often metres wide. Their leaves are usually deep green and shiny, as though lacquered. The tallest trees of the forest, the great red cedars and Moreton Bay figs, grow 50 metres tall, and the mighty hoop pines that poke through the tree canopy like skyscrapers above a city's smog are as high as 70 metres. A more common height is 30–40 metres, for species including red carabeen, flame tree, white beech, the booyong with its winged seeds, silky beech and mararie.

But it is not enough to list only the trees: in the rainforest they are bedecked with vines, garnished with delicate epiphytes, daubed with a myriad mosses, lichen and fungi, so that at times the tree's real form is almost completely obscured. Some 70 vines grow in the forest: some, like the blood vine, are content to coil around the trunk of a tree like giant hawsers; others, such as the strangler fig (actually an emergent, not a vine), tend to strangle their hosts. The strangler fig germinates in the crown of the tree, then drops to the forest floor long roots which thicken to envelop the tree. Ultimately, the host tree, hideously disfigured, may succumb to the unequal contest, die and rot away.

Moss and lichen encrust the cooler, wetter southern sides of the trees, which in exposed positions will also lean towards the north. On the ridge tops the trees may grow so close to one another, interlaced with leafy vines, that they lock together in one continuous canopy, creating a gloomy half-light. Epiphytes, like the beautiful bird's nest fern, cling to tree trunks and forks, drawing their nutrients from leaf litter. The forest floor may be relatively open, or choked with lawyer vines armed with sharp hooks. Feather-like tree ferns dot the southern slopes of the ridges.

The forest has its peculiarities: luminous fungi so bright one can read a book by them at night; a variety of potentially lethal stinging trees with leaves as big as dinner plates and coated with spines that inject an excruciatingly painful poison; and tiny leeches that seize onto warm-blooded animals as they pass, opening a wound that will bleed for almost half an hour after the creature has been removed. There is a purple worm known as the squirter that, when alarmed, ejects for up to a metre fluid from minute pores in its body; a blue, white and orange crayfish lives in the mountain streams; and there is a snail that grows up to 10 centimetres tall.

On the ridge lines above 950 metres stand the gnarled, decayed trunks of Antarctic beeches, a tree which is endemic to Australia, New Zealand, and Patagonia, and remains of which have been preserved in the Antarctic icecap.

As if the vegetation itself were not sufficient obstacle to travel through the forest, the plateau has been cleft by creeks fed by the drenching rain. Some cliffs fall 600 metres sheer into the valleys, the grey rock brushed by wisps of cloud no more substantial than puffs of smoke from a camp fire.

It was in the unexplored country south of O'Reillys' that a Stinson aircraft with seven people on board crashed in February 1937. Eyewitnesses reported having seen it go down off the coast near Sydney, but Bernard O'Reilly, who knew it had not called as intended at Lismore in northern New South Wales, thought differently. Acting on a hunch, he set out to hack his way through the forest, eventually being attracted by the sight of a single splintered tree on the far side of a valley. The aircraft had come down there in one of the fierce storms that lash the ranges in summer. O'Reilly reached the wreckage some hours later and found two men alive beside it; a third person had died trying to walk out for help.

To these men the trackless rainforest was as hostile a place as any to be found on the planet. Even the Wangerriburras stayed mainly in the lowlands, making only day trips into the mountains in search of game. Yet for city people wanting to slough off the plastic wrapping of an urban lifestyle, the McPherson Ranges hold a magnetic attraction.

OPPOSITE, TOP LEFT **The strangler fig (*Ficus watkinsiana*) starts life in the crown of another tree. Its roots eventually envelop the trunk of its host.**
OPPOSITE, TOP RIGHT **Bracket fungus grows from a tree stump. Fungi help to recycle organic debris.**
OPPOSITE, BELOW **The verdant green of the rainforest contrasts starkly with the greyer tones of the surrounding wet sclerophyll forest. Less than 1 percent of Australia's landmass is covered with rainforest.**

Carnarvon Gorge

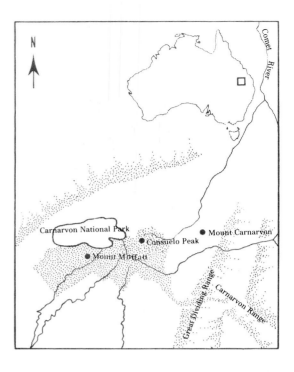

CARNARVON was gazetted as a national park more than 50 years ago, for the qualities that make it a natural wonder meant it had no pastoral potential. It had been part of Upper Carnarvon station since 1863, when John Peter and Company applied to the Crown Lands Office for a lease, but neither Peter nor his successors found much use for the inaccessible sandstone gorge slicing 200 metres deep into the Carnarvon Ranges, a high point in the Great Divide north of Roma. On the northern boundary of the park looms Consuelo Tableland, more than 1000 metres high; its tallest mountain, Consuelo Peak, soars 1219 metres into the clear blue sky of south-central Queensland. To the south is a rugged jumble of hills that eventually opens out into more gentle grazing country watered by the infant Maranoa River and its tributaries.

This is normally a semi-arid land, poorly watered and supporting only sparse woodland. But the ranges act like a giant sponge, soaking up the rains of the summer wet season, releasing them into the permanent waters of Carnarvon Creek, then absorbing them again, downstream, into the aquifers of the Great Artesian Basin. For more than 20 million years, since a period of massive earth movements and fierce volcanic activity that uplifted the ranges and left a hard basalt capping on top of the Jurassic and Triassic sandstones, the stream has been digging down into the vertical faults in the rock. Along the creek grows a lush vegetation that quite belies the poor nature of the surrounding countryside. Here soaring white-barked flooded gums rub shoulders with swaying cabbage palms while, beneath the tree canopy in the protective shadow of the cliffs, grow brilliant white and pink orchids and dark green ferns. Cycads sprout like sentinels from the plains and open forest country at the entrance to the gorge; baked in ashes and soaked in water to remove toxins, their seeds formed an important part of the Aboriginal diet.

Microclimates, each a new treat, flourish in the smaller gorges leading off the main stream. Light rarely filters through into the luridly named Hell Hole Gorge, a narrow chasm 100 metres deep, its walls verdant with slimy moss, lichens and fungi interspersed with the delicate fronds of climbing ferns. In the Amphitheatre, reached via a steel ladder 10 metres tall, silence reigns supreme. The floor of this natural hole in the rock is covered with ferns and grass, from which sprout golden wattles, palms, figs and tree ferns. Beyond it, the fine spray of a waterfall marks the entrance to Angiopteris Ravine, named for the handful of large, primeval ferns found here, hundreds of kilometres from their normal habitat on Fraser Island.

A stucco of moss covers the walls and floor of the Moss Gardens, a cavern near Koolaroo Creek, sharing this moist environment with ferns, a few other small plants and the red and orange splash of lichen. Water seeps perpetually through the sandstone ceiling of the cave, dripping in a cold, light shower.

In many parts of these side gorges lives a large spider, *Dolmedes*, which darts from its home in the rocky crevices to catch tiny fish and water beetles in the clear, cool pools. The local Aborigines, the Karingbal, caught fish, too, stringing nets across the streams or spearing the silver perch and bony bream in the ageless fashion of their forebears. There were about 500 of them when white men first visited the Carnarvon Ranges, but they were soon decimated by diseases to which they had no immunity.

Ludwig Leichhardt travelled to the east of the gorge in 1844, but it was the controversial New South Wales Surveyor-General, Sir Thomas Mitchell, who first visited the ranges, in 1846. He noted: 'The hills overhanging that valley surpass any that I have seen in picturesque outline. Some resemble Gothic Cathedrals in ruins, others forts. It was a discovery worthy of the toils of pilgrimage . . .'.

Mitchell named the ranges after the rugged Caernarfon Mountains of north-western Wales. White settlers soon followed in his footsteps; a personal friend of his, Allan McPherson, took up a 17 000 hectare holding near the present site of Roma in 1847. For the Karingbals, it was the beginning of the end, although internecine warfare between tribal sub-groups had already killed many younger men. But they did not vanish without a trace. On the walls of caves and overhangs in the gorge they left more than 5000 paintings and engravings, including hand stencils similar to those found to the south-west at Mootwingee in outback New South Wales. The artist would place his hand or arm (or, in one case, a steel axe) on the rock surface and then spray an ochre paste over it from his mouth. When the hand or other object was removed, a perfect stencil of it was left outlined on the wall. The rock art tradition may date back 15 000 years or more at Carnarvon Gorge; it is a heritage worthy of fastidious preservation.

OPPOSITE, LEFT **A Karingbal art gallery, comprising an unusual mixture of freehand net patterns, V-shaped killer boomerangs, hand stencils, and carved female symbols.**
OPPOSITE, TOP RIGHT **Primitive cycads (***Macrozamia moorei***) line the gorge floor. A paste formed from the seeds, after treatment to remove toxins, formed an important foodstuff for the local Aboriginal tribes.**
OPPOSITE, CENTRE RIGHT **Violet Gorge, one of the numerous small defiles branching off the main gorge.**
OPPOSITE, BOTTOM RIGHT **Rough tree-fern (***Cyathea australis***).**

The Channel Country

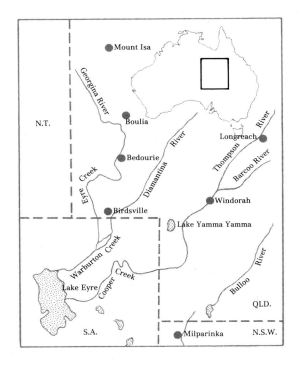

I N Queensland they have a saying: it takes two rivers (the Thomson and the Barcoo) to make one creek (the Cooper). This statement is as misleading as the anomaly to which it refers. For the Thomson, the Barcoo, the Cooper, and the other watercourses of the Channel Country, the Diamantina, the Georgina and the Bulloo, all defy conventional classification. Between them, they drain one-eighth of Australia, a catchment area of almost 1 million square kilometres, stretching from the southern slopes of the Barkly Tableland to the Great Divide between Hughenden and Charters Towers. Yet, in all this vast region there is not one perennial stream, just sandy channels lined with river red gums and coolibahs, cotton threads stringing together the permanent waterholes that are the pearls of the Channel Country.

To the north, there is the Georgina River, which rises on the Barkly Tableland south of Arnhem Land. The Diamantina takes its rise on rugged Swords Range, west of Winton. The headwaters of the Thomson lie in the Great Divide, east of Hughenden. The Bulloo has already travelled more than 100 kilometres from its source by the time it passes the small town of Quilpie.

Yet despite their great lengths and the volume of water that sometimes flows down them (the Diamantina and Cooper in flood may be more than 80 kilometres wide), not one of these streams reaches the sea. All, apart from the Bulloo, end their run in the crescent of salt lakes ringing the Flinders Ranges in South Australia. The Bulloo's passage is halted by the low series of silcrete-capped 'jump-ups' known as the Grey Range, and it dissipates itself in a group of lakes and swamps known as the Bulloo Overflow on the New South Wales–Queensland border.

The myriad smaller streams into which each watercourse diverges, and the hundreds of minor tributaries which feed them, constitute the Channel Country. After prolonged heavy rain, much of this country is interlaced with shining streams of brown and colloidal white water, a sight which Lord Casey, flying over it in 1950 when Minister for National Development, described as 'the world's only example of a vast irrigation scheme created by Nature'.

Lord Casey was right: for much of their length the Diamantina and the Cooper and their tributaries water the so-called 'black soil plains', fertile, basalt-derived, grey, self-mulching soils with up to 80 per cent clay content. The soil may be 1 metre or more deep and it supports a mixed vegetation of gidgee and brigalow, and nutritious pastures that rarely require fertilising. North-west, around Longreach, Hughenden and the Queensland headwaters of the Georgina, the soils are of similar composition, but red and brown, and grow tall tussock bush and saltbush. When dry, these soils crack naturally and break into clods known as peds. But after rain, as many motorists will attest, the soil becomes a cloying, glutinous 'goo' that has to be scraped off an upside-down shovel and that makes movement across the plains impossible.

The first white men to pass through this country found the fertile black soil as difficult to cope with as the sand dunes and gibber plains with which it intermingles. In August 1845, Charles Sturt and four companions pushed across Strzelecki Creek into the heartland of the Channel Country. Commented Sturt, 'The singular and rapid succession of these watercourses exceedingly perplexed me, for we were in a country remote from any highlands'. A week later he passed onto the bed of a dry lake—it had been a year of fearsome drought ...

> ... its surface was absolutely so rent and torn by solar heat, that there was scarcely room for the horses to tread, and they kept constantly slipping their hind feet into chasms from eight to ten feet deep, into which the earth fell with a hollow rumbling sound, as if into a grave.

The next party to pass this way suffered as much from the sticky nature of the wet soil as Sturt had done from the crevasses of the dry. Burke, Wills and King, struggling to reach Mount Hopeless in the northern Flinders Ranges after their frantic dash back to Cooper Creek from the Gulf of Carpentaria, lost their only sound camel, Landa, to the mud of a waterhole. 'All the ground beneath the surface was an impossible quicksand,' wrote the dying Wills, 'through which the beast sank too rapidly for us to get bushes or timber fairly beneath him.' They were forced to shoot the camel, destroying their only chance of salvation.

From the air, the myriad streams that water the Channel Country form an intricate network of green threads.

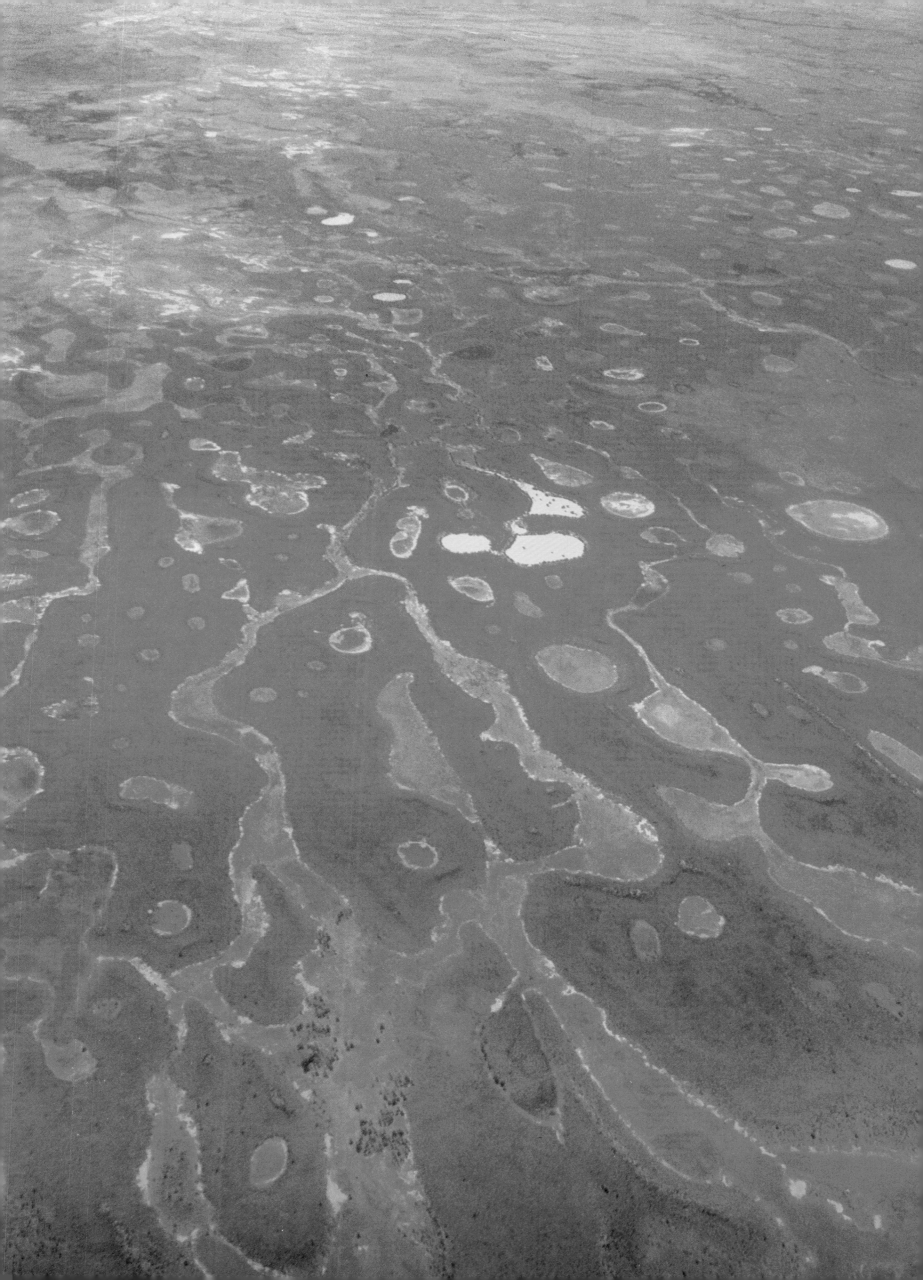

Yet stony desert and longitudinal sand ridges, tending north-south, are more typical of this country. Through the stony plateaux and the red, orange and white dunes wind the creeks and channels that give this country its name, life-giving arteries that, ironically, also bring down the sand that is pushed into dune fields by the prevailing winds. Most of the hundreds of small and large playas, or claypans, filled by the Cooper are, unlike their larger cousins to the south-west, free of salt. There are also big, deep waterholes in the beds of the rivers, many of them permanent and filled with fish—bream, callop, catfish and yellowbelly—indications that once the rivers flowed into the open sea.

One of the largest waterholes is Cullyamurra, near Innamincka: it is 10 kilometres long, nearly 30 metres deep and has never dried up in white man's memory. It is one of a string of waterholes along this stretch of the creek beside which the tragedy of Burke and Wills was played out. Forty-eight kilometres upstream from Innamincka is the famous 'Dig Tree', under which the base party, having left only hours before the exhausted trio returned from the Gulf, had buried a few meagre supplies. The local Aborigines, the Yantruwantas, would have succoured the explorers but Burke inexplicably chased them away with his gun. Burke and Wills perished here, in the midst of plenty, fish and freshwater mussels theirs for the taking, birds and mammals to be shot and trapped on the banks. King was eventually rescued by a relief party under Alfred Howitt: the Aborigines had kept him alive after the death of his companions.

Sturt explored right along the banks of this river, up into Queensland until the permanent waterholes vanished. He named it Cooper's Creek, after the Chief Justice of South Australia, and commented that he would 'gladly have laid this creek down as a river, but as it had no current I did not feel justified in so doing'. Mindful perhaps of those two rivers making one creek, by 1858 the explorer Augustus Gregory had dropped the possessive 's' and today it is most commonly called, simply, 'the Cooper'. Similarly, the Diamantina which, 130 kilometres south of Birdsville beyond Goyder Lagoon, becomes Warburton Creek, is then known as 'the Warburton'.

BELOW The tranquil oasis of Yidniminckanie waterhole, on Cooper Creek near Innamincka.

John McKinlay, searching for Burke and Wills in 1861, was quite favourably impressed with the Cooper flood-out country west of Cullyamurra. 'If this country had permanent water and rain occasionally, it would do well for stock of any kind,' he wrote. A member of his party, John Davis, described the area as 'this fine lake country' although, with summer temperatures of up to 73°C in the sun, it was clearly too hot for comfort. Davis recorded that,

> the Aborigines seemed to pour out from every nook and corner where there was water. They were in companies of fifty or a hundred and sometimes in considerably greater bodies. They were mostly an athletic, hearty, well-conditioned people.

This latter comment seems to prove that the local tribes enjoyed a relatively leisurely lifestyle, and is further evidence for the psychological nature of Burke and Wills' death.

When the Cooper 'comes down', the great chain of lakes, channels, lignum swamps and waterholes fills inexorably, the water swirling past the outstations, covering the tracks of the rabbiters who work the Channel Country, trickling between the fiery red dunes, on towards its meeting with the greatest playa of them all, Lake Eyre. The inland sea has filled twice in living memory: once in 1950 and again, following record rains, in 1975. Here the Channel Country fulfils its destiny as the waters of the Cooper mingle with those of the Warburton.

More frequently, though, the flood-out country through which the rivers have to pass soaks up the water before it ever reaches Lake Eyre. Many of the freshwater lakes remain full for years at a time, and are home to countless thousands of waterbirds: pelicans, black swans, egrets, spoonbills, herons, marsh terns and others. Then, as the lakes slowly dry up, the birds start to leave until finally only a few muddy pools are left. In time, even they vanish, and the grass dies and the willy-willies dance across the dusty plains. Just below the surface, the seeds of plants lie dormant and there are tiny fish burrowed into the cool earth, waiting for the cycle to begin anew.

BELOW, LEFT Coongie Lakes are filled when the Cooper 'comes down'.
BELOW Everlastings (*Helipterum* spp.) splash colour amongst the dunes and gibbers.
BOTTOM Most desert animals are nocturnal, and their tracks (like these of a small mammal) may be seen crisscrossing the dunes in the morning.

The Glasshouse Mountains

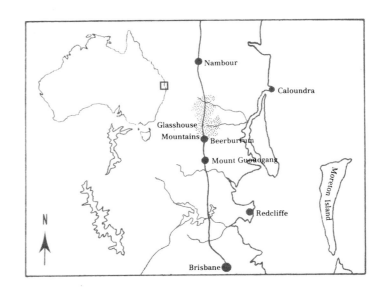

THE Aborigines from the Kobi tribe knew these peaks well, and feared them. For beneath the greatest of them all, Beerwah (556 metres), lives Brocalpin, the great spirit who transported the mountain from Durundoo station and who jealously guards his sacred spot. It is forbidden for anyone to climb the mountain, and he who breaks the taboo shall be afflicted with blindness. So it was for Andrew Petrie, the first white man to stand on top of Beerwah: he climbed the mountain in 1838 and became permanently blind eight years later. His son John, however, proved the legend a fable—or, at most, true only of the first man to stand on the peak—by retaining his sight after accompanying Andrew on the climb. John later returned to scale others of the nine peaks in the group, although the steepest of all, Coonowrin (375 metres), was not conquered until 1911.

Coonowrin is also known as Crookneck and, again according to legend, is the son of nearby Tibrogargan (282 metres) who struck him on the back of the neck because he refused to help his mother escape with the other children during a flood. So disgusted was Tibrogargan with his son that he turned his face away from him and remains today impassively staring out towards the coast. Certainly it is possible to believe in the legend on dark nights, when the moon is half hidden by scudding cloud. Tibrogargan's face, with its cavernous eyes and fixed leer, glares menacingly from the rock face: Queensland's answer to Mount Rushmore. Even when speeding up the nearby Bruce Highway, cocooned in steel, it is impossible not to feel a little uneasy at the sight of that frightful countenance.

The trachyte plugs of the mountains break the flat expanse of the coastal plain north of Brisbane.

The names of the mountains are grim and primeval: Mickeeteebumulgrai, Tunbudla (the twins), Tibberawacum, N'Gun-Gun, Beerburrum (after which a town is named), Cochin. Why are they here? What tumultuous event caused them to appear above the straggling stringybark and tea tree of the low coastal plain?

Perhaps 25 million years ago, during the Oligocene epoch, a series of volcanoes erupted through the Lower Mesozoic sandstone, spewing out rock and molten lava as they forced their way upwards. But the eruptions could not last for ever. Eventually, and perhaps after repeated explosions, the vents became choked with fast-cooling trachyte, the eruptions subsided, and the weathering processes that had begun with the first shower of rain upon the new mountains set to work. When the soft outer cones of the volcanoes had worn away, only the trachyte plugs remained as the singular group of hills and mountains we see today.

'Remarkable' was the adjective used to describe them by James Cook, who sailed this stretch of coast on 17 May 1770. Cook mentioned only three hills in his log—almost certainly Tibrogargan, Coonowrin and Beerwah—plus 'several other peaked hills inland to the Northward of these', probably the nearby Conondale Range. It was Cook who called them the Glasshouse Mountains, 'on account of their Singular form of Elivation [sic]', and it has been suggested that they either reminded him of Yorkshire glass-furnace chimneys or of burial mounds on Cleveland Moors (one of which is called Glasshouse).

The name was perpetuated by visitor Matthew Flinders, who in 1799 sailed up Bribie Passage in the *Norfolk*, then took to the ship's boat and finally walked through the scrub to the base of the nearest peak, Tibrogargan. Settlement began in the area in 1840. Flinders claimed Tibrogargan could not be climbed, and certainly scaling any of the three tallest of the Glasshouse Mountains is a challenge. Beerwah, by far the most massive peak, is a classically shaped mountain, its steep grey-brown slopes rising abruptly from a mixed forest of eucalypts and casuarinas. Toeholds chiselled into the bare rock trace a precarious path up the first pinch beyond the tree line. Above, on the hill's northern side, an overhanging cliff face looms threateningly above a small copse of stunted gums sprouting from a narrow ledge.

It is a steep and dangerous climb that has claimed more than one victim. But the view from the top is ample compensation. Far to the east, the sun glints off the waves breaking on the sand bars beyond North-West Channel. Spread out below, like the giant chessboard in *Through the Looking-Glass*, are the squares of pineapple plantations, interspersed with market gardens and the green gleam of grapevines. Smoke rises sluggishly from the kitchen chimneys of the twin towns of Glasshouse Mountains and Beerburrum on the highway. To the north and south run serried lines of pine trees, first planted in the area in 1925.

Four small national parks protect Beerwah, Coonowrin, N'Gun-Gun and Tibrogargan from commercial development. Unfortunately, too much of the surrounding land has been opened up for forestry or farming to make practicable a large national park encompassing all of these extraordinary peaks.

The tallest mountain is Beerwah, home of the great spirit Brocalpin.

QUEENSLAND

The Undara Lava Tubes

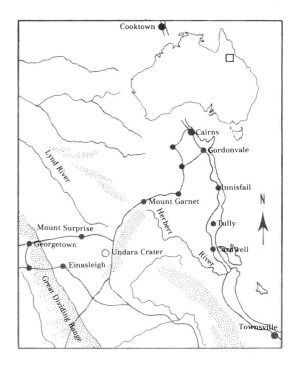

Fifty kilometres east-south-east of the small town of Mount Surprise in north Queensland, just inland from the Atherton Tableland, a subterranean network of tunnels, like shallow mine workings, snakes out from a 48 metre high volcanic crater. It is impossible to trace just how far these tunnels or tubes run, but it is thought the system may be more than 100 kilometres long, making it the largest feature of its type in the world.

Lava tunnels occur beneath the surface of smooth lava flows, known as pahahoehoe, over which forms a glassy skin like that covering the surface of warm custard. This skin is so elastic that before hardening to glass or slag it is wrinkled and folded by the differential currents flowing beneath it. The lava is more fluid in the centre of the flow than it is at the edges, and frequently ends up occupying cylindrical tubes when much of the mass has solidified.

Initially, the tubes are completely full of molten rock which exerts a hydrostatic pressure, causing the tunnels to change levels and even to turn upwards for short distances. As the amount of lava flowing through the tubes diminishes, the space it has vacated is taken up by gas and air. A trip down this river of fire would have been the ride of a lifetime. The gases given off by the lava would be burning fiercely, sucking in air as they escaped through cracks in the tunnel roof. The result would be something akin to a blast furnace, with temperatures greater than 1200°C fusing the tunnel walls and constantly forming and reforming stalactites ranging in size and shape from tiny currant-like blobs to long stems like walking-sticks. A bright yellow light would suffuse the tube, pulsing with energy, the intense heat glazing the surface of the tunnel walls. Hopefully, the traveller would be spat out at the end of the tunnel before the lava began to gell; otherwise, he or she might become trapped by the hardening rock sealing off the tube. As the lava ceased to flow, stalagmites would start to form on the floor beneath the dripping stalactites.

All these features are exhibited in the Undara lava system, which was created 190 000 years ago, during a period of volcanic activity which characterised the Late Pleistocene epoch in north Queensland. The Undara crater, from which the pahahoehoe flows emanated, is only 340 metres across, but the longer of the two tubes which once drained it, the Yarramulla section, is possibly more than 70 kilometres long, evidence of the immense quantity of molten rock which once poured out across the countryside.

As far as is known, a single tube leaves the crater, but divides in two and branches west and north 4 kilometres away. The north branch continues for at least 16 kilometres and possibly more than 35 kilometres, well beyond the Mount Surprise road, while the Yarramulla section runs slightly north of west, towards Mount Surprise and a unique geological feature known as 'The Wall'. This flat-topped ridge, up to 20 metres high and 70–300 metres wide, is thought to mark the course of an undrained lava tube connected to the Yarramulla section.

These tunnels resemble gigantic mine adits, but nature's pit props gave way millennia ago, so that only relatively short stretches of tunnel are accessible, via the collapses. The longest section of uncollapsed tunnel in the system is Bayliss Cave, 901 metres long. Better known is 561 metre long Barkers Cave, which is nearly 20 metres across at its widest point and has a height of 13.5 metres, making it substantially bigger than a two-track railway tunnel. These tubes would originally have been circular or oval: their floors were once the surface of the lava streams. From the air, dark patches of collapsed tunnel, often covered with vine scrub, mark the paths of the lava tubes across the surrounding open woodland.

It is not recorded which European first noted the existence of these remarkable landforms, but it was probably a boundary rider from nearby Mount Surprise station. This property was taken up in 1864 by Yorkshireman Ezra Firth, a gold digger from Ballarat who had surprised a group of about 100 Aborigines (probably from the Ewamin tribe) at the spot when travelling north-west with his family and sheep in search of suitable land.

Fossilbrook, the outstation Firth established on the Lynd River 40 kilometres to the north, was for some years the most northerly outpost in Queensland. Life for the pioneers in this, the Kennedy district was difficult in the extreme. As well as a lack of ready markets for their wool and meat, the squatters had to contend with disease, isolation and hostile blacks. One man estimated that up to 15 per cent of the European

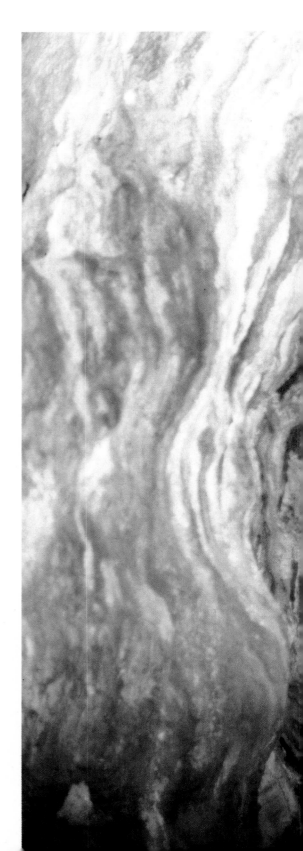

population lost their lives to the Aborigines in the first ten years of settlement, although eventually, of course, the white man won by sheer weight and superiority of arms. Ezra Firth certainly had a hard time, occasionally having to walk barefoot alongside the bullock dray which carried his wool clip the 300 kilometres to the new port of Townsville (established in 1865) because he could not afford to buy boots.

His luck, and that of north Queensland, changed in June 1872, when a party led by fellow squatter William Hann left Mount Surprise for the north. Three hundred kilometres away they found 'flattering indications of a goldfield' on a river they named the Palmer after the then Premier of Queensland. When followed up by adventurer James Venture Mulligan, this modest discovery led to the biggest, and most dangerous, goldrush in Queensland's history and the opening up of the far north.

Diggers, including thousands of Chinese, flocked to the new field from the disappointing Gilbert and Etheridge fields to the west of Mount Surprise and from as far south as Bendigo and Ballarat. Many of them were killed by Aborigines, who were reportedly cannibals. The blacks' resistance was better organised and stronger than it had been anywhere else in Australia, and legion are the tales of their cruelty to hapless travellers they captured on the lonely road to the Palmer.

Firth was quick to cash in on the goldrush, driving all his sheep to the diggings and selling them at a huge profit, then buying cattle, for which demand was high, with the proceeds. Other pastoralists soon followed the miners to the north. One of them, John Atherton, settled in 1877 on the 32 000 square kilometre tableland behind Cairns that bears his name.

Firth, whose remote property had played such an important role as a staging post in the push to the far north, gave his name to Mount Firth, a well-known landmark near the Yarramulla section of the lava tubes.

Barkers Cave is 13.5 metres tall and 20 metres across at its widest point. (James Cook University)

Evening sun bathes the eastern face of the Three Sisters.

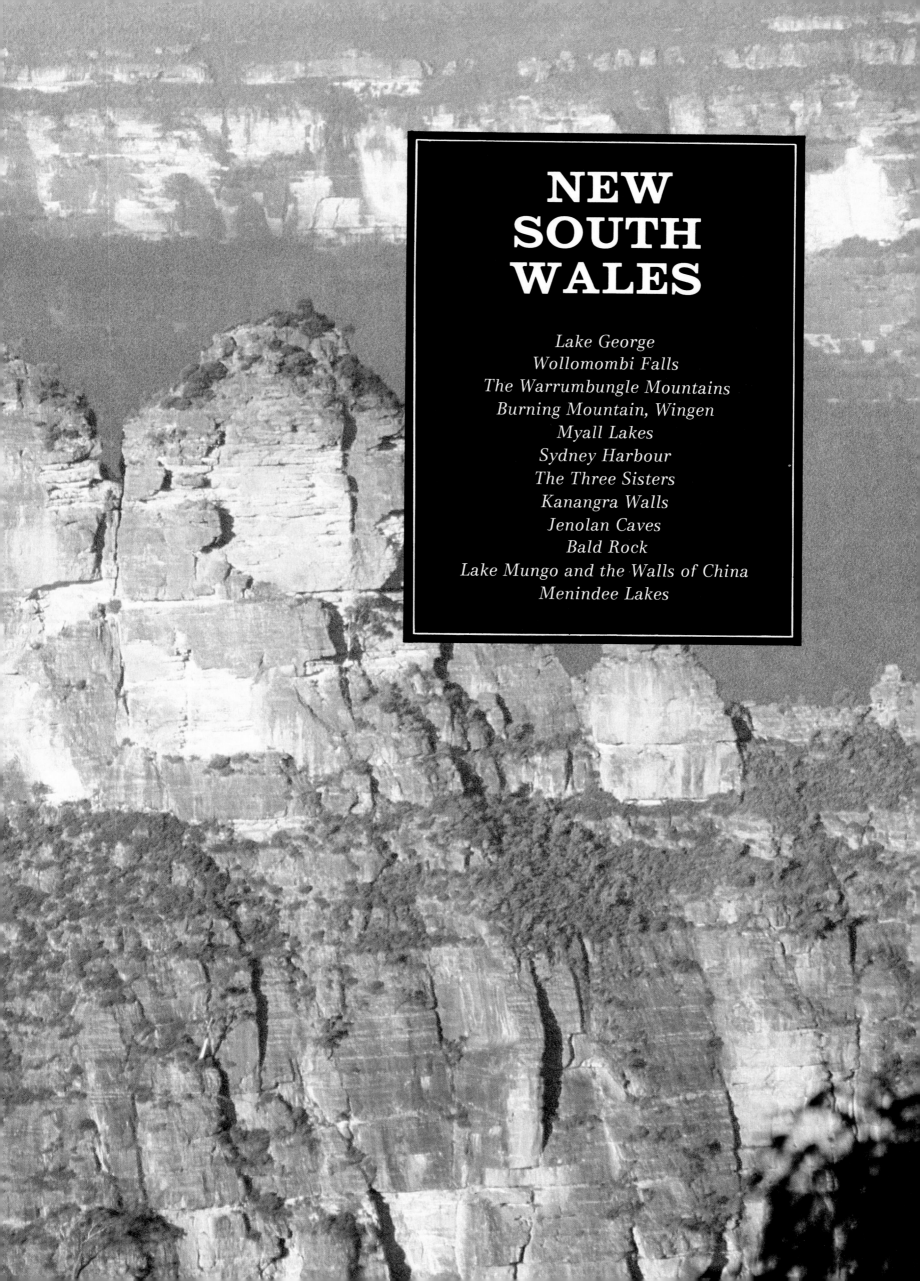

NEW SOUTH WALES

NEW SOUTH WALES

Lake George

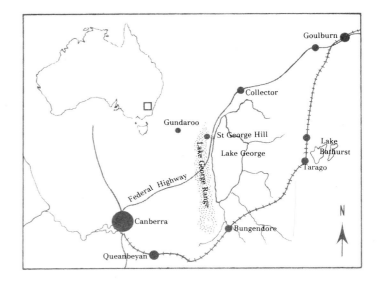

EVER since its discovery in 1820, Lake George, on the New South Wales southern tablelands between Goulburn and Canberra, has been the subject of mystery and debate. The reason: the freshwater lake, said by some to be Australia's largest, periodically vanishes, the water level sometimes dropping almost before the onlooker's eyes.

In 1874 the waters of the lake reached such a level that two steam launches operated there, in waters which were well stocked with Murray cod and other fish. Both the fish and the launches suffered an unpleasant fate when the lake dried up about the turn of the century. In the 1930s motorcycle racing on the dry lake-bed was common and racing driver 'Wizard' Smith considered making a land speed record attempt on the flat surface. Thus the legend of the mysterious 'vanishing lake' was born—even though no one has ever queried similar fluctuations in the level of the ephemeral lakes of the inland.

Like its cousins in the arid centre, evaporation exceeds precipitation at Lake George. The lake bed is also 673 metres above sea level, or only 237 metres below the highest peak in the surrounding ranges, and its catchment area is a mere six times the maximum size of the lake. In other parts of Australia, there would be no mystery about Lake George: its comings and goings would be taken for granted.

The lake was created in late Tertiary or early Pleistocene times, perhaps 2 million years ago, when movements of the earth's crust created a number of fault blocks, including the Lake George fault along the western shore of the present lake. The uplift thwarted the flow of a number of tributaries of the Yass River, principally Taylors Creek, which had previously flowed through what is now Gearys Gap, where the Federal Highway swings south-west across the Lake George Ranges. Denied an alternative outlet, the streams filled the natural basin at the foot of the new range.

When it is full, the lake extends 18 kilometres north to south and 8 kilometres across, with a maximum depth of about 5 metres. In the 1870s, however, it was considerably larger than this, and flooded the road which parallels the western shore of the lake for 13 kilometres. Traffic was diverted from Collector, north of the lake, across the ranges to Gundaroo. The water is quite brackish, particularly at low levels, the suggestion being that easterly winds have carried the salt inland from the Pacific Ocean 105 kilometres to the east.

Twenty thousand years ago, the climate was much cooler, and grinding glaciers were gouging chunks from the Snowy Mountains to the south. Although the average annual rainfall may have been less than today's 625 millimetres, the evaporation rate would have been below the current 1250 millimetres, with the consequence that the lake was all but permanent, reaching a maximum depth of 35 metres. A few metres more and it would have overflowed through Gearys Gap into the Yass River.

The lake was at a peak depth of nearly 7 metres when it was first glimpsed by Joseph Wild and his two companions in August 1820. Wild was under instructions from surgeon-settler Charles Throsby to find the lake, called by local Aborigines Lake Weereewaa and subsequently renamed after King George. He recorded that 'strong westerly wind occasioned a heavy rolling surf like the ocean' (common on large lakes) and noted that overnight the level of the water near their campsite fell by 15 centimetres. This was the beginning of the legend of the evanescent lake, yet Wild had already noted its cause: the strong westerly wind had created a seiche, or oscillatory movement of the water. On the opposite bank, the water would have risen 15 centimetres.

Neither seiches nor evaporation provided satisfactory explanation for one John Gale. In his book, *Canberra*, published to coincide with the opening of the new Parliament House in 1927, Gale postulated the incredible theory that water vanished through a volcanic fissure in the rock near Kennys Point on the north-eastern shore of the lake, feeding an easterly tending subterranean river. The fissure was eventually blocked by soil dislodged by browsing cattle, only to open again the next time there was an earth tremor. Today bores put down into the lake bed confirm the existence of underground water, but the rest of the theory is too absurd to be given any credence. It did, however, enjoy some currency until recently.

Gale also challenged the notion that Wild was the discoveror of Lake George, causing a lively debate in the letters column of the *Sydney Morning Herald* in 1919 with his contention that the real discoveror was none other than Governor Lachlan Macquarie!

Gale claimed that Robert Cartwright, the late parson of Collector (founded 1841) had told him that he accompanied Macquarie's party to the Breadalbane Plains in 1812, and thence south to Lake George. There is nothing in Macquarie's copious journals to validate the story, although he does record visiting the lake in 1820, two months after Wild's journey, accompanied by Robert Cartwright.

The lake was partially full right through the 1950s and 1960s, when an annual swimming race across it was held. In 1902 it was considered as a possible site for the national capital, but its vagaries would surely have given Walter Burley Griffin, Canberra's architect, apoplexy.

Thickset stringybarks line the lake's shore, but the mushy black silt of the lake bed—it dried up again in July 1982—is devoid of trees and shrubs. A constant mirage creates the illusion of water where there is none and elongates to giraffe-like proportions the legs of sheep grazing on the lush green grass. Much of the lake bed is fenced off as pasture, and local farmers must curse the rains that flood some of their best land. To the north and south the beaches and dunes of the shore line are being mined as material for Canberra's expansion, while the eastern ranges are scarred by the grey-brown tiers of the Woodlawn lead-zinc-copper open-cut mine, begun in December 1978.

Development may mar the idyllic picture captured by artist Joseph Lycett in 1824, but it cannot alter the rhythmic cycle of the lake, which will continue until the next major change in global climate. That will either convert Lake George into a brimming lake, teeming with fish, or a cracked earthen plain, rent with fissures, like the crab-hole flats of the outback.

Lake George periodically dries up; its catchment area is too small for it to be perennial.

NEW SOUTH WALES

Wollomombi Falls

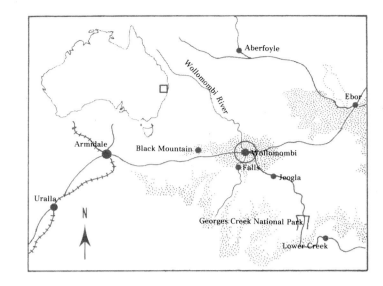

THE great waterfalls of the world have always held a fascination for explorers and the general public alike. There is something irresistible about the thought of a bustling river, flowing from perhaps hundreds of kilometres distant, suddenly coming to a steep precipice and pouring unchecked over the lip, the water racing and dancing in the sunlight, the spray pluming upwards in an eternal rainbow . . .

Australia, being both the driest and the lowest of the inhabited continents, has no Niagaras, no Victoria Falls, with their awesome might. But in the gorge country of the New England Tableland there are literally dozens of major waterfalls, no fewer than 13 feeding the Macleay River alone. Among these, Wollomombi Falls, highest in Australia and, it is said, fifth highest in the world, are pre-eminent.

The Wollomombi River (also known as Rockvale Creek) rises on rugged Chandlers Peak, at 1470 metres the highest mountain near the town of Guyra. It flows 50 kilometres, picking up tributaries on the way, before running under the bridge on the Armidale–Dorrigo road, just west of the hamlet of Wollomombi. Here the river is a gurgling, shallow highland stream, its banks lined with sedges, sheep browsing on the surrounding rich green herbage.

A few kilometres downstream, the character of the river changes. It enters a steep, narrow gorge, quickening its pace. From now on, this is a river of no return. A bushwalker slipped and fell into the gorge a few years ago—he was lucky: it had been a dry season and the stream was barely flowing. Had it been raining in the high country, causing the stream to rise, he would have been swept away, to the edge of the precipice, to plunge 457 metres into the valley below.

Below, so far down that the wattles clinging precariously to the cliff edges seem like tufts of Mitchell grass, is a pool of water enclosed on three sides by rock walls. The wall on the opposite side to the falls is part of a rugged spur separating the Wollomombi from the Chandler River. So massive is the gorge carved by the twin rivers that visitors tend to misjudge its scale. From the western lookout there is no way down without ropes and pulleys. Some who have tried to make the descent on foot, one an experienced mountaineer, have fallen to their deaths on the bleak, cheerless rocks below. Others have been trapped on the narrow ledges and had to wait out long, sub-zero nights before being rescued. To reach the base of the falls in safety, you must clamber down the Green Gully Spur, several kilometres downstream, then scramble up the boulder-strewn riverbed and swim through the broadest pools.

Like that most celebrated of all river gorges, the Grand Canyon in the United States, this is a relatively young landscape. The grey rocks themselves are slate and greywacke, probably formed beneath a shallow sea 250–290 million years ago, but the streams did not begin their work until 6 million years ago when the plateau began to be gradually uplifted. As the tablelands rose, as much as 800 metres, the speed of the streams flowing east across them increased, so that eventually they were slicing into the soft rock at the rate of 8 centimetres every 1000 years.

None of this was evident to the Aboriginal tribe, the Anaiwan, who inhabited the cold highlands for millennia before white men arrived. They knew the falls as Walamumbi, simply meaning 'great falls', but they left no artefacts in the shadowy gorge, no creation myths to be passed down through the generations. Their sparse occupation of the highlands was shattered when John Oxley and his party passed by in 1818 en route to the coast. Oxley did not glimpse Wollomombi Falls.

The first property taken up in the district was Wolka (Walcha), claimed by Hamilton Semphill in 1832, and by 1840 there were 66 stations dotted across the tablelands. William Chandler was an elusive figure, a stockman who worked for Peter McIntyre of Guyra. Did he, following on horseback the tracks of some straying cattle, hoofs crunching the frost-draped grass, stumble across the falls that now bear his name and gaze in awe down into the abyss? Or was it simply a 'flow-on' from his naming the river and the nearby peak after himself? The answer appears to have been buried with him.

Today Ron Edgar, owner of Rosewood station, uses the gorge as a natural fence for his sheep. His grandfather, John, took up the property in 1898. In the early years, says Ron, the sheep had to be mustered every night to protect them from marauding dingoes which climbed out of the gorge at dusk.

One hundred kilometres to the south-east, the waters of the MacLeay River, born on the slopes of Chandlers Peak, mingle with the Pacific Ocean at Trial Bay, the message of their eventful journey lost in the rolling breakers.

Falls' 457-metre sheer drop is amongst the highest in the world. Most waterfalls of similar height drop in stages.

The Warrumbungle Mountains

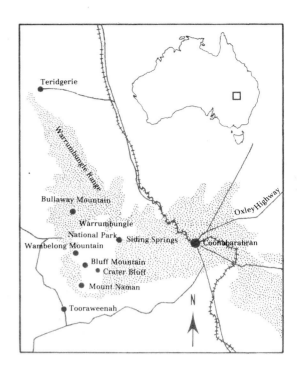

FOR those who believe that, once west of the Great Divide, the plains roll on unchecked to the Indian Ocean, the jagged, Tolkienesque Warrumbungle Mountains, 520 kilometres north-west of Sydney, must come as a rude awakening. The name, given to the rugged range of volcanic bluffs, spires and domes by the local Kamilaroi Aborigines, has outlasted the prosaic title, Arbuthnots Range, coined by explorer John Oxley who, in June 1818, was the first white man to glimpse the mountains, from a granite hill 110 kilometres distant.

Oxley had been following the westward-flowing Macquarie River, which he was convinced must lead to an inland sea. And it was from the west that he glimpsed the jagged skyline of the Warrumbungles, in his words 'a stupendous range of mountains'.

Beyond them, the river petered out in the impenetrable Macquarie Marshes, running through only in good seasons to join the Darling River and, ultimately, the deeper ditch of the Murray. Oxley turned back, crossed another tributary of the Darling, the Castlereagh, and came face-to-face with the mountain range, 'its elevated points . . . of a dark, barren and gloomy appearance'. He paused to climb one of the high peaks, which he named Mount Exmouth but which from his description was probably present-day Mount Bullaway, then moved on to the north. It was left to the settlers lured to the district by Oxley's tales of the rich grazing country of the Liverpool Plains to clamber amongst the grey-black peaks, spires and bluffs.

This is a landscape born in fire. Seventeen million years ago a volcano erupted through the much older Pilliga sandstones, festering for another 3 million years. Its legacy was a series of dark basalt cones concealing harder trachyte 'plugs' and 'dykes' (former cracks). As the basalt eroded away, the pieces of light-coloured trachyte were exposed, gigantic, invulnerable, soaring like gods amongst the pantheon of the main range.

When conservationist Myles Dunphy first visited the mountains in the late 1930s, he was struck by their mystic presence. 'There is a strong atmosphere of Stonehenge in England, Carnac in France, and of the cairns, dolmens and barrows of Carromore and Knockarea in Ireland,' he mused. And so he named the outstanding features of the Warrumbungles after Celtic gods and goddesses: Balor of the death-dealing eye; Dagda, who slew the hundred-legged Mata; Danu; Nuada of the silver hand; Ogma and Sreng. Dunphy wanted to see a national park created, incorporating the major points of interest. His wish was granted in 1953 when 3759 hectares of land, most of it donated by local grazier Alf Pincham, was set aside for preservation. Since then the National Parks and Wildlife Service has acquired another 14 316 hectares, quintupling the size of the park.

The 14 kilometre trail across the Grand High Tops boasts some of the most spectacular views in Australia. The track skirts the Breadknife, a 100 metre high freestanding trachyte dyke only 2 metres thick at its top. Once the western face of the Breadknife was one of the prime rock climbs in Australia, but fear of erosion and of falling rocks striking walkers below closed the Breadknife to climbers in 1962. Today, to avoid detection, climbers risk scaling the steep western face at night.

Beyond the Breadknife looms Belougery Spire (1061 metres), a neck on the outer rim of the volcano. To the south soar Crater Bluff (1087 metres), Bluff Mountain, Mount Wambelong (1205 metres), and cone-shaped Tonduron Spire (1130 metres). Most of the trails were built in the early 1960s, a labour of love for the first ranger, Carl Dow. Materials for the huts along the trails were carried in by men and horses. For three years, prison teams worked on the trails, improving drainage and surfaces.

These mountains occupy a strategic position between the inland and the coastal zone. They have an annual rainfall of 500–600 millimetres and are an important habitat for wildlife, in particular the rare brush-tailed rock wallaby, a colony of which inhabits Belougery Split Rock.

Since 1965 new domes have joined the ancient plugs of the volcano: a complex of giant telescopes atop Siding Spring Mountain on the road to nearby Coonabarabran. The observatory, operated by the Australian National University, has made many major discoveries, taking advantage of the unusually clear night skies. Did the previous custodians of the Warrumbungles, the Kamilaroi, try to pre-empt these scientists? Did they try to make sense of their universe from the forbidding grandeur of the mountains? The evidence suggests not. Few artefacts, rock carvings or paintings have been found. Perhaps this sinister landscape was sacred to them, or—a less romantic interpretation—maybe, living amongst plenty on the adjacent plains, they had no need to penetrate the towering ramparts.

OPPOSITE, TOP LEFT **Belougery Spire.** (Trevern Dawes)
OPPOSITE, TOP RIGHT **The Breadknife, a volcanic dyke.** (Trevern Dawes)
OPPOSITE, BELOW **Bluff Mountain.** (Trevern Dawes)

Burning Mountain, Wingen

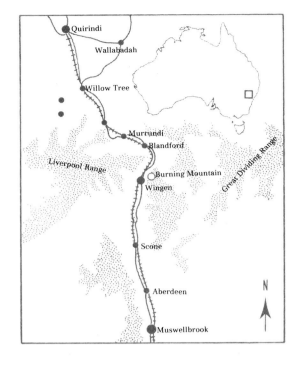

THE blast of heat can be felt almost before the fire and smoke are seen rolling off the hillside like the searing heat of the desert in summer. Closer up the heat is even more intense, beating through the soles of your boots until it becomes impossible to stand in one place. What a spot this would be for tyro fire-walkers! Yet even their seniors would find it impossible to withstand the scorching heat emitted by the cracks and vents on the hill top. Below, where the fissures cut so deeply into the earth that a dropped stone barely touches bottom, the temperature reaches 1700°C. The mountain is alive—and has the stench of a snorting steam train.

This is Burning Mountain, one of the most curious natural wonders in Australia. Running through the 518 metre high hillside is a seam of lignite, ignited it is thought by natural causes—lightning, bushfire, or even by an unwitting Aborigine camped for the night—hundreds or perhaps thousands of years ago. As the coal turns to ash, the earth subsides, opening up great rifts and chasms in the hillside.

The mountain, known to the Wonarua people as Win-jen, is located just north of Scone on Glengarry station, a brisk 20-minute walk from the roar and bustle of the New England Highway. Beyond the kurrajongs and casuarinas, the hill lies stripped bare, the dry earth stained sulphur-yellow, the Permian sedimentary rocks metamorphosed by the fire. A smoke haze drifts lazily across the valley, down where the sheep are grazing. As at the mud pools of Rotorua in New Zealand, it is easy to imagine oneself being sucked down into that Hadean inferno. It happens sometimes to straying sheep and, presumably, to small animals, too. Droppings indicate that kangaroos and other mammals come to sit on the warm earth at night, when the vents glow orange-red.

Yet the sheep have, in the past, benefited from the fiery mountain. As far back as 1830 the Reverend Pleydell Wilton, assistant chaplain of Newcastle, recorded how 'its sulphurous and aluminous products combined' had been 'successfully applied in the cure of the scab in sheep'. If the sheep did not appreciate its miraculous healing properties, several generations of humans did. Winjennia ointment, manufactured in Melbourne from sulphur mined on the mountain until 1964, was a universal panacea. Sulfazone 'hypertonic' was another, claimed to be suitable for wounds, cuts, sores, scalds, burns, sore eyes and throats, sprains, bruises, blisters, sunburns, bites and stings, carbuncles, sore legs, bruises, crusted sores, corns and tinea. It is surprising the modern pharmaceutical industry has stood a chance!

Wilton was the first person to bring the mountain to scientific notice. Predictably, his story of a fiery mountain was distorted into rumours of a volcano. There is some debate over which European actually 'discovered' the phenomenon, though. A sign at the site claims it was Major Thomas Mitchell, in 1829; others suggest a station hand named Smart was first on the spot.

Both Wilton and Mitchell made several trips back to the mountain, in its strategic location on the route north from the Upper Hunter Valley. It is changing gradually, although neither the clergyman nor the surveyor-general would have noticed it. The fire is consuming the 3.5 metre thick coal seam at the rate of perhaps 1 metre each year. One day, maybe within the lifespan of the saplings growing nearby, the fire will go out, new growth will cover the area, and Mount Wingen will become just another minor peak in the Liverpool Range.

Sulphur from the burning coal seam encrusts the rocks of the bare hillside.

NEW SOUTH WALES

Myall Lakes

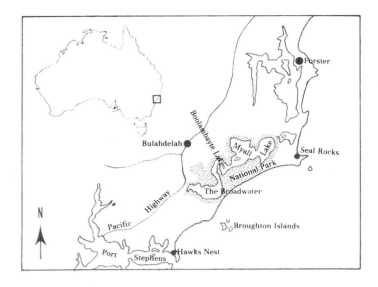

JUST south of the sleepy New South Wales town of Buladelah, the bustling Pacific Highway crosses a gently flowing stream. Most travellers do not give it a second glance, yet this river, the Myall, is the key to the fishing and prawning industry of the New South Wales mid-north coast. It is the largest tributary of three tranquil lakes which are the breeding ground for 95 per cent of the commercial fish and crustaceans taken between Newcastle and Kempsey.

Incorporated into a national park in 1972 and since extended, the Myall Lakes—The Broadwater, Myall Lake (the largest), and the S-shaped Boolambyte Lake—are the most beautiful of the string of lakes that parallel this stretch of coastline. Relative difficulty of access, despite their closeness to Newcastle, has kept them free of much crass commercial development, although Port Stephens, into which the Myall River ultimately flows, was discovered by James Cook in 1770 and named by him after the Secretary to the Admiralty.

Governor Macquarie had intended to establish a convict settlement on the port but he abandoned the idea because of the infertility of the surrounding countryside. Still, this did not stop the Australian Agricultural Company in 1824 from acquiring 400 000 hectares of land bordering on Port Stephens and the Myall Lakes for raising sheep. The block stretched north beyond Gloucester to the Manning River and incorporated the same rugged mountains that have inhibited development ever since. The sheep died by the hundreds of fluke and other diseases, and by April 1828 the company had suspended its Commissioner, Robert Dawson, and was importuning the government for alternative land. In 1834 more than 200 000 hectares of land was exchanged for blocks west of the Great Divide, although the company retained more than 185 000 hectares bordering to the south on Port Stephens, the lower Myall River and The Broadwater.

Much of the land surrounding the lakes is composed of giant, stable sand dunes up to 120 metres high. Large trees are rare and the lakes area escaped extensive logging, even though Port Stephens was used as a shipping base for the valuable red cedar and the timber-getters sailed up the Myall River beyond The Broadwater in search of suitable trees.

The local Aboriginal people, the Worimi, lived well on a rich and varied diet of fish, shellfish, crustaceans, and a variety of plants, reptiles, mammals and birds. They left their middens right along the coast. But the arrival of the Europeans destroyed this apparently idyllic lifestyle for ever. By 1859, 34 years after Agricultural Company settlers had come to the district, enlightened colonists were expressing concern that the company's employees had ruined 'the matrix of future generations' by bedding Worimi maidens, thinning the ranks of the graceful and athletic blacks to such effect that there was only a handful of pure-bloods left.

White fishermen were quick to realise the lakes' potential and built holiday shacks along the coastline. Two permanent holiday resorts have grown up since World War II, at Seal Rocks north of the National Park, and at Tea Gardens–Hawks Nest on Port Stephens. Seal Rocks, originally known as Seals Rock but corrupted over time, is actually the name of an island offshore. The seals have long since vanished, killed off by lobstermen who cut up the meat for bait.

Most of the fish in the lakes are saltwater species: whiting, flathead, bream and blackfish. A surface layer of fresh water overlies a deeper layer of denser salt water and, by and large, the two do not mix. Prawns as well as fish spawn in the unpolluted waters of the lake system. The young prawns swim up the tidal, mangrove-fringed Myall River to the lakes, mature, spawn, and return to the sea. They run on dark nights to escape the lurking bream, but another, more efficient, predator may be waiting for them: man. Local prawners draw lots to see who shall get to cast his funnel-shaped nets across the best part of the river.

The western shores of the lakes were laid down 270–340 million years ago, as deposits of sand in a wide, submerged valley. There were also volcanic intrusions on what is now the eastern shore. Then, in the great Tertiary uplift, the land was raised to form a coastal tableland. Streams cut into the rocks, creating valleys and ridges. The Myall River may have run out onto a wide plain before reaching the sea.

During the Ice Ages the ocean level rose and fell substantially. As it rose, the valleys were flooded, leaving the peaks—Broughton, Violet Hill and Johnsons Hill—as islands. Sand washed up by the sea joined together most of these former islands, with the

exception of Broughton Island which remains isolated (it was used as a testing ground for myxomatosis in 1952). About 15 000 years ago, the sea level rose again, flooding the depression behind the frontal dunes and forming a lagoon.

Resembling the sand ridges of the inland, the dunes ran parallel to each other, like ripples on the seashore magnified ten thousandfold. But the largest dunes in central Australia are only a quarter as high as some of the older dunes north of the headland known as the Big Gibber. Like their inland cousins, the seaward dunes are stabilised by spinifex, a species related to the canegrass found atop the central Australian sand ridges and not to the spiky *triodia* species popularly called spinifex.

This spinifex cover represents the least exotic of the area's many plant communities. Inland, on the first line of dunes, grow tea trees and coast wattles, banksias and lilly-pillies. Wet and dry heaths of banksias, bottlebrushes and blackboys crowd the low dunes while, on the higher dunes, forests of blackbutt and smooth-barked apple up to 35 metres high overshadow a diverse understorey. At Mungo Brush and Chinamans Knob are rainforests dominated by palm trees and containing the fearsome stinging tree. Reeds and bullrushes fringe the lakes to a depth of 1.5 metres; behind them stand melaleucas with their characteristic papyrus-like bark, and further back grows a sprinkling of swamp oaks and swamp mahogany. Predictably, the lakes attract a large variety of waterbirds; and 76 different species of birds, including the gleaming satin bowerbird, have been noted in the rainforests.

The sand dunes are a rich source of the space-age minerals rutile and zircon and have been mined since the early 1950s. Conservationists fought against the granting of leases because the mining process involves stripping the dunes of vegetation, although Mineral Deposits' reclamation work is exemplary. Sand mining is to continue at three locations within the park, Big Gibber, Bridge Hill Ridge and Bombah Point, until reserves are exhausted.

The characteristic tree of the lakes' edges is the broad-leaved paperbark (*Melaleuca quinquenervia*).

NEW SOUTH WALES

Sydney Harbour

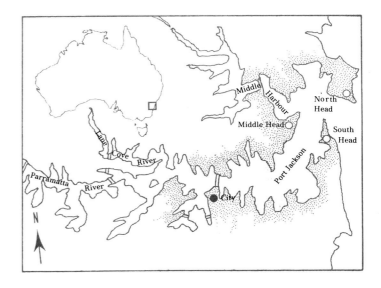

THE official account of the voyage of the First Fleet (published in 1789, the year after the establishment of Sydney Town) described it as a harbour where 'a thousand ships of the line might ride in perfect security'. Surgeon John White of the First Fleet wrote that it was 'without exception, the finest and most extensive Harbour in the Universe', a view shared by Marine Captain Collins, who called it 'equal if not superior to any yet known in the world'. All this might have been a little easier to swallow a century or so earlier, when much of the world remained to be discovered by European mariners, but, at the end of the eighteenth century, there was very little left—except Antarctica.

'What about Rio?' the doubting Thomases still cry. Well, what about Rio? The First Fleeters called there en route to Botany Bay, and they were under no illusions about the comparative merits of the two harbours. To them, Sydney Harbour (or Port Jackson, as it is officially known) was, quite simply, without peer. One great advantage the harbour offered ships' captains of the day was that there was sufficient room and depth of water inside the heads for their unwieldy sailing vessels to manoeuvre. This made it both a convenient and a safe port for them.

The statistics are impressive enough. The average width of the harbour is 1.6 kilometres; its tidal waters extend as far as Parramatta, 29 kilometres from the ocean, and they are navigable by large ships for at least 16 kilometres of that length. More than half the harbour has a depth of over 9 metres at low tide, its greatest depth being 47 metres. The distance between the heads is more than 1.6 kilometres; the average depth, 24 metres.

But mere numbers cannot do justice to the reality of the harbour. It dominates the city of Sydney in the way the Himalayas do the Tibetan capital, Lhasa. Sydney's traffic jams are not so much the product of inadequate street planning or traffic control systems as of the harbour, which creates bottlenecks at the major crossing points: Ryde Bridge, Gladesville Bridge, Iron Cove Bridge, Glebe Island Bridge and, of course, the famous 'Coathanger'. Yet no Sydneysider would be without his or her harbour. It would be like asking New Yorkers to make do without Manhattan Island.

Arthur Phillip, first governor of New South Wales, described Port Jackson as 'the Bay of a Hundred Coves'. Since then, successive naming parties have labelled as 'bays' 66 indentations on the harbour's 400 kilometre shoreline, 15 'coves' and three 'creeks'; many others are not named at all. Equaly anomalous is the categorisation of the four main arms of the harbour: the Parramatta River, the Lane Cove River, Middle Harbour and North Harbour. The major tributary of the Parramatta River, Toongabbie Creek, rises at Seven Hills, 25 kilometres west of the Sydney Post Office, while the Lane Cove River rises as Coups Creek in the northern Sydney suburb of Wahroonga. Middle Harbour also is fed by a stream, Middle Harbour Creek, but North Harbour is a simple inlet of Port Jackson.

Of course, today's tiny streams, all polluted by sewage and other runoff, are not the rivers they once were. During the last Ice Age the sea was 135 metres below its present level and the estuarine arms of Port Jackson were all river valleys. The minor streams which today individually flow into the harbour would have combined with the major tributaries to have formed considerable watercourses, cutting into the Sydney peneplain, an undulating plain of Hawkesbury sandstone formed under a shallow sea during the Triassic period. When the last Ice Age ended, 8000 years ago, sea levels rose and the river valleys were flooded, leaving isolated peaks protruding as islands. Broken Bay, Port Hacking and Botany Bay were formed at the same time as Sydney Harbour, but none has the same depth of water. Silt from the Blue Mountains, which might otherwise clog the harbour, is diverted by the Hawkesbury River into Broken Bay. A sandbar near the heads, which reduced clearance to only 6 metres, once posed a danger to large ships, but it was dredged long ago.

Even though they are surrounded by a city of more than 3 million people, the waters of Port Jackson are clean enough to support 570 species of fish, more than the total for the waters surrounding the whole of Great Britain. Bream, blackfish and leatherjackets are the fish most commonly taken by anglers (net fishing is banned), but species include tropical gobies and wrasse, more frequently found in the warmer waters of the Great Barrier Reef. Corals live on the floor of the harbour, too, and sea fans, sea pens, soft corals and sponges. The large number of habitats within the harbour, coupled with the flushing effect of the wide entrance, has maintained the species diversity.

A mighty city has grown up on the shores of the drowned river valley that is Sydney Harbour.

Sydney Harbour's range of habitats includes mangroves (on the upper reaches of Middle Harbour, the Parramatta River and the Lane Cove River), sandy beaches, rocky promontories, mud, seagrass and heavy kelp beds. Waterbirds are common. A surprising amount of the foreshore remains as it did 200 years ago, before Arthur Phillip founded a nation on the shores of Sydney Cove. In sheltered pockets, forests of gums, banksias, wattles and smooth-barked apples grow; beautiful, buttressed Port Jackson figs ring the water's edge, while close-cropped scrub and heath cap the exposed headlands.

Acting upon his instructions, Phillip sailed his motley fleet of two naval vessels and seven merchant ships into Botany Bay on 19 January 1788, but he soon realised that the open bay, with its marshes and sand dunes, was unsuitable for settlement. He decided to examine the 'bay or harbour' which Cook had noted and named after a Secretary of the Admiralty 18 years earlier, and sailed up the coast in three ships' pinnaces. He was understandably elated by what he found, and transferred the fleet to Sydney Cove, 7 kilometres from the harbour entrance, on 26 January 1788.

Captain John Hunter, the fleet's second-in-command, conducted the first survey of the harbour, naming many of its prominent features, including the infamous Sow and Pigs Reef, one of the only navigational hazards. Few Aboriginal names have survived 200 years of colonisation: Phillip noted the Aborigines' 'confidence and manly behaviour' when he stepped ashore at Manly Cove, and so named it after them, but in a British way. Woolloomooloo, Kurraba, Kirribilli, Parriwi and Curraghbeena are still in use, but the pioneers seemed more at ease with the English names they stuck on their maps. In any case, the Sydney tribes did not last long after the advent of 'civilisation'—many died of an epidemic, thought to have been smallpox, 14 months after the arrival of the First Fleet.

As well as being the port of Sydney, Sydney Harbour is the main fleet and support base of the Royal Australian Navy. Surface ships berth in Woolloomooloo Bay, submarines across the harbour in Neutral Bay, the 'mothball' fleet in Athol Bay; Garden Island, site of the first vegetable plot in Australia, now boasts one of the biggest dry docks in the world. Yet, surprisingly, the naval presence is not obtrusive. It is possible to scrape oysters off the rocks only a few hundred metres from a 'mothballed' minesweeper.

Harbourside land fetches a fearsome price in the Sydney real estate market, but many people over the years have contrived to live in caves and sheds and on houseboats around the harbour foreshores for very much less. The millionaires and the paupers share the same view: that magnificent stretch of blue water, dancing in the sunlight, speckled with brightly coloured sailboards and yachts and the bobbing hulls of dinghies. If it is not the finest harbour in the world, it takes a lot of beating.

OPPOSITE, TOP LEFT Grey mangroves (*Avicennia marina*) grow in a backwater of the Lane Cove River, less than 9 kilometres from the Sydney GPO.
OPPOSITE, TOP RIGHT The Harbour was formed by streams which cut into the surrounding Hawkesbury sandstone.
OPPOSITE, BELOW The distance between the Heads is more than 1.6 kilometres.
BELOW Sandstone cliffs guard the harbour entrance. Cook noted a possible opening in the ramparts, but did not explore further.

The Three Sisters

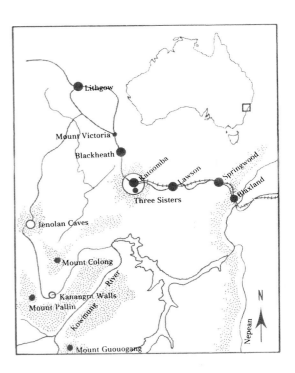

THEY stand like the crumbling buddhas of Borobudur at the end of the curving cliff face that sweeps south-east from Echo Point lookout at Katoomba. More than 600 metres below, the radial fronds of tree ferns swirl like green snow crystals amongst the drifting forest of the valley floor. Eight kilometres to the south looms the massive bulk of Mount Solitary, proud and aloof, guarded by the lonely fortress of Ruined Castle to its west and, beyond, the ramparts of Narrowneck, the sandstone peninsula that divides this valley, the Jamison, from the gentler grasslands of the Megalong.

It is a landscape of astonishing grandeur for a range of hills—or, rather, a tableland—so low as on most continents to be almost inconsequential (the highest point, near Lithgow, is little more than 1100 metres high). Nowhere else except perhaps in south-eastern Victoria are the brooding grey-green eucalypt forests that are for most people synonymous with the word 'bush' so impenetrable, so overpowering, broken only by the orange slashes of unscalable cliffs. The impression of impassibility is heightened by the blue haze that hangs, like the smoke from a bushfire, over the mountains, the product of the light-scattering effect of oil evaporating from the eucalypts.

Most of the sandstone and shale that form the mountains were laid down in the Triassic period (247–212 million years ago), beneath a shallow sea that once covered an area stretching from Yass to Bathurst and north to Newcastle. Earlier, freshwater lakes and swamps had provided a fertile environment for the growth of slimy forests which came to form some of the most extensive bituminous coal beds in the world, deposited in Permian times along with more sandstone and shale, on top of granite and quartzite bedrock. Much more recently, perhaps only 15–20 million years ago, basalt lava erupted through fissures and poured out over the ground.

These rocks were uplifted in a monoclinal fold under enormous pressure from the east during the late Tertiary period, 2–3 million years ago. Streams running off the plateau so formed began to carve out deep valleys. Then the earth convulsed again, tilting the new tableland, pushing the western edge up to a height of 900–1100 metres and depressing the coastal fringe, allowing the sea to flood the seaward valleys and create the bays and harbours of Port Jackson, Broken Bay and Port Hacking.

The tableland became fretted and dissected by a series of V-shaped valleys. As the resistant Hawkesbury sandstone was worn through, it was undercut by the erosion of the softer underlying Narrabeen shales, causing it to fall away in huge slabs along vertical joint planes—one of the most recent being a great landslide which altered the shape of the Malatia Point headland near Katoomba in 1931—and rimming the valleys

The Three Sisters, "...like the crumbling Buddhas of Borobudur". (Trevern Dawes)

with awesome cliffs. More than half the plateau has already been washed down the streams and, eventually, out to sea, even though its height has not altered appreciably.

Erosion on this scale has created many isolated mountains, hills and columns, including Orphan Rock, Mount Solitary and Ruined Castle which, like the Three Sisters, border the Jamison Valley. The sisters once formed a continuous point reaching out into the valley, but have long since been separated by the action of water seeping into cracks in the rock.

Although the mountains were not high, they remained until 1813 unconquered by the colonisers of New South Wales, prohibiting all westward expansion. The successes of men like Blaxland, Lawson and Wentworth, and William Cox were hard won: crossing the mountains and building roads and railways called for bravery, patience and skill, and the sweat of many a convict brow.

The penetration of the creaking bullock wagons and snorting locomotives shattered the tranquillity of the Daruk Aborigines, who had lived in these mountains for more than 12 000 years. The Daruk left few visible signs of their long occupation but relayed some of their creation myths before their passing. One concerned the Three Sisters, which they believed to be the three daughters, Meenhi, Wimlah and Gunnedoo, of a witchdoctor named Tyawan. Beneath them, in a cave in the Jamison Valley, slept a bunyip, terror of the bush. So whenever Tyawan ventured into the valley to gather food he built a rock wall behind which his daughters would shelter.

One day when Tyawan had gone down into the valley, Meenhi knocked a rock off her lofty perch, breaking an important law of her people. The crash silenced the creatures of the bush and caused the wall of rocks to break away, leaving the girls exposed on a narrow ledge. Worse, it awoke the sleeping bunyip, who emerged angrily from his cave to see the three girls cowering above him.

Tyawan saw the danger his daughters were in and as the bunyip advanced towards them, he pointed a magic shin bone at them and turned them into stone. The bunyip wheeled round and gave chase to the witchdoctor, who soon found himself trapped against a rock face too steep to climb. A small cave in the cliff appeared to offer safety but it was too small for a man to squeeze into. So Tyawan changed himself into a lyrebird and hid in the cave until the bunyip grew tired of the pursuit and returned to his cave to sleep.

Unfortunately, in his haste Tyawan had dropped his magic shin bone into the valley below and he consequently lacked the means with which to turn his daughters, and himself, back into people. He can still be seen, scratching about the forest floor in search of the all-important bone.

The bunyip apparently remained asleep when white men arrived in the Jamison Valley in the 1870s and began to mine the rich coal and oil shale deposits underlying the orange sandstone. They built a double-cable railway down a 45-degree slope to the valley floor, and a flying fox through the bush to carry oil shale from the Ruined Castle. The flying-fox rope snapped in 1890, putting it permanently out of action, so a horse-drawn tramway was built around the base of the cliffs, also servicing the coal mine that burrowed 1.5 kilometres into the hillside below Katoomba Falls. The mining operation made good money for a time but ran into economic difficulties during the Depression; after World War II the mine railway was converted into a scenic joy ride for tourists.

From the base of the railway one track leads west, past the abandoned coal mines and through lush rainforests and eucalypt stands to Narrowneck and the Ruined Castle, while another branches east, across Katoomba Creek and along the great cliff face of Echo Point to the base of the Three Sisters. Here a series of about 750 steps, the so-called Giant Stairway, winds upwards to the cliff top. The steps were cut into the crumbling rock more than 50 years ago by one Ranger McKay; recently, many of them have been replaced by less attractive but more practical galvanised-iron steps.

Just below the top of the stairway a small bridge leads across a chasm to a shallow cave scooped out of the side of the first 'sister'. The formations have now been closed to rock climbers and this is the closest anyone can get to the summit of any of the three pinnacles. Below, the rock face falls away sheer for more than 100 metres to the first phalanx of gum trees, which grow almost horizontally. The Three Sisters themselves, and the West Wall that tapers off beyond them into the valley, are crowned by a light scrub of wattles, boronias, banksias and the occasional blackboy, while ferns and mosses grow in pockets of moisture amongst the rocks.

It is a vista that changes with the seasons in a peculiarly Australian way. In spring and early summer, the ridges and rock ledges burst into colour as the yellow wattles, red mountain devils and pink boronias bloom; later, the dancing tongues of bushfires may lick the immobile bodies of the sisters, as they did in 1977 when the flames were only halted by a firebreak cut below Echo Point. In autumn, it is the turn of the yellow-bronze banksias, while in winter snow may dust the sisters' heads and shoulders.

A concrete pathway follows the cliff line around to Echo Point on the outskirts of Katoomba. The town, the largest in the Blue Mountains, takes its name from the Daruk word *kedumba*, meaning 'falling water'. Settled originally because of the nearby mines, by the 1890s Katoomba was a fully fledged holiday resort. The majestic Carrington Hotel, then called the Great Western, opened its doors to its first train-load of mountain-air-loving city dwellers in 1882; other, less lavish, hotels and guesthouses followed. In one of the delicious ironies of nineteenth-century Australia, the mountains that, for the first 25 years of settlement at Sydney Town, had formed such a barrier to westward expansion had become a destination in their own right.

OPPOSITE, TOP LEFT **Moss-covered rocks at the base of Katoomba Falls.** (Trevern Dawes)
OPPOSITE, TOP RIGHT **Wentworth Falls plunge over the precipice.** (Trevern Dawes)
OPPOSITE, BELOW **Morning mist fills the Jamison Valley, leaving Mount Solitary floating like an island.** (Trevern Dawes)

Kanangra Walls

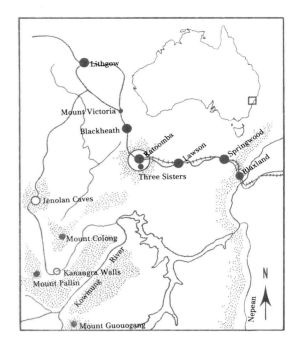

IT is as though the world has ended. And, in a sense, it has. One moment you are striding across an undulating heathland, the tough, tenacious bushes clawing at your leggings, the next, there is nothing beneath you, nothing for 600 metres but the air and the occasional gliding hawk.

This is where the world of the Kanangra-Boyd plateau ends and the valley of the Kanangra Creek begins. The junction is seemingly well defined as the event horizon of a black hole, except that there is no problem about light escaping: it glints off the trickling water of the creek, glares through storm clouds gathering over the aptly named Cloudmaker, 6 kilometres to the north-east, and in late afternoon lights up the straggling walls of the historic Hydro-Majestic Hotel, 40 kilometres distant at Medlow Bath.

Described by some commentators as 'the most dramatic area of wilderness in the whole of Australia', Kanangra Walls are but part of the 67 881 hectare Kanangra-Boyd National Park, which is virtually the south-western annex of the much larger Blue Mountains National Park. It was the Kanangra area which the conservationist, Myles Dunphy, suggested in 1932 should become the first stage of a Greater Blue Mountains national park. But in fact the northern and central sections were proclaimed first, in 1959, and it was 1969 before Kanangra Walls were incorporated in a national park, extended in 1977 to include the 10 000 hectare Konangaroo State Forest on Boyd Plateau.

The walls themselves had since the turn of the century been included in a reserve, in recognition of their scenic splendour. The view from the plateau edge—actually a narrow, two-pronged spit of land jutting out from the much larger Boyd Plateau—is amongst the most spectacular in Australia. The scale of this landscape is rivalled only by the gorge country of the New England Tableland. A topographical map, which reduces these mighty ramparts to a shaded line and the roaring waterfalls and rapids to a network of sinuous threads, makes a mockery of nature's handiwork.

The sandstone walls glow orange and gold in the late afternoon sun, a seemingly impregnable fortress when seen from the confines of the narrow, moist gorge below. Yet two tracks lead over the lip of the plateau. One takes walkers on to Mounts High and Mighty (1015 metres), Stormbreaker (1042 metres), Rip, Rack, Roar and Rumble and the Cloudmaker to the Coxs River; the other follows Gingra Creek to its junction with the Kowmung River, the only unpolluted stream flowing into Warragamba dam.

Although the cliffs are composed of Megalong conglomerates, capped with Permian sandstone and shale and chert overlying Upper Devonian quartzites, much of the Boyd Plateau and upper Kowmung River valley is volcanic: granite, porphry and diorite broken down in less dramatic fashion to create rich soils which support extensive forests of brown barrel, mountain gum and manna gum. For more than 50 years, from 1921 to 1977, the stands of hardwoods in Konangaroo State Forest were logged, and at one stage plans were proposed to replant the forest with non-native *Pinus radiata*.

Such a move would have been tragic. The plateau provides an important link between the flora of Kosciusko National Park in the south of the state and Barrington Tops to the north. Winter snow, high winds and moist conditions all contribute to this phenomenon. Most of the 13 000 hectare plateau is more than 1000 metres in height, with some points, including Mount Emperor, Mount Whalan and Ben Lomond, reaching over 1300 metres.

The deep valleys and gorges of the mountains were created by fast-flowing streams given impetus by a great uplifting along the eastern seaboard perhaps 6 million years ago. Cliffs were formed where the sandstone resisted weathering, and the great blocks of stone broke away along vertical fault lines, as at Kanangra.

Wild and woolly as the plateau is, it proved useful to generations of landowners following the first push into the area in 1802, 11 years before the first successful crossing of the Blue Mountains. That early explorer was French ensign Francis Barallier, and he and his party scrambled west along Christies Creek, a tributary of the Kowmung, only to be halted by sheer cliffs more than 30 metres high down which flowed a waterfall today known as Baralliers Falls. Had they managed to climb the cliffs, it would have been a relatively simple matter for them to have crossed the plateau and skirted past the present location of Oberon to the Bathurst Plains.

In 1819, Charles Throsby, a former Assistant Colonial Surgeon, proved that the Blue Mountains did not extend in an impassable chain all the way to Bass Strait by crossing the Great Divide from Moss Vale to Bathurst. A stock route was subsequently blazed from the Burragorang Valley (now submerged beneath Lake Burragorang) past what was to become the silver-mining town of Yerranderie to the Boyd plateau. This proved a boon to the graziers of the Bathurst district, who had despaired of overlanding cattle along the poorly grassed ridge tops followed by the Great Western Highway. In the late nineteenth century several freehold blocks were cleared as holding paddocks for stock along the plateau.

Much of the Aboriginal history of the area has been obliterated by the twin scourges of insensitivity and disease. The Burragorang Valley was home to the Gundungara tribe, who hunted grey kangaroos (plentiful in the area and on the Boyd Plateau), swamp wallabies and wallaroos on the grassy flats and in the surrounding ranges. They bequeathed their name for wombat, *colong*, to the system of limestone caves burrowing into the Silurian limestone beneath Mount Colong, and *bindook*, meaning artificial waterhole, to the Bindook Highlands and Bindook station, on the Colong stock route.

Perhaps the most extraordinary thing about this remote, rugged and inaccessible area is that it is so close, as the crow flies, to Australia's largest city—just 95 kilometres due west of Botany Bay. Clearly, there are physiographic limits to Sydney's growth, undreamed of by Arthur Phillip, the city's founder.

The great vertical cliff-line of Kanangra Walls has been formed by erosion along a vertical fault-line.

NEW SOUTH WALES

Jenolan Caves

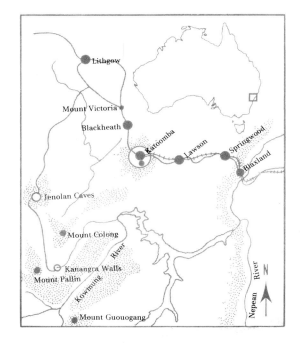

SOME idea of the ruggedness of the country surrounding Australia's best known cave system is given by the fact that a landowner named Archibald Hood took up land just 16 kilometres south-west of the caves 12 years before they were officially 'discovered'. One of Hood's men, roaming the maze of ridges and gorges at the western edge of the Blue Mountains may have glimpsed the great arches that betray the presence of the caves. If so, he told no one. A bushranger named McKeown, who made one of the caves his hide-out and farmed the adjacent valley, was understandably reticent about revealing their whereabouts. But it was he who unwittingly led the outside world to them.

In 1838, a Tarana grazier named James Whalan tracked the prints of McKeown's horse to his mountain lair. The following day he arrived with reinforcements, his brother Charles and two troopers, and arrested McKeown. Charles then set about exploring the gloomy open caverns with their intriguing side passages. He and his two sons were to act as honorary guides until 1867. The caves were not known as Jenolan Caves then, nor even as Binoomea, their Aboriginal name, but popularly as the Fish River Caves (after the tributary of the Macquarie most visitors followed to reach them) and officially as Binda Caves, a corruption of Mount Bindo, a snow-gum-topped peak 20 kilometres to the north. The trouble was that the Fish River rose on the other side of the divide from Jenolan's three streams, so in 1884 an official decision was taken to change the name to Jenolan, the name of the parish in which they were situated and of a high point overlooking the broad Coxs River valley.

The caves lie in some of the wildest country in New South Wales, hidden in a deep gorge cut by the Jenolan River, a tributary of the Coxs. Here a 90 metre high ridge of Silurian limestone is interbedded with softer slates which have been eroded away in the several million years following the uplift which created the eastern highlands. The limestone was built up by billions of coral polyps and other animals beneath a primeval sea, and outcrops also appear at Wellington, Mount Colong, Wombeyan Caves and Bungonia Gorge, near Goulburn.

Over the past 500 000 years or so three streams bearing carbon dioxide dissolved from the atmosphere and from rotting vegetation have trickled into bedding planes and joints in the limestone, chemically excavating giant caverns and tunnels. A similar process has decorated the caves with a rich variety of coloured calcite formations, as dissolved calcium carbonate (the major constituent of limestone) trickles down through the caves and is deposited at an imperceptibly slow rate on the originally bare walls. It is the richness and variety of these formations—dripstone stalagmites, stalactites, straws and columns, flowstone shawls, canopies and 'cave corals', strangely twisted helictites and the oddly named moonmilk—rather than the size of the caves that have made Jenolan world famous.

The limestone belt is up to 300 metres thick and runs north for about 8 kilometres from the Grand Arch and south for 3 kilometres; there is a separate outcrop some distance down the Jenolan River. It contains 22 known major, and hundreds of minor, caves, none more than 4 kilometres from the Grand Arch. One stream, Camp Creek, has carved the Grand Arch, described by one nineteenth-century British author as 'like the portico to some great castle of Grand Despair', through the ridge.

The roof of the largest cave, the open Devils Coach House, is a great canopy 50 metres overhead; a sinkhole acts as a natural skylight. The Coach House (named either by James Whalan or by an inebriated cattle duffer who hallucinated whilst camped in the cave) is 130 metres long and up to 40 metres wide, but it would form a mere antechamber to the 800 metre long, 107 metre high Carlsbad Cavern in New Mexico. Yet the great chamber, with its green-coloured walls perforated with mysterious openings, is reputedly big enough to accommodate the Sydney GPO, presumably with the clocktower poking through the sinkhole.

Few of the dark caves were explored before 1867, when Fish River farmer Jeremiah Wilson was appointed 'keeper'. During his custodianship, the 90 metre deep Bottomless Pit, Mammoth Cave, Glass Cave, Frenchmans Cave, Imperial Cave, Jersey Cave and Jubilee Cave were all discovered. Legend has it that Wilson came across Imperial Cave by accident, being lowered 16 metres down a hole from the Elder Cave to recover a lost smoking cap. Many of these new caves were subsequently opened to the public.

But it was at the beginning of J. C. Wiburd's term as caretaker, in 1903 and 1904, that the most outstanding caves of all were discovered. Wiburd found the River and

Skeleton caves in his first year on the job, then followed the passages above them to stumble into the great domed cavern of the Temple of Baal, 45 metres high, and the Orient Cave with its magnificent Egyptian Chamber. These caves are the oldest on the south side of the Grand Arch, and contain the most spectacular formations. Even more importantly, they are painted in rich shades of yellow, brown and red, overcoming earlier criticism that the cave calcite was 'monotonously white'.

No new caves were discovered then for 50 years, until speleologists using comparatively sophisticated equipment arrived on the scene. In the early fifties, cave divers, breathing air pumped through a hose by bellows, explored underwater passages. Wiburd had blocked off the entrances to certain caves he had found, one of which he said contained a lake large enough to float a Manly ferry. It is not certain whether this has yet been rediscovered. One interesting find was the humid Spider Cave, which is home to large numbers of spiders and wetas and is littered with the bones of dead marsupials and dingoes.

Whilst interest in most of the caves centres on the limestone formations, the major attraction in Skeleton Cave is the remains of an unfortunate Aborigine who died there, perhaps from a fall caused through his blundering about in the Stygian gloom. His final moments may have been as horrific as those of the marsupials in Spider Cave, whose claws dug grooves in the rocks as they scrabbled desperately to get out.

Before 1872, when breaking of dripstone was made a punishable offence, it was said that the route to Jenolan Caves was signposted by discarded souvenirs. Vandals destroyed four out of five major columns in one cave. Of those caves discovered early on, only Lucas is still regularly inspected. Paradoxically, control over vandalism improved with road access to the caves. For many years Wilson had lived 32 kilometres away from the caves, so that many visitors had come and gone without his knowledge. In 1878, a team led by Surveyor-General P. F. Adams (after whose daughter Carlotta Arch was named) surveyed the caves and the road in from Oberon (finished in 1879). The first guesthouse, a wooden structure, was erected in 1880 and access to the caves was more rigorously policed. A second road was constructed from Mount Victoria to within 400 metres of the east side of Grand Arch in the late 1880s, and this soon became the more popular route from Sydney. It was extended through the Grand Arch to the guesthouse in 1896, the year after most of the original building was destroyed by fire.

The edifice which arose in stages on the site of the old guesthouse was sufficiently luxurious to ensure that henceforth the caves would be one of the major tourist attractions in the state. Smoke blackening caused by the use of tallow and sperm-oil torches (the guide would illuminate highlights with a magnesium flare) ceased from 1887 with the progressive introduction of electric lighting. Although the passage of so many visitors through the nine caves open for public inspection, coupled with the cutting of access tunnels and alteration of stream patterns, has had a deleterious effect on the formations, many other caves discovered more than a century ago are still not open to the general public and are preserved intact.

They remain as they were when a flickering candle threw the first light ever to illuminate their glittering arrays of calcite *objets d'art*: as magnificent a treasure trove as any buried with an Egyptian pharoah.

BELOW The Music Hall and Broken Column, Lucas Cave. The Lucas, opened for public inspection in 1860, incorporates the highest and widest dark caves at Jenolan. (Trevern Dawes)
OPPOSITE, TOP LEFT The Mosque (centre), one of the rich flowstone formations in the Egyptian Colonnade, Orient Cave. (Trevern Dawes)
OPPOSITE, TOP RIGHT The Angel's Wing (l.), White Altar and Gabriel's Wing (r.) are spectacular formations in the Temple of Baal. (Trevern Dawes)
OPPOSITE, BELOW Straw stalactites hang from the roof of the Lucinda Cave. (Trevern Dawes)

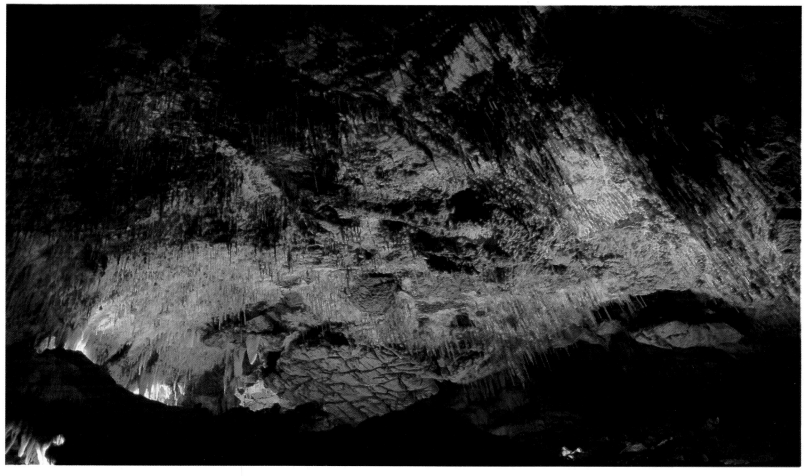

Bald Rock

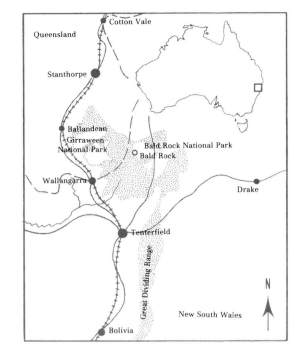

IF it stood in the centre of a desert, Bald Rock would be acclaimed as another Ayers Rock. But this is not the case: so closely does the forest crowd its base that it is only when one has broken free of the dense tree canopy that one realises there is a massive grey rock face beyond. It is like emerging from the tangle of London streets to see the dome of St Pauls soaring in breathtaking splendour above.

Not that Bald Rock is on the same scale as Ayers Rock, which rises 348 metres above the desert sands. Bald Rock surges 200 metres out of the grey-green forest, reaching a height of 1341 metres, the highest point in this section of the Great Divide, right on the New South Wales–Queensland border and 140 kilometres from the coast at Ballina. It is also the biggest of Australia's four Bald Rocks (one in every state except Tasmania and South Australia). In fact, the local Jukambal people knew this rock as Boonoo Boonoo, meaning 'big rock', a name which has now been applied to a new national park nearby. Bald Rock's ritual significance is not known.

White men recognised the uniqueness of the rock as long ago as 1906 and set it aside as a recreational reserve, although it was not gazetted a national park until 1974. One nearby area was selected as a possible site for a tuberculosis sanatorium; another, as a wattle plantation (wattle bark is a good tanning agent). Some of the bushland now contained within the 2104 hectare national park was once partially logged, and Bald Rock has gazed down on these intrusions with lofty disdain. Well it might, for, like Ayers Rock, it dominates life around it, creating micro-environments and habitats that would not otherwise exist. Runoff from the rock keeps the sclerophyll forest immediately fringing it always moist. The black soil squelches underfoot; ferns grow bright green beneath the messmate and mountain gum canopy.

The climb up the orange- and black-streaked grey rock is neither as steep nor as arduous as that up Ayers Rock, but it nevertheless defeats many visitors. They should persevere: the climb to the trig. station on top is in many ways more rewarding than the crazy scramble to the Ayers Rock cairn. The surrounding landscape falls into sharp relief as you climb, and many other exposed rock surfaces are evident, particularly to the south. They were all formed at the same time, around 225 million years ago, during the most recent intrusions of the New England batholith. (The rock is actually Stanthorpe adamellite, closely related to granite.) To the north-east, the prancing masses of the McPherson Ranges cavort across the horizon. To the north, the country is partially cleared and there are houses, with tin roofs glinting, and a television tower.

From here, too, it becomes obvious that Bald Rock is not a true dome. To the east, a gentle spur connects it to the surrounding forests; from the south the wind sweeps hard and chill up the rock face, bending before it a lone snow gum near the summit. Belying the rock's name, a low heath of white beard and tea tree springs from the humus around the trig. station. To the east, on a shoulder below the summit, perch four large granite boulders, seeming to need only a push to send them crashing into the tree tops below. The adjacent wood is a shadowy copse of stunted native cypress pines, Mr Badger's Wild Wood in miniature.

Like Ayers Rock, this tablelands landmark is gradually crumbling away. The adamellite is flawed and along its cracks erosion is accelerated. Exfoliation, the peeling off of layers of rock from the surface, is common, as is spalling, the lifting away of thinner flakes of rock. Rain channels have formed beneath the cypress wood. Imperceptibly, the giant rock is being worn down to the level of the surrounding countryside.

Thick forest crowds the base of Bald Rock. (Michael Richardson)

NEW SOUTH WALES

Lake Mungo and the Walls of China

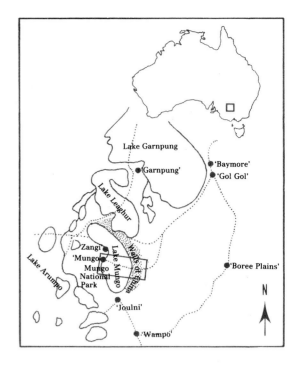

AUSTRALIA was not always as it is today: scorched brown by the sun, lashed by fiery desert winds, a land where saltbush and spinifex form the most widespread ground cover, and water is a scarce and precious commodity. For more than 30 000 years, until the end of the last Ice Age about 8000 years ago, average temperatures in Australia were perhaps 3°C lower than they are today. There were glaciers on the Snowy Mountains, and rainfall was higher. Even more importantly, the evaporation rate was lower, and lakes which today are ephemeral, or even predominantly dry, were full of water and supported a rich diversity of wildlife. Many of these lakes provided idyllic living conditions for generations of Aborigines, for a period many times longer than recorded history.

A major freshwater lake system existed at this time 100 kilometres north-east of the junction of the Murray and Darling rivers. Fed by Willandra Creek, a distributary of the Lachlan flowing from a spot near present-day Hillston, the Willandra Lakes system once straggled over more than 110 kilometres of the flat western plains, covering an area of more than 1000 square kilometres to a depth of up to 10 metres. Such a lake system, if it existed today, would eclipse in size even the Menindee overflow lakes on the Darling. But the creek is no longer strong enough to reach beyond the upstream end of the lakes, and local runoff only remains fleetingly as shallow pools on the cracked clay surface of the great flat basins.

Low, mallee-covered sand ridges roll across the unyielding emptiness round about, interspersed with saltbush and bluebush flats that mirror the appearance of the dry lake beds. The average rainfall of the region is around 200 millimetres a year, although evidence from the past—when mighty Gol Gol station (203 000 hectares) covered most of the lakes region and groundwater was never too far away—suggests that last century was considerably wetter. On the eastern (windward) margin of the lakes, crescent-shaped sand dunes known as lunettes formed. The composition of these dunes altered according to climate. When the lakes were full, white quartz sands were blown up from wave-lapped beaches, and they were eventually stabilised and overlain by reddy-brown soil. As the lakes dried up, strata of clay and gypsum-rich sediments covered the dunes, capped off in turn by 10 000 years of drift sand.

In recent times erosion has carved sections of the lunettes into a fantastic series of canyons and gorges, spires and minarets. The best known group of erosion formations is the Walls of China on the eastern shore of Lake Mungo, named for the Chinese labourers who built the nearby Gol Gol woolshed in 1869 from Murray pine logs. Part of the Walls of China is contained in Mungo National Park, named after the property which the National Parks and Wildlife Service acquired in 1978 and resulting from the division of Gol Gol in 1922 into 16 000 hectare holdings. Here, wind and water have scoured the sand from the underlying red clay, creating a rugged topography like the Flinders Ranges in miniature, and leaving isolated hillocks, each surmounted by a clump of bluebush, a twisted hopbush, or sandhill wattle: Lilliputian buttes and mesas casting their shadows across the playa of Lake Mungo. Beyond, the great white dune is marching east at the rate of 4 metres a year, impelled by hot westerlies from the inland.

Incredibly, it is this erosion—expedited, no doubt, by more than a century of grazing and by the undiscriminating teeth of thousands of rabbits—that has placed Mungo on the World Heritage list. For it has uncovered traces of the most ancient occupation of our island continent, dating back almost 40 000 years. Conditions on the eroded lunette are ideal for the preservation and discovery of remnants of this ancient culture. The lake shoreline was for millennia the home of Aboriginal people, and the alkaline sediments tended to mineralise their remains. Because of the continuous construction of the dune system, a stratigraphic sequence was built up over tens of thousands of years.

This is one of the most important archaeological sites in the world. Only a small portion of the dune has been excavated, although some 70 tonnes of sand and soil have been shifted, but the three skeletons found have thrown new light on prehistoric man's lifestyle and intellectual capacity. The body of the woman known as Mungo One, discovered in 1969, had been cremated, then the bones smashed and buried in a conical pit. The cremation, which occurred about 26 000 years ago, is the earliest recorded anywhere in the world. A male skeleton dating back 30 000 years was covered in ochre; red pigment was also discovered in the ashes of a fire lit 32 000 years ago.

The Lake Mungo region once provided idyllic living conditions for generations of Aborigines. The oldest recorded Aboriginal remains in Australia have been found here.

These people were of modern stock. Their diet included freshwater mussels, Murray cod, golden perch, marsupials, reptiles, frogs and emu eggs, as well as plants, the remains of which have not been preserved. As the lakes dried up, people adapted to the changing environment. Water was still readily available, collecting in clay pans in the lake bed and in freshwater soaks. Grass seeds may have become a more important source of food, as indicated by the numerous large grinding dishes found on the lake bed.

One of the most intriguing discoveries at Lake Mungo has been that of a major deviation of the earth's magnetic field 30 000 years ago. The north magnetic pole swung first east, then south-east, before returning to its normal position, leaving evidence of its 'excursion' in the fireplaces of Mungo man.

Clearly, other Aborigines lived out in the bush, away from the lake system, but much less evidence remains today of their existence. Perhaps they adapted better to the changing environment. It is impossible to tell. One thing is certain, however. The rate of ecological change within the area has been much more rapid since Sturt first sailed down the Murray from the Murrumbidgee in 1830. So much has the vegetation changed that no one is quite certain of the exact composition of the original flora. The Murray

The erosion formations on the eastern side of Lake Mungo are known as the Walls of China.

pines, valued by the early settlers for their resistance to white ants, are no longer regenerating; the seedlings are being eaten by rabbits. Barley grass, a foreign species, has become dominant over the native spear grass. Only a handful of indigenous mammals remains: dunnarts, red and grey kangaroos, echidnas. The hare wallaby, once abundant in the region, has been supplanted by the ubiquitous rabbit. The birds and reptiles have survived, though. Once, probably contemporaneously with man's earliest occupation of the site, the monstrous flightless bird, genyornis, roamed the lake shore. There were also giant short-faced kangaroos, Tasmanian tigers and devils, bettongs and hairy-nosed wombats.

The potential for discovering more of the prehistory of Aboriginal man in the windswept lunettes of the Willandra Lakes is great. Already, the bones and artefacts unearthed have helped today's Aboriginal people regain much of their lost self-respect. White Australia is just 200 years old; to put it into perspective, a mere 36 hours compared to a full year of Aboriginal occupation of Lake Mungo. And this cannot be the Aborigines' first home in this country. How, one wonders, will Australia look when white man's first year is up?

The lakes fill only partially from local run-off; the climate is drier today than it was even last century.

NEW SOUTH WALES

Menindee Lakes

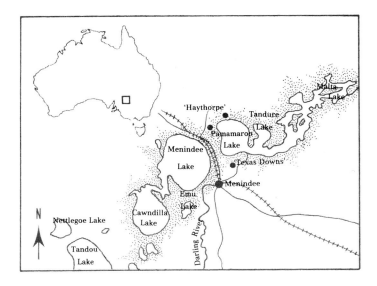

THE dead trees that are the symbol of Menindee Lakes are symbolic also of man's intrusion into this bountiful region, 100 kilometres south-east of Broken Hill. For they are the victims of our desire to harness the water resources of the outback—in this case, the series of overflow lakes stretching for 80 kilometres along the west bank of the Darling River.

Before the great interlocking network of weirs and channels was built between 1949 and 1967, the lakes filled only in times of flood, when the Darling spread out 50 kilometres and more beyond its banks and last century the more daring of the paddle-wheeler captains steamed cross-country to collect the wool clip. For more than 30 years the scheme has assured the citizens of Broken Hill of fresh water. The price has been the death of thousands of eucalypts, drowned by the waters that once gave them life.

The largest lake, Menindee, is more than 16 kilometres across. Yet this is country where a dry saltpan would seem more appropriate; the average rainfall is only 216 millimetres a year and away from the river flats red sand, bluebush and prickly wattle predominate. South-east of here the great shimmering plains, intersected only by non-perennial streams lined with red gums and coolibahs, stretch to the saucer-like horizon.

The river is the life-giving artery of this land: a narrow, muddy, snag-filled artery, to be sure, but one which impacts decisively on the landscape. Fertile black-soil floodplains fan out from the river, supporting a black-box woodland, home of the western grey kangaroo. Along the river banks the red gums wave welcome like old friends.

The two largest lakes in the system, Menindee and Cawndilla, are encompassed within the boundaries of 44 000 hectare Kinchega National Park, named after a sprawling, 400 000 hectare sheep station that predated the park. For more than a century, from the early 1850s, Kinchega sheep competed for feed with the red and grey kangaroos, the euros and hairy-nosed wombats. Feral animals—pigs, cats, foxes, rabbits and house mice—as well as the livestock took their toll.

The Aboriginal population dwindled fast, too. When the first white men, a party under New South Wales Surveyor-General, Thomas Mitchell, visited Menindee (which the Aborigines called Wottenella) in July 1835, a quarrel began between some of his men and the local tribespeople, three of whom were shot and killed. They retaliated by firing the bush around the explorers' camp site, milling around it waving their weapons. Mitchell, far from home, turned back, having failed to prove or disprove that the Darling flowed into the previously discovered Murray.

Mitchell called the shimmering sheets of water Laidley's Chain of Ponds, a rather unimaginative title that has not stood the test of time. Sturt used the 'ponds' as a staging point for his terrible journey to the centre in 1844–45. By the time Burke and Wills passed this way in 1860, the riverboat captain Francis Cadell had established a trading store at Menindee on the west bank of the Darling, pastoralists had settled in the nearby districts, and Maiden's hotel at Menindee was thriving. In its heyday Kinchega station ran 143 000 sheep; the large timber shearing shed had stands for 60 shearers.

Less striking reminders of the gentler inhabitation of the original owners of the land are scattered around the crescent-shaped lunettes piled up on the north-eastern shores of the lakes by the prevailing winds: middens, burial grounds and campsites. The traditional lifestyle of the Aborigines quickly vanished after European settlement; most of the population has now been moved to Lake Cargelligo, 400 kilometres to the east.

The bulldozers and scrapers that arrived in 1949 were to change the lake system forever. A major weir was thrown across the Darling, backing up the river for 160 kilometres. Water is diverted from this artificial lake to the natural lakes Malta, Balaka, Bijijie and Tandure, while a regulator allows water to flow into the much larger Lake Pamamaroo, connected to Lake Menindee via Copi Hollow and a man-made channel.

In the gaunt grey limbs of the dead gum trees fringing the lake shores roost thousands of waterbirds: kingfishers, ibises, egrets, spoonbills, and cormorants with their wings hung out like washing to dry. Pelicans sail in majestic splendour on the glistening lake waters. The river red gums are home to corellas, cockatoos, yellow rosellas and noisy friarbirds. Like the people of Adelaide and Broken Hill, the waterbirds have cause to be thankful for the presence of these great freshwater reservoirs, truly among the paradoxes of the inland.

An angry sky looms over Lake Cawndilla.
(Michael Richardson)

The tranquillity of Wilsons Promontory

VICTORIA

VICTORIA

The Bogong High Plains

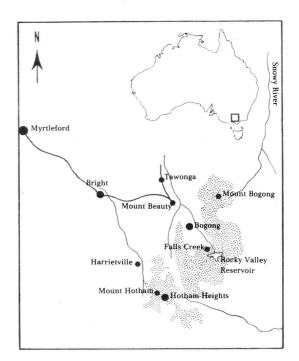

Myrtleford

Bright

Tawonga

Mount Bogong

Mount Beauty

Bogong

Falls Creek

Rocky Valley
Reservoir

Harrietville

Mount Hotham

Hotham Heights

Snowy River

ABOVE the treeline snow clouds threaten, sullen, angry tendrils raking the ground. It is late autumn; soon this rolling expanse of snow-grass and dark green heath will disappear beneath a thickening mantle of crisp snow, with only the unkempt, windswept shapes of the snow gums and the red flashes of the snow poles breaking the white crust.

The snow cover will last for four months or more, then start to melt, feeding the rivers, the Mitta Mitta, the Kiewa, the Cobungra and Bundara, the Dargo and Ovens, that rise on the Bogong High Plains and its peaks. When the snow vanishes so, seemingly, will the snow clouds, although even at the height of summer a heavy rainstorm laced with sleet may sweep up unexpectedly from the south. The average precipitation on the high plains tableland is more than 2 metres a year, a fact which was not lost on the engineers who in the 1930s started work on the Kiewa Valley Hydro-Electric Scheme, an engineering project which was the forerunner of the massive Snowy Mountains project to the north.

It was the hydroelectric scheme which opened up the high plains to tourists. Previously, only a handful of intrepid bushwalkers and skiers, and the cattlemen and shepherds who valued the nutritious herbs and snow-grass for summer grazing, visited the area. Cattlemen from as far away as Hay had been using the high plains for pasture since the 1850s, soon after their 'discovery' by John Mitchell of the Kiewa Valley in 1843. For millennia beforehand, since the ending of the last Ice Ages, Aboriginal people had climbed above the snow line in spring to feast on the plump brown bodies of the Bogong moths that breed on the western plains of New South Wales.

The undulating tableland has an average height of 1700 metres and is wholly above the snowline. Here soar nine of the state's ten highest peaks, including isolated Mount Bogong (1986 metres), Victoria's tallest. From the plateau, many of these peaks, like Mounts Cope and Nelse, which are only 100 metres or so above it, seem like nothing more than minor rises. Incredibly, 450 million years ago this land was under a sea. Later, earth movements buckled and rent the sandstones, shales and siltstones that had been laid down underwater. Pressure and heat metamorphosed the rocks, forming gneiss, phyllite and schist. Igneous granite intruded 430 million years ago. Erosion, particularly along the fault lines, continued for the next 390 million years, until the Oligocene epoch, when there was a period of volcanic activity which created mountains like Mount Jim (1838 metres). Finally, during the late Tertiary uplift along the Great Divide, the Bogong High Plains and Mount Bogong were raised up, increasing exponentially the speed of the streams and the rate of erosion.

'Bogong' is an Aboriginal word meaning 'the big one', but few other natural features here have native names, perhaps because the Aborigines did not permanently occupy this land. Cattlemen Jim Brown and Jack Wells named many of the most prominent features in 1851, including Mounts Feathertop and Fainter. Naturalist Ferdinand von Mueller, who explored the area on horseback in 1864 and was on occasion so short of supplies that he was forced to eat Bogong moths, named Mount Hotham after the Governor of Victoria.

These visits by the devil-may-care cattlemen and the earnest botanist von Mueller symbolise the conflict that thas raged between graziers and conservationists for decades. The environmentalists claim that grazing causes soil erosion; the cattlemen, that it reduces fire risk. The conservationists seem to be winning the battle. Sheep, which tend to nibble closer to the ground than cattle, have been totally banned from the high country, while cattle grazing has been controlled since 1945. In 1955, Mount Bogong became off limits to grazing; Mounts Loch, Feathertop and Hotham followed

Snow covers the Rocky Valley catchment area, highest in Australia, in late autumn. Later, the reservoir will ice over, and water drawn from beneath it will leave a dangerous suspended table of ice.

in 1958. Bogong National Park was proclaimed in 1981 and it is expected that more closures will follow. Eventually, the curtain may be brought down on one of the most colourful events on the Australian rural calendar: the December long-horn cattle drive up onto the High Plains.

The cattlemen's legacy will be the timber, stone and iron huts dotting the high country—if the huts are allowed to remain. Built in the late nineteenth and early twentieth centuries—a few were added later by ski associations and the State Electricity Commission—they are havens for cross-country skiers caught out late or in bad weather. Cleve Cole hut, on the slopes of Mount Bogong, commemorates a skier who died from exposure following a ski trip from Hotham Heights to Mount Bogong. Two years after its construction, the solidly built stone hut sheltered cattleman Wally Ryder from a totally different type of peril: the firestorm that swept through Victoria in 1939, unmatched in intensity until the brutal bushfires of 1983.

Like the Rocky Valley catchment area, Hotham Heights and Falls Creek ski resorts form enclaves within the national park. Skiers were visiting the peaks and high plains as early as the 1880s and by the 1920s permanent accommodation had been erected at Mount Hotham. Falls Creek came later, started in 1946 as a recreational facility by State Electricity Commission workers on the Kiewa Valley scheme. At that time nearly 4000 men were working on the Rocky Valley reservoir, highest in Australia, most of them housed in a new town called Mount Beauty at the head of the Kiewa Valley. But the full scheme, envisaged as far back as 1911 and approved by Parliament in 1937, was never finished; the Pretty Valley reservoir, which was to have been the lynchpin of the project, became a holding pond, and in the early 1950s the work force was cut to one thousand. Three power stations now generate 184 megawatts of electricity, but the Kiewa scheme is only a peak-load sytem; used every day in summer, the waters would run dry in a matter of weeks.

In summer, when the snow melt is exhausted, stream flow is maintained by water released from sphagnum moss bogs up to 2 metres thick. Like the alpine herb fields, grasslands and sedge lands, the bogs are sensitive to user pressure and over-snow and other vehicle use is strictly controlled. The road to Rocky Valley dam was extended to join up with the Omeo Highway in 1965 but is closed to through traffic during the snow season. Threading across the plateau are the yellow markers delineating the Alpine Walking Track, 400 kilometres of unparalleled scenery stretching from Walhalla in Gippsland to Tom Groggin on the New South Wales border.

In December, the grassy slopes come alive with colour as the snow daisies, buttercups, sundews, sunrays and everlastings burst into bloom. Several plants, including the Bogong daisy bush and Australia's only native dandelion, are found in few other places. Native fauna is not plentiful in the high country. The mountain pigmy possum was thought extinct until it was discovered beneath a ski lodge at Mount Hotham in 1966. In winter, marsupial rats and bush mice live in warm burrows underground, without hibernating. Occasionally wombats may be found above the snow line, but they prefer the timbered country below 1600 metres, where woollybutt, manna and candlebark gums provide a valuable commercial resource (and clear felling arouses conservationists' ire). Above 1600 metres, no more than 20 bird species are found, including the orange-breasted flame robbin, the yellow-faced honeyeater, and strutting flocks of emus, clearly among Australia's most adaptable birds. Like the miner who digs for gold in the Red Robin mine beneath 1875 metre high Mount Loch, at the onset of winter most of the birds leave the high country for warmer climes, their songs replaced by the revelry of après-ski entertainment and the schuss of skis.

BELOW Snow dusts the vertical columns of Ruined Castle. Oligocene basalt outcrops in several places on the High Plains.
RIGHT The only tree growing on the High Plains is the beautiful, varnished snow gum (*E. pauciflora*).

VICTORIA

Mount Elephant

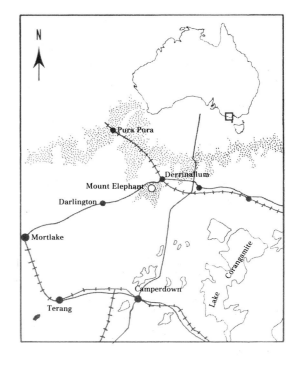

THERE is little that is remarkable about Mount Elephant itself: a small, 238 metre high, volcanic scoria cone rising abruptly from the lush green grazing country just west of the small town of Derrinallum. But Mount Elephant is merely the biggest of an immense chain of 350–400 volcanoes that began to erupt in western Victoria in late Pliocene and early Pleistocene times. The basalt plain created by the molten lava they spewed forth is the third largest in the world, after the Snake River Plains in the United States and the Deccan Plateau in India. It stretches 260 kilometres from Mount Gambier in South Australia to Port Phillip Bay, and covers an area of 23 000 square kilometres.

No one has yet been able to give a satisfactory explanation for the extraordinarily large number of points of eruption in the region, although it seems certain the volcanic activity was triggered off by tectonic movements. Few of the volcanic hills reached more than 150 metres in height; only 94 of them are significant enough to have been named. Some 34 of them are unusual tuff-ring volcanoes, crater-like accumulations of bedded 'tuffs' from 500 metres to more than 3 kilometres in diameter, and 15 rise to nearly 150 metres.

The volcanic soil is rich and black and would be ideally suited to growing root crops, such as potatoes, except that it is too rocky for planting. So the Derrinallum area has become the province of the grazier, and the surface rocks have been scooped up from the grasslands and used to build low stone walls between the paddocks.

This was the country Surveyor-General Major Thomas Mitchell called 'Australia Felix' when he passed through in 1836. He named one of the small hills jutting out of the grassy plain Mount Clarke, after his friend Major Shadwell Clarke, but the name did not stick. Thomas Learmonth of Boninyong renamed it Mount Elephant because, when he viewed it from the east, he imagined it resembled an elephant lying down.

The peak is actually a classic example of a breached scoria cone: the lava broke through the north wall of the crater and flowed down the hillside onto the plains, covering them with basalt to a depth of 60 metres. The volcano began to erupt perhaps 2 million years ago, drilling through the underlying hornfels and quartzite, clay, limestone and marls. The activity culminated 100 000 years ago in a series of eruptive explosions which built up much of the cone. As well as scoria, the mountain consists of some small interstratified basalt flows and a large number of 'bombs', spindle-shaped masses of lava up to 2.5 metres long wrapped around a rock core and shaped by twisting in mid-air while the lava was still plastic.

As well as ousting the local Aboriginal tribes, the Wathaurung and the Kirrae, the white settlers altered the ecology of the plains, chopping down the native eucalypts and replacing them with orderly rows of European trees, displacing the kangaroos and emus with sheep and cattle. Mount Elephant, too, suffered from this onslaught. It was once covered with honeysuckles and blackwoods, and there was a grove of she-oaks, the only one for hundreds of square kilometres roundabout, growing in the 90 metre deep crater. Today, only a lone grey skeleton remains on the north-west slope of the crater and soon it, too, will probably fall before the bitter south-westerly winds. The native grasses are interspersed with lichen-encrusted scoria and thistles and other exotic weeds.

Once, three landholders each owned part of the mountain and it was divided up by fences meeting in the crater. Today, it is all owned by Mount Elephant station and the fences have gone, but an ugly car track leads up the north slope to the crater and the west side of the mountain is scarred by a road metal quarry, part of which has been turned into a rubbish dump. This is not the first time the black scoria has been quarried. In 1913 a railway line was built up to the north-east side of the mountain to transport ballast out for the Gheringhap–Maroona branch line. The scoria proved too coarse for maintenance requirements and so the pit was abandoned in 1917.

Since 1973 Mount Elephant has had a National Trust recorded landscape classification and it is also listed on the National Estate register. The volcano is thought to be extinct now but the story persists in Derrinallum that once a shepherd who had dug a hole near the mountain was terrified by a rumbling sound from beneath the ground. Apocryphal though this tale may be, if the mountain were to erupt again it would swiftly obliterate all signs of man's incursions into its domain.

OPPOSITE A grove of she-oaks once grew in the 90-metre deep crater of Mount Elephant. (Michael Richardson)

VICTORIA

The Organ Pipes

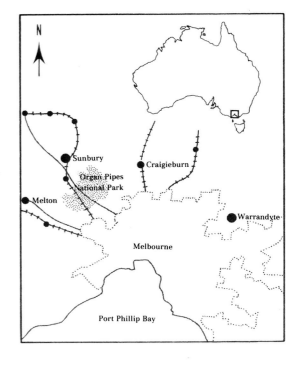

ONLY 20 kilometres west of Melbourne, and connected to the city by the bitumen artery of the Tullamarine freeway, the Keilor Plains are as unlikely a location for a natural wonder as any in Australia. This was once grazing country, dotted with market gardens and orchards, most of which have now been supplanted by rib-roofed factories and bland new housing developments. Sandwiched between the roar of Tullamarine Airport and the snarl of Calder Raceway is an oasis of tranquillity, a tiny, 65 hectare national park that preserves several intriguing geological features.

Through the centre of the park meanders winding Jacksons Creek, formerly known as the Saltwater River. This polluted stream was until 1972 choked with noxious weeds, but since then the weeds have been cleared away and the creek now runs free, continuing the work of erosion which has exposed the 22 metre high basalt columns known as the Organ Pipes.

The car park above the creek valley sits on top of a small scoria cone. The volcano which created it about a million years ago was one of many: the Keilor Plains lie on the edge of the third-largest lava plains in the world.

The molten rock covered the pre-existing Ordovician, Silurian and Tertiary sediments, in places to a depth of more than 70 metres. There was a river valley running at right angles to Jacksons Creek, and it, too, was filled with fiery lava. The surface of the molten rock was the first to cool and solidify; beneath it, tensions developed within the lava mass, tensions which split the rock into vertical, and usually hexagonal, columns. Horizontal cracks developed as the basalt continued to cool. Then rain came and Jacksons Creek began its work of peeling away the layers of rock hiding the columns.

For thousands of years, since a time before the Greeks and Romans raised their great temples of stone, the local Aboriginal tribe, the Woeworung, camped on the river flats beneath the looming grey columns of the Organ Pipes. Yet within 16 years of Melbourne being settled these people had gone, vanished like the native animals and leaving behind them only scattered stone tools.

The settlers brought pests with them: boxthorn, horehound and artichoke thistle which soon became dominant species. The plains are in a rain shadow and their 500 millimetre annual rainfall proved better suited to grazing than agricultural purposes, although the creek was once a handy source of water for orchards and tomatoes which grew in the bend opposite the Organ Pipes.

In the late 1960s there was a suggestion that the area should be quarried for road metal. Alarmed environmentalists prevailed on the landholders to present the land as a gift to the Crown for preservation. The national park was gazetted in 1972. Then began the work of weeding out the exotic species and replanting trees and shrubs known from earlier reports to have grown there.

Upstream from the Organ Pipes, at the edge of the park, is a tesselated pavement, actually the top of a second set of basalt columns. Between the two similar formations the stream flows past a very different one: Rosette Rock, an odd grey wall of radiating basalt, patterned like the starburst of an exploding gunpowder rocket. Geologists seem fairly satisfied with their explanation of how the Organ Pipes and similar formations, such as the Ruined Castle on the Bogong High Plains, were formed, but to them Rosette Rock is a mystery. What fantastic forces were at work, deep beneath the cooling basalt mass? The search for an answer will probably intrigue scientists for years to come.

TOP AND BELOW RIGHT Hexagonal basalt columns of the Organ Pipes were formed as the lava mass cooled. BELOW LEFT Even geologists are bemused by the strange starburst pattern of Rosette Rock. (Michael Richardson)

VICTORIA

Wilsons Promontory

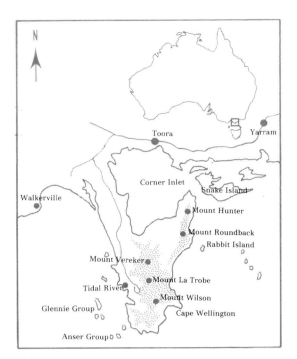

Ｔ IDAL River is bedlam any fine weekend when the wilderness spirit takes Melburnians, and at Easter and Christmas it resembles a refugee camp on the Thai–Cambodian border. By bus, car, lorry, even bicycle, they descend in their thousands on 'the Prom', as they affectionately call the wedge-shaped peninsula 225 kilometres south-east of the Victorian capital. Tidal River is the headquarters of this 49 000 hectare national park that preserves the most southerly part of the Australian mainland, for just these people.

A kilometre or so away are places so quiet, so tranquil, that the teeming camp sites at Tidal River seem as distant as Rome or London. From Mount Oberon, two seas may be glimpsed before the mist swirls in from Bass Strait and blankets the grey-green hills. The timber stepping-blocks of the lilly-pilly forest lead through an exquisite garden of tree ferns, watered by a shallow stream of the utmost purity. Heavy surf pounds a beach made of grains of sand so nearly spherical they squeak underfoot. Further north, timorous crabs scurry across the mud flats of Corner Inlet, amongst the stunted shapes of the most southerly mangroves in Australia.

Few places in Australia can boast such a diversity of moods or habitats as Wilsons Promontory. It is a microcosm of the south-eastern landscape, encapsulating in one compact area everything from golden beaches to windswept mountain tops. Small wonder it is one of Victoria's oldest national parks, proclaimed in 1905 and extended to include the coastline in 1908, and the Yanakie Peninsula (as well as several important offshore islands) in 1969.

Only 8000–10 000 years ago this peninsula formed part of the land bridge to Tasmania. Then the last Ice Age ended and the rising ocean flooded across the low-lying land to the south, probably making Wilsons Promontory, with its high spine of granite mountains rising to 754 metres, an island. Sand gradually piled up across the narrow channel which separated it from the mainland, until it was an island no more.

Thus Wilsons Promontory has much in common with the north coast of Tasmania and with the islands that mark the one-time high points of the land bridge: Flinders, the Kent Group, the Hogan Group, Rodondo and the Moncours. The Tasmanian state border is, in fact, only 7 kilometres to the south of the promontory.

Granites which intruded into an overlying rock mass in the Devonian period (416–367 million years ago) form the backbone of the Prom. The overlying rocks have long since been eroded away, exposing the granites as a prominent range of high hills dominating the landscape. Granite boulders, rounded by erosive forces, dot the coastline, like hunters seeking prey.

The hilly promontory, with its grey granite headlands and clothed with more than 700 species of plants, made a powerful impression on 27-year-old surgeon George Bass, the first white man to sight it, on 29 January 1798. He wrote:

> Its firmness and vast durability make it well worthy of being, what there is great reason to believe, it is, the boundary point of a long strait and a cornerstone of this great island, New Holland.

Bass sailed his open whaleboat around the promontory, naming it Furneaux Land in the mistaken belief that it had already been seen by Tobias Furneaux, captain of the barque *Adventure*, which had accompanied Cook on his second voyage. Governor Hunter renamed it after Thomas Wilson, an English friend of Bass.

But one name Bass bestowed on a part of the Prom has endured: Sealers Cove, a sheltered bay on the east coast where Bass's crew shot some fur seals for food. By 1809 a sealing station had been established here and within 17 years the defenceless animals had been all but exterminated. Whalers, based at nearby Refuge Cove, succeeded the sealers. Timber-cutting followed in the 1850s and 1860s, and was briefly revived in the early 1900s when a long jetty was built out from Sealers Cove beach. In the mid-1800s,

The west coast of Wilsons Promontory, from Mount Oberon, overlooking Tidal River and Norman Bay.

much of the Prom was taken up by pastoralists, but the deceptively lush-looking grasslands they coveted proved to be suitable only for seasonal grazing, which is still permitted in the area north of Darby River. From 1920 until 1925 a tin mine operated on the slopes of Mount Hunter, on the remote north-eastern Singapore Peninsula.

None of these activities impacted greatly on the Prom, although the white man's presence proved costly to the local Aborigines, the Brataualung, a sub-group of the Gippsland Kurnai tribe. They knew this place as Wamoom, the home of Looern, a good spirit who protected them from their enemies, and they collected shellfish along the shore and hunted kangaroos, koalas, possums and wombats in the thick forests. The possums furnished warm skins with which to ward off the chill winds of winter. Brataualung middens are plentiful along the shoreline.

The offshore islands, often visited by the Aborigines, are important breeding grounds for many sea birds, including mutton birds, giant petrels and Cape Barren geese. They are off limits to the general public. For a short time the entire Prom was out of bounds when, from 1940 to 1942, commandos trained in the hilly terrain, pushing through the open eucalypt forest that was characteristic of most of the high country. In 1961 much of this woodland was destroyed in a devastating bushfire and has since been replaced by acacias. Eucalypt regeneration should follow in time. Without fire, the lilly-pilly, a rainforest species with dark, shiny leaves, would come to dominate the lowland forest.

Not every visitor to the Prom has welcomed its beauty and grandeur. All ships sailing between Sydney and Melbourne pass close by its shores, and more than 40 of them have foundered on the treacherous coastline. As early as 1859 a lighthouse (since modernised twice) was erected on South-East Point to warn ships of danger.

'What danger?' you may feel entitled to ask in the serene world of the gully rainforests, or running barefoot along the warm sand of the eastern beaches. But that, after all, is part of the Prom's mystique.

BELOW Yanakie Peninsula, joining The Prom to the mainland, has formed since the ending of the last Ice Age.
OPPOSITE, TOP LEFT Bracken (*Pteridium esculentum*) forms a common groundcover because it can survive both fire and slashing necessary to reduce the fire risk.
OPPOSITE, TOP RIGHT Pippies strain nutrients from the rich tidal flats of Corner Inlet.
OPPOSITE, CENTRE LEFT A crimson rosella (*Platycercus elegans*) feeds on a scrap of bread.
OPPOSITE, CENTRE RIGHT The pure white quartz sand of Squeaky Beach. Quartz sand predominates on the west coast of The Prom; calcareous sand on the east coast.
OPPOSITE, BOTTOM The stunted white mangroves (*Avicennia marina*) of Corner Inlet are the most southerly in the world.

The Grampians

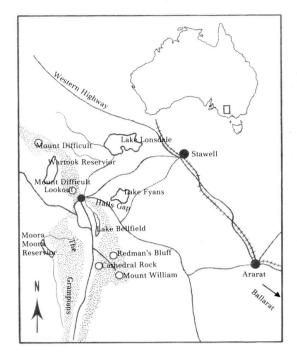

MOST of Australia's explorers who saw lakes glimmering in the distance advanced on them full of hope, only to find that the 'water' was nothing more than a sheet of salt-encrusted mud. Not so Major Thomas Mitchell in his 'Australia Felix'. From the top of a high peak he called Mount William, he saw to the north a lake which he named Lake Lonsdale after the first administrator of Port Phillip, Captain William Lonsdale.

It was July 1836, and Mitchell and his companions were forced to spend a night on top of Mount William, unable to find their way back down again in the dark. It was so cold that the ends of the twigs burning in their small fire were still white with frost, and the health of two of Mitchell's best men was seriously impaired by the experience.

Lake Lonsdale now is one of a dozen reservoirs, some natural, some man-made, supplying water to the towns and farms that sprang up after Mitchell returned to Sydney and filed his report. They are fed by the 88 kilometre long mountain range Mitchell named the Grampians because they reminded him of the range of the same name in his native Scotland and which forms the western extremity of the Great Divide.

Mount William, at 1164 metres, is the highest point in the range, which has the distinctive shape of a cuesta, an escarpment with one side much steeper than the other. Cuestas, the result of differential erosion, develop in tilted rock formations where a hard, resistant rock layer (quartzose sandstones, in this case) overlies softer, more easily weathered rock.

The Grampians are very old geologically: a geographical island where plants and animals have been able to evolve over more than 250 million years, while much of the surrounding countryside has lain under the sea. The Grampian sandstones and siltstones were laid down in layers underwater in Carboniferous and Devonian times, then tilted. Stresses in the rocks have caused them to fracture vertically, and erosion has been swifter along these joint planes, carving out deep gorges and canyons where the sun is a stranger.

Magma from deep beneath the earth's crust has also intruded into the sandstones, in places becoming exposed by the erosion of the overlying rock. Many of the high waterfalls along the McKenzie River and elsewhere have been created by volcanic porphyritic dykes which have prevented even erosion along a stream bed, while in places gold has been discovered locked in granite outcrops. The most significant strike was made in 1900 south of Mount William, at a place called Mafeking after the besieged South African town.

But gold mining has had a much less significant effect on the Grampians than forestry and tourism. The first permanent settlers in Halls Gap, gateway to the Grampians, were timber-getters. Control of the Grampians has since 1907 been vested in the Forests Commission of Victoria, and 152 000 hectares of the mountains are permanently dedicated to forestry purposes. More than 100 years of harvesting hardwood species, including messmate, yellow box and manna gum, have inevitably altered the composition of the forests, despite a Plan of Management, adopted in 1938 and designed to prevent wildfires and preserve the environment. (In 1939 the Grampians, along with much of the rest of Victoria, exploded in the worst bushfires ever to afflict the state.) Forestry tracks criss-crossing the Grampians provide access to many otherwise difficult to reach parts of the ranges, but inevitably this also increases user pressure and erosion. Obviously, the Forests Commission's liberal attitude towards tourism is a mixed blessing.

As well as the commercial trees, the Grampians are home to more than 1000 different plant species, some of which are found nowhere else. Species unique to the area include the Grampians gum and Grampians snow gum; various bush peas; the bush heath-myrtle; the showy bauera; and the narrow-leaf trymalium. There are more than 100 species of orchid in the ranges. Several Tasmanian plants found here, including the shiny tea tree, grow nowhere else in mainland Australia, while the pincushion lily is found only in south-western Australia and on one small rocky ledge on a peak of the North Grampians. Victoria's floral emblem, pink heath, is common. In the springtime the mountains are a Mecca for hundreds of amateur naturalists, keen to record existing, or new, species of wildflowers.

The Grampians' wide range of habitats—grassland, heath, scrub, savannah woodland, stringybark forests, dry and wet sclerophyll forests, and a sub-alpine zone—supports a varied fauna. The rare tiger cat was last seen here in 1960, while in 1970

Broken Falls, on the MacKenzie River.

brush-tailed rock wallabies were identified for the first time in the Red Rock area. The delicate potoroo was found on the eastern slopes of Mount William in 1964. The koala population, seriously depleted by farming and timber-getting, was boosted in 1957 by the introduction of 500 animals to the Dairy Creek area. Of the introduced species, only the red deer are not regarded as pests.

Before the first dams were built in the 1880s, nature had already thrown her own weirs across several streams, creating swamps along the Wannon River, on Mason Creek, at Ming Ming north-west of the Victoria Range, and at Moora Moora on the Glenelg River behind the Serra Range. Moora Moora is the largest swamp by far, extending more than 30 kilometres along the headwaters of the Glenelg River, a wild and desolate place criss-crossed by forestry tracks and surrounded by high peaks. This was the lair of the legendary Moora Savage, a dangerous white bull that led a rampaging mob of wild cattle into adjacent farmland in the 1890s. West of the swamp, across 960 metre high Mount Thackeray, clusters of fine paintings adorn several caves and overhangs.

There were three Aboriginal tribes inhabiting sectors of the Grampians: the Bunganditji to the west, the Tjapwurong to the east, and the Jaadwa in the north. As elsewhere in Australia, they were treated shamefully by the early squatters. Some of the Aboriginal people were assimilated into the white community as station hands and domestics, but eventually they died out or moved away.

Most visitors to the Grampians pass through Halls Gap en route to the rugged Wonderland Range south-west of the township. Here the weathering processes that have moulded the Grampians have carved a singular assemblage of fantastic formations from the sandstone. Water the colour of strong tea runs through the Grand Canyon after heavy rain, gouging ever deeper into the soft Devonian sandstone. A steel ladder leads up and out of the canyon, past the Whales Mouth, Ladys Hat and Echo Cave to Silent Street, a box canyon so narrow at its exit point that a man of generous girth would find it impossible to proceed. Beyond it are the Pinnacle, a look-out point high above Fyans Valley; the Fallen Giant, an enormous chunk of rock that has sheered off a cliff face; and the Nerve Test, a narrow promontory of rock surmounted by 'stepping stones' along which the agile scramble to prove their courage.

South, along the ridge top, is the incredibly fashioned Mushroom Rock, a boulder undercut by running water so that its only contact with the ground is a single 'stalk' of rock centimetres thick. The gloomy stringybark forests, lit by the occasional flicker of a yellow wattle, are sometimes devastated by fierce gales that sweep through the mountains. The southernmost point of the range is Sundial Peak, so called because the sun shines on it first thing in the morning and again last thing in the evening and now graced by a real sundial installed by boys from the Stawell Technical School. Below lies Lake Bellfield, created in 1966 by damming Fyans Creek; to the south, Mount William is wreathed in cloud, its slopes dark green like pine forests.

The Wonderland Range was incorporated into the Wonderland Forest Park, a sort of forestry-run national park, in 1962. It encapsulates the wild and splendid grandeur of the Grampians, a grandeur given emphasis by the names bestowed on many of the mountains' most prominent features: the Battlements, Valley of Mystery, the Jaws of Death, Asses Ears, Abrupt Peak, Mummy Rock, Gate of the North Wind, Grand Stairway, Wild Sheep Hills, Cathedral Rock, Sheet of Water Creek and Chimney Pots, amongst others.

There is always something new to discover in the Grampians. Many people have devoted a lifetime to studying its flora and fauna, yet new species await recording. But the lure of botanical or zoological fame does not attract everyone who makes the 250 kilometre trip from Melbourne. For many, it is enough to wander, like Milton in *Paradise Lost*, 'where the Muses haunt clear spring, or shady grove, or sunny hill'.

BELOW The Grand Canyon, cynosure of the Wonderland Range.
OPPOSITE, TOP LEFT Foam in mountain stream is caused by tannin leached from the plant cover.
OPPOSITE, TOP RIGHT The amazing Balconies, two protruding ledges of rock in the Mount Victory Range.
OPPOSITE, CENTRE LEFT Mushroom Rock, in the Wonderland Range, has been undercut by two streams. (Michael Richardson)
OPPOSITE, CENTRE RIGHT The Grampians are home to more than 1000 different plant species, some of them unique to the area.
OPPOSITE, BOTTOM The Elephant's Hide, near Halls Gap.

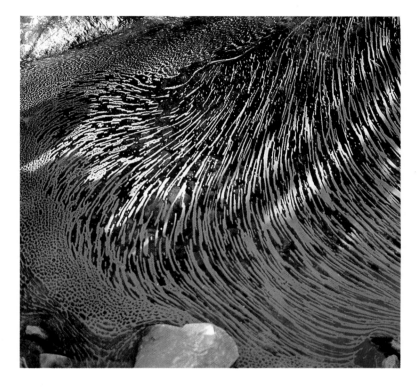

VICTORIA

The Port Campbell coastline

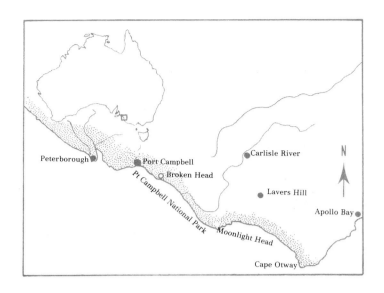

$\mathbf{M}$ORE than 30 ships have been wrecked on the 70 kilometre stretch of coastline between Curdies Inlet and Cape Otway, at the western entrance to Bass Strait. The cape was often the first part of Australia new arrivals would glimpse after leaving Cape Town in South Africa, and ships sailing eastward had to navigate between King Island and the mainland, a passage less than 80 kilometres wide. There was no light on King Island until 1861, so for the 13 years after the completion of the Cape Otway lighthouse vessels hugged the mainland coast, their crews keeping a sharp lookout for the light. Before 1848 the ships' safety was in the hands of God and their masters; the standard of navigation was often woeful and the charts inadequate (the first survey of the coast was not made until 1846–47), so that captains of ships with limited ability to manoeuvre against the fierce westerlies were often 50 kilometres or more out in their reckoning.

Frequently the survivors of shipwrecks died a more agonising death than those who drowned. The smooth, vertical cliff faces were up to 150 metres high and offered no toeholds. Some bodies found at the foot of the cliffs, perhaps where a narrow beach offered sanctuary from the sea, had their fingertips chafed raw by desperate attempts to climb to safety. According to one report, a shipwrecked Negro sailor managed to scale one of the tall stacks offshore, where he sat, trapped by the angry sea and within sight of onlookers, until he eventually died and his body was blown off the rock and into the water.

BELOW **Angry seas pound the London Bridge peninsula...**
RIGHT**...and eat away the base of one of the Twelve Apostles.**
PAGE 144.**Muttonbird Island, near which the** *Loch Ard* **sank in 1878, drowning 52 passengers and crew.**
PAGE 145. **Sunset silhouettes one of the Twelve Apostles.**

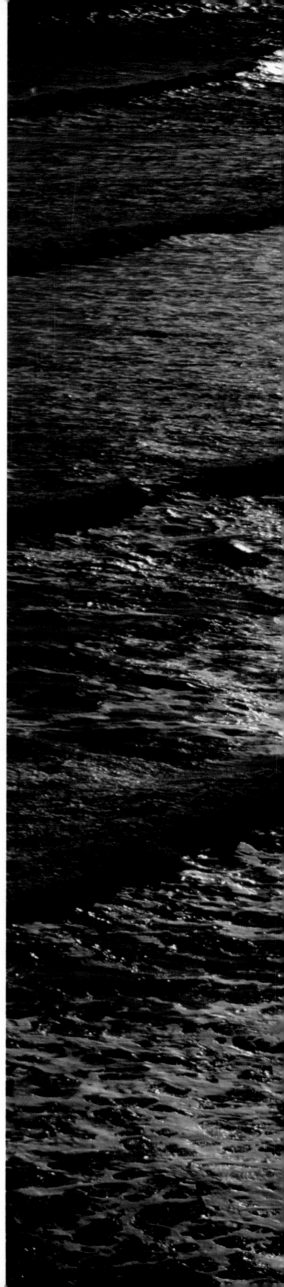

One of the more notable shipwrecks was that of the *Loch Ard* under Captain George Gibbs. The 1594 tonne, three-masted iron clipper, carrying 54 passengers and crew, hit a submerged reef off Muttonbird Island, just after 4 o'clock in the morning on 1 June 1878. Bad weather had previously prevented Gibbs from fixing the ship's position, and a thick haze obscured the coastline. When the haze lifted, it was too late to stop the ship from running ashore.

Within 15 minutes of striking the reef, the clipper had vanished, slipping off into deep water. She broke up too quickly to launch the lifeboats. An apprentice named Tom Pearce floated on and under an upturned boat into the mouth of a narrow gorge, 50 metres across, and managed to struggle ashore. Some time later he heard a cry for help and saw a girl, Eva Carmichael, clinging to a spar at the entrance to the gorge. He threw off his clothes, swam out to her and brought her, unconscious by this time, into the beach.

Tom left Eva in a nearby cave while he went to seek assistance. He climbed the steep walls of the gorge with difficulty, not realising that some 'rude steps' marked an easier path. Walking west, he met two men from Glenample station who were mustering sheep. While the men rode for help, Tom returned to what would henceforth be known as Loch Ard Gorge. Eva had vanished, terrified apparently at the thought that her rescuers were murderous blacks. One of the station hands eventually found her cowering under some bushes.

Tom was subsequently awarded the Royal Humane Society's first gold medal for bravery. He and Eva were the only two survivors of the shipwreck (she lost eight members of her family in the disaster) and many Australians hoped they would marry. But within three months Eva had returned to Britain and she never saw Tom again. Pearce's next ship, the *Loch Stuart*, sank the following year off the Irish coast; again he survived, and went on to gain his own command.

Only five bodies were recovered from the sea. Four of them were buried in a tiny cemetery above the cliff-lined gorge. Loch Ard beach looks pleasant enough, but it is swept by winds that seem to carry the voices of the dead, and visitors do not stay long. The undersurface of the water is a swirling mass of rips and undertows.

In fact, the whole coastline is treacherous. Hidden reefs as well as the offshore islands transform the giant Southern Ocean swells into a maelstrom of swirling white water. For any lesser swimmer than Tom Pearce to plunge into that sea when it was running would be to go to certain death.

The fine-grained limestone which confronts the sea for more than 50 kilometres, from the Bay of Islands south-east to the more resistant sandstones of the Otway Group beyond Moonlight Head, was formed beneath a sea which covered much of south-western Victoria during the early Miocene epoch. Over a period of millions of years, the calcareous remains of marine invertebrates compacted to form a soft white limestone which was subsequently uplifted. The land's interface with the ocean would have changed according to sea level: during the Pleistocene Ice Ages, the limestone would have sloped down to the lowered shoreline. Today's perpendicular cliffs and offshore stacks and pillars have been created since the last rising of the sea level, 6000–8000 years ago.

The forces of erosion at work here are rapid. Wave action, worrying away at points of weakness in the rock, is constantly undermining the cliffs and, in places where deep water occurs right up to their bases, the cliff tops are sometimes stripped bare of protective vegetation by salt spray. Rain works down through joints and cracks in the rock or tends to eat away larger areas in the 'stripped zones' along the cliff edges. Stacks and offshore islands are left where the waves and rainwater have cut through a headland; arches form where the waves have undercut opposite sides. Sometimes the roof of a sea-cave or tunnel partially collapses, creating a blowhole. The most spectacular example of this is near where the *Loch Ard* sank; 11 bodies (never recovered) were said to have been washed into the blowhole shortly after the disaster.

Further east, the famous group of high stacks known as the Twelve Apostles makes a defiant stand against the sea. But there are many others, some fat, some thin, some bald, some wearing a green cap of salt-tolerant heath and grasses. Many of the stacks and islands are nesting sites for muttonbirds, remarkable fliers that spend the southern winter in the region of the Bering Sea, between Alaska and Siberia.

Isolated bays and many of the beaches and offshore islands also form suitable sites for fairy penguin rookeries. These little birds emerge from the sea in late afternoon and clamber up to their burrows. Some never make it: the wanton sea hurls them to their destruction on the rocks. Even for creatures as well adapted as penguins, this coast, with its unpredictable rips and currents and freak waves, can be a dangerous place.

Port Campbell, the only relatively safe anchorage on this coastline, was named after a Scottish whaler, Captain Alexander Campbell, who in the 1840s sailed his ship past the reef guarding the entrance to the bay. Squatters had already taken up runs around nearby Heytebury Forest, and sealers probably used the bay intermittently over the next two decades, but it was not until 1865 that the first permanent settlers arrived. The rutted tracks across the thickly wooded hinterland were very slow and difficult to traverse, so for a long time all supplies came into Port Campbell by sea.

Despite the problems of access, by 1886 there were 300 people living in the settlement and its environs. Then, in 1892, the railway reached Timboon, 15 kilometres to the north, and it was the safe and reliable trains, not the coastal ships using Port Campbell, that won the business. Port Campbell's inevitable decline was arrested by the expansion of the tourist trade. Until 1932 Melburnians came mainly by train to Timboon; then the Great Ocean Road, a memorial to the fallen of World War I, was opened, allowing those wealthy enough to own cars to motor down. The 320 kilometre former tollway, built largely by men and horses, winds down the coast from Geelong through the resort towns of Anglesea, Aireys Inlet, Lorne and Apollo Bay, across the foot of the densely forested Otway Ranges, and on up the coast to Port Campbell, Peterborough (on Curdies Inlet) and Nirranda. It is probably the best known scenic drive in Australia.

A treacherous undertow makes Loch Ard Gorge unsafe for swimming.

The Pink Lakes, Underbool

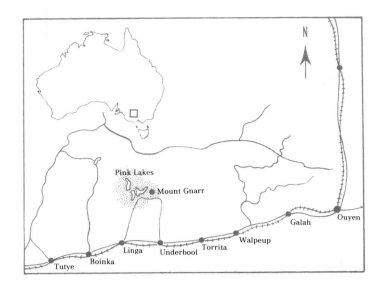

VICTORIA, the smallest and most densely populated of the mainland states, boasts relatively few areas of true wilderness, where traces of man are unknown and the visitor can feel totally alone with nature. The most extensive wilderness area in the state is the 113 500 hectare Big Desert National Park in the north-west, bisected by just one rough track and bordered to the north by the Ouyen Highway. Beyond this road is an almost equally large tract of land known as the Sunset Country, partly grazed, partly farmed for wheat, criss-crossed by tracks and dotted with bores. Too settled to be called wilderness, it is nevertheless lonely and isolated, a dry, hot region of low sand ridges and mallee scrub that contrasts markedly with the fertile green plains of Victoria's Western District.

Most of the lakes in this area of 312 millimetre annual rainfall are saline and ephemeral. The Pink Lakes, which form part of a state park 11 kilometres north of the village of Linga, are no exception, as a history of more than 60 years salt harvesting attests. They are named for their characteristic pink hue, for decades thought to be caused by pink salts in the water. In the 1930s it was proved that the colour is, in fact, due to the presence of tiny flagellates of the *Dunaliella* genus, about 40 per cent of the dry body weight of which is red pigment. The colour changes with the season and rainfall. Usually rose-pink, it deepens after heavy rain to a rich mauve. It is more than a tinge of colour: the lakes are actually bright pink in any light, and their shores are rimmed with white crystals of drying salt streaked with red *Dunaliella* like an unravelled barber's pole.

The pinkish hue is not uncommon in the salt lakes of the Mallee and Wimmera, nor along the south-eastern coast of South Australia or in Western Australia. But nowhere is the colour as striking, as vibrant, as here. It takes a little time to adjust to the fact that the water is not blue, as it should be, even the salt-tolerant samphires that thrive in the mud of the lakes' shorelines are red-green.

The first white settlers in this district took up their holdings in the 1850s, grazing sheep initially and swiftly displacing the Aboriginal landowners, the Latjalatji tribe. Closer settlement began with the surveying of the railway line from Ouyen to Cowangie and on to Murrayville and South Australia in 1908 (it was completed in 1912). Blocks were thrown open in a 5 kilometre strip on both sides of the railway line, the authorities issuing settlers with a map of the district showing each numbered block, marked out on the ground by a metre-wide strip pegged at the corners. They cleared the land for cultivation by dragging, with bullocks or horse teams, heavy logs or iron rollers through the thick mallee scrub, but had great trouble digging up the tough mallee rootstocks, or lignotubers (the mallee eucalypts control evaporative water loss by storing it underground in the bulbous lignotuber, sending up numerous thin stems instead of one large trunk). By the time the wheat industry was under way an enterprising entrepreneur from Underbool named Ebenezer Jones was already bringing in another, rather incongruous, harvest—salt from the Pink Lakes.

Begun in 1916, this industry survived until 1978. The salt was scraped into piles using a buck scraper dragged between two horses, and taken by wheelbarrow and drags to the edge of the lake, where it was bagged and carried in wagons to the railhead. By 1922 the sandy roads had become too chopped up for conventional horse-drawn transport and camels were imported from Broken Hill; they survived for 13 years until superseded by motor trucks. A tramline to Linga functioned for only a few years. In 1939 Eb Jones, the only operator still working the leases, merged with the Melbourne chemical company Hart & Co. ICI took over the business after the war, assigning leases to Cheetham Salt. Harvesting ceased at Lake Becking in 1971 and at Lakes Kenyon and Crosbie in 1978, although huge grey piles of salt, like concrete blockhouses, still dot the shore of the biggest lake, Lake Crosbie.

The lakes are of recent origin, precipitated from saline groundwater which percolates down from the surrounding countryside during winter. To protect them from wind-blown debris, the result of over-clearing on surrounding land, an 1850 hectare reserve was declared around them in 1925. The reserve was later licensed for grazing, and a combination of drought, stock and hungry camels prevented regeneration of important species such as native pine, which grows alongside bull-oak in the grassy savannah away from the lakes.

In 1979, the year after salt mining ceased, the lakes were incorporated into the 50 700 hectare Pink Lakes State Park.

The characteristic pink colour of the lakes is caused by the presence of red flagellates of the *Dunaliella* genus.

The gaping maw of Admirals Arch frames the surging Southern Ocean.

SOUTH AUSTRALIA

The Coorong

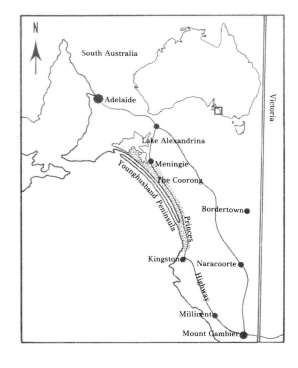

MOST of South Australia is all but uninhabitable. Even the south-east, which contains the state's greenest pastures and the bulk of its dairy farms, is a mixed bag, an intermingling of wetlands, volcanic cones and plains, arid scrublands, salt flats, and the 100 kilometre long strip of water that is the Coorong.

Formed by the global fluctuations in sea level during the past 120 000 years, the Coorong, at the mouth of the Murray River, is a drought refuge for waterbirds from all over the world. Enclosed to the west by the rolling parabolic dunes of the Younghusband Peninsula and to the east by low hills, dunes and farmland, the shallow waterway is rarely more than 3 metres deep; more often, little more than 1 metre. Its maximum width, near Woods Wells, is just over 4 kilometres; at Hells Gate, a promontory which divides the Coorong into North and South lagoons, the water flows through a narrow passage only a few hundred metres across. The Princes Highway, one of Australia's major arteries, runs along the eastern shore of the Coorong for more than 60 kilometres, and Adelaide is only 70 kilometres distant as the crow flies. Yet it is possible to stand on the debris-strewn Ninety Mile Beach, buffeted by a howling onshore gale, enveloped in the roar of the booming surf, and imagine oneself the last person on earth.

This was, of course, the setting for one of the best loved and most widely read of all Australian children's books, Colin Thiele's *Storm Boy*, a story which explored many of the threats to the survival of the Coorong. The first of these is duck shooting. Some 6800 hectares of the Coorong form a game reserve, splitting the 38 200 hectare national park in two. Clearly, the two concepts are incompatible. During the season, from mid-February to the end of June, thousands of duck shooters descend on the reserve in boats and four-wheel drives. Most obey the rules, but inevitably some shoot protected species (like Mr Percival, the pelican murdered in *Storm Boy*), and others drive off-road and disturb the delicate web of plants binding the dunes together. Where livestock grazing, timber cutting and earlier unrestricted vehicular access have killed off the ground cover, massive sandblows up to 20 metres high encroach on the tea tree, mallee and she-oak scrub fringing the shoreline. Some of these are natural, for the dune system is an active one, constantly forming and reforming under the agency of the south-westerly winds. When clouds threaten, the sun sweeps its golden waves across the hummocks and hollows of the dunes, momentarily bringing a clump of bush, a sand ripple, or a piece of driftwood to life, and the spinifex flashes messages as it catches the light.

This is where the Aboriginal people, the Tanganekald, lived, hunted and fished, and left enormous piles of empty sea shells on top of the silent dunes, unprotected from careless footprints or wheel tracks. It was, and still is, a place of plenty, with numerous freshwater soaks along the shoreline.

The Aborigines' first contact with Europeans was far from friendly. Many of the whalers and sealers who had operated out of nearby Kangaroo Island since the beginning of the nineteenth century kidnapped Aboriginal women from the mainland and from Tasmania, and treated them abominably, reportedly cutting off one gin's foot to prevent her escaping. Inevitably, this prejudiced the tribes living near the mouth of the Murray against Europeans, and so they speared the first white man to set foot on the Younghusband Peninsula, Captain Collett Barker, who had swum across the mouth of the Murray, and threw his body into the sea. Nine years later, in 1840, the 26 survivors of the brig *Maria*, shipwrecked on Ninety Mile Beach, suffered an even more horrific fate: a rescue party under Captain Pullen discovered their dismembered and partially eaten bodies, including those of several children, lying on the ground, 'dreadfully bruised about the face and head', more than 130 kilometres from where the party had come ashore. Two men were hung for the crimes, and subsequent settlers, who found that the Aborigines had begun to develop a taste for beef and lamb, killed many more. Yet the Tanganekald people had been very kind to the survivors of an earlier shipwreck, that of the *Fanny*, in dramatic contrast to the murderous actions of the Milmenrura clan. The Aborigines were forced to abandon their traditional way of life in the 1880s, leaving the fishing to the professionals who even today pull hundreds of tonnes of fish each year from the shallow waters of the Coorong.

To the Aborigines this was Kurangh, or 'narrow neck of water', formed during a titanic struggle between hunters and the giant cod which created the tortuous course of the Murray as it swam from the Darling towards the sea. Because the cod

The Spirit of the Coorong.

152

reached the ocean, the legend has it, the mouth of the Murray was not properly formed and is constantly shifting, as much as 2000 metres this century and occasionally, during periods of drought, closing completely. Scientists believe there was a time when the great sand dunes of the Younghusband Peninsula did not exist, and the coastline lay along what is now the inland shore of the Coorong. Stabilised former barrier islands, like stranded whales, run in waves parallel to the coast for up to 65 kilometres inland.

There is a hard core to the peninsula, formed during another warm period when the sea level was high, perhaps 80 000 years ago. The sea retreated during the last Ice Age, when Tasmania was joined to the mainland, and the Coorong was simply an interdunal corridor. Then the seas began to rise again, flooding across the sand bar, gradually filling the Coorong and heaping up a protective wall along its western edge, piling up sand swept northwards by the prevailing winds and halted by the seaward sweep of the mighty Murray.

For more than 40 years now, the Murray has been partially tamed by a series of five barrages which segregate it from the sea. Inevitably, this has also had an effect on the composition of the Coorong. The water at the southern end of the lagoons, where tendrils of land snake out into the water like the embankments of rice paddies, is three times saltier than the sea. Old timers say water quality has deteriorated since the south-eastern drainage scheme was begun in the 1920s. It is considerably less brackish to the north, where the lagoon once merged with giant Lake Alexandrina, and this is where most fish are caught. Flushing occurs during floods and when the barrages are opened but during 1982, a year of record drought, they remained closed. Local runoff and reduced evaporation swell the southern lagoon by an extra 15 kilometres or more during winter, but at the end of the long, hot summer the stench of dead fish is almost unbearable. Local rains also fill a series of lakes straggling down towards the coastal town of Kingston, most of them freshwater, but a few saline, tinged with the pink of algae and bordered by the red succulent samphire. Carbonate

sediments here are creating, agonisingly slowly, limestone and dolomite, the characteristic rocks of the south-east and of the north-eastern shore of the Coorong.

Salinity problems notwithstanding, more than 200 bird species have been recorded at the Coorong. The most common, in summer at least, are the red-necked stints and sandpipers, but there are also plovers and egrets by the thousand, herons and ibises, banded stilts, spoonbills, black swans and grey Cape Barren Geese. Six islands are declared prohibited areas. Here pelicans (and other species) breed in huge numbers. Even without *Storm Boy*, the pelican would have been the symbol of the Coorong: heavyweight bombers droning in perfect V-formation through the onshore winds, often accompanied by a fighter escort of black cormorants.

Vehicular access is restricted to a few tracks through the park, and to the ocean beach. But here, where the sea daily deposits new flotsam, is a place of prime importance for the pied oystercatcher and the endangered hooded plover. Both birds nest behind the frontal dune, sheltered from the battering wind, and their chicks, when hatched, spend much of their time walking on the beach. Inevitably, some are run over and killed by drivers who just do not see them.

Boats, preferably rowing or sailing boats, seem more in keeping with the spirit of the Coorong. In water so clear that it is hard to believe the Coorong is connected to the muddy Murray it is possible to glimpse and spear the bottom-hugging flounder by spotlight. Nearby, in complete contrast, the tracks of waders lie imprinted on the surface of mysterious weed-choked black pools pulsing with the croaking of frogs.

This is the spirit of the Coorong, and inevitably it infuses itself into everyone who takes time to pause a while—even shooters. The Coorong's very accessibility is at once its greatest strength (in that so many can gain peace from its solitude) and major weakness (in that too many visitors would destroy it). Fortunately, if it has managed thus far to escape the desecration of mass tourism, there remains hope that it will continue to do so in the future.

The Coorong flooded when the last Ice Age ended. This century, a local drainage scheme has caused water quality to deteriorate.

SOUTH AUSTRALIA

Remarkable Rocks and Admirals Arch

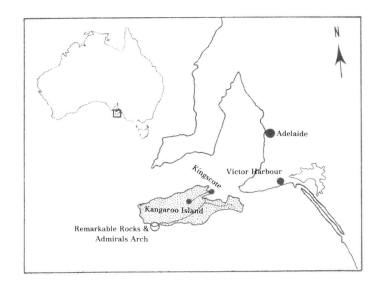

GRANITE outcrops, of themselves, are nothing unusual: they occur in many parts of Australia as, indeed, they do throughout the world. But nowhere do they form a more fantastic assemblage of natural sculptures than at Kirkpatrick Point, on the south-western tip of Kangaroo Island. Here Nature proves 'what fools we mortals be' to imagine that our puny attempts to coax form and beauty from stone could ever compare with hers.

From nearby Cape Du Couedic, the great weathered boulders affect the unorthodox shapes of a 'sci-fi' space colony, established on high ground above a seething sea. Close-up, they assume the status of sculptures: Henry Moore reclining figures; the great hooked beak of a wedge-tailed eagle; improbable 'boulder bubbles', their scooped out centres large enough to accommodate a man. There are caves protected from the elements by sharp-edged overhangs, like awning fringes, and narrow winding passage-ways where the sun rarely penetrates, and rock walls furrowed like a freshly ploughed field. Vivid orange and yellow lichen daub the rocks, merging into brilliant splashes of colour when seen from the two granite 'viewing platforms' poking through the surrounding heath.

All this, and perhaps the most magnificent natural setting in Australia. The granite dome slopes steeply down below the rocks into the ocean, where giant swells from the Antarctic ceaselessly scourge its flanks. There are more boulders here, worn smooth and round by the sea. To the east and south-east, the white lines of reefs break the rolling blue of the water, and lines of limestone cliffs run away from Kirkpatrick Point like the back-stretched arms of a high diver.

The granite of which Remarkable Rocks are formed intruded into the surrounding sedimentary rocks about 500 million years ago. Xenoliths, blocks of impure sandstone deposited in the sea 50 million years earlier, have been changed by heat and incorporated in the granite. Until comparatively recently, these rocks were covered by glacial deposits from the Permian period (247–289 million years ago), but erosion has worn away the overlying surface, re-exposing the granite, uncovering it for the sculpting of the deft chisels of the elements.

As the sedimentary rocks were being worn away, water seeped into cracks in the granite, creating a cluster of partially rounded boulders sitting on top of a round tor. Weathering on the surface was fastest in the sheltered corners, away from the sun and wind, where water could collect. Small depressions formed by trickling water became even more protected and hence eroded more quickly. As a result, many of the caverns face north-north-east, away from the prevailing winds.

Similar granite outcrops occur on the mainland, for Backstairs Passage, which separates Kangaroo Island from the rest of South Australia, was created only at the end of the last Ice Age, about 8000 years ago. There is evidence that Aborigines once lived on Kangaroo Island, but they were gone, extinct or absorbed into the mainland tribes, many thousands of years before white man came to these shores.

The first ship to sail off the coast of Kangaroo Island was the *Investigator* (1802), commanded by Matthew Flinders, whose crew killed for food many of the large, tame kangaroos they saw. Flinders' route took him only along the north coast and through Backstairs Passage, and it was left to a Frenchman, Nicholas Baudin, whom Flinders met in Encounter Bay, to sail along the rugged west and south coasts in his ship, *Le Géographe*. Baudin's journal contains many references to the island's rugged limestone cliffs, and it was he who bequeathed a French flavour to many of the more prominent landmarks he noted, including Cape Du Couedic.

Six kilometres along the coast from Kirkpatrick Point, Kangaroo Island's other great natural wonder has been formed. You stroll down a well-kept pathway, through a natural garden of yellow daisies and purple pigface divided by irregular borders of meandering limestone. To the south, the two small Casuarina Islets are deluged by spray from big seas which roar like a river in flood through a narrow channel and meet with a mighty clap of waves in the bay to the east of the point. The path winds downwards, around the end of the point, along a sloping cliff line. Then, suddenly, the cliff vanishes; there appears a great gaping cavern, rimmed by ancient black stalactites like the fangs of a yawning monster and framing a picture straight out of the Maelstrom. Admirals Arch is huge: more than 20 metres high and at least 30 metres across, its floor a smooth, sloping shelf of granite. Elsewhere the rock is all limestone, pitted and eroded by wind and tide, heaped in jumbled piles, as wild and violent as the sea.

Orange lichens colour the granite of Remarkable Rocks.

A vague feeling of uneasiness creeps over you, and a voice calls from deep inside, 'Come away! Come away!' Then you look around and notice the green succulents growing out of small, sheltered pockets in the cliff face and, squinting against the sunlight, glimpse the bullet head of a New Zealand fur seal playing in the swirling surf. The disquiet vanishes.

Yet perhaps that first, indefinable trace of fear is not out of place after all. For this coast has claimed more than its share of ships, forced onto the rocks by wind and storm. It was for this reason that the lighthouse on Cape Du Couedic was built between 1906 and 1909, with its cluster of three stone houses. The lighthouse was once one of the most inaccessible in Australia, manned by three families who took it in turn to work the giant clockwork mechanism. There were no roads in through the thick bush of Flinders Chase in those days, so supplies were brought in by boat once every six months and pulled up the cliff by a horse-powered winch at nearby Weirs Cove. The first motor car did not reach the lighthouse until 1936. In 1958 the clockwork mechanism became obsolete when electricity was brought out to the point.

The lighthouse, Remarkable Rocks and Admirals Arch are all located in Flinders Chase National Park, 59 000 hectares of undeveloped bushland at the western end of Kangaroo Island. It was the thick mallee scrub, broken along the creek lines by forests of sugar, pink and swamp gums, which proved such an obstacle to the early lighthouse keepers—even though Kangaroo Island itself was the first part of South Australia to be settled, in 1806, 30 years before Adelaide, by an unsavoury group of sealers, whalers and escaped convicts. The farmers who followed these misfits found little use for the high plateau area to the west, and Flinders Chase was proclaimed a reserve in 1919, a 'sanatorium and playground for tired workers suffering from brain fag or other forms of overwork'.

BELOW Admiral's Arch undercuts a small point below Cape Du Couedic lighthouse. Supplies for the lighthouse were originally shipped in and winched up a nearby cliff.
OPPOSITE Remarkable Rocks have been formed by the erosion of granite boulders sitting on top of a round tor.

Wilpena Pound

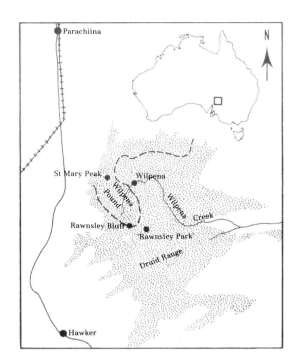

To many people, Wilpena Pound *is* the Flinders Ranges: it is, after all, their most striking natural feature; it encompasses the highest peaks; it is located almost exactly at the mid-point of the ranges, close to where Sir Hans Heysen painted his best landscapes; and it is, significantly, where the bitumen road ends. The Pound is also the most fertile spot in the central ranges, attracting a 350 millimetre annual rainfall (100 millimetres more than the surrounding countryside) and containing some of the best grazing country in the Flinders Ranges.

It is not easy to farm Wilpena Pound, ringed as it is with 600 metre high walls, broken only in one spot by the creek which rises there. When the Hill family acquired the Wilpena lease in 1889, they decided to take advantage of the favourable conditions to grow wheat on the floor of the Pound; with difficulty they constructed a road alongside the creek and, later, a small stone hut just inside the Pound. The road stood for nearly 25 years but was washed away in a torrential downpour in 1914 and was never rebuilt.

Previously, the grass-covered Pound had been a naturally fenced sheep paddock. Discovered in 1850 by stockman William Chace, it was taken up as part of Wilpena Run the following year. The station prospered until the Great Drought of 1864–66, which shattered the hopes and fortunes of many of the pastoralists who had taken up land after Edward John Eyre's journey to the ranges' northernmost point, Mount Hopeless, in 1840. Yet few learnt the lesson of the Great Drought—that rain cannot be counted on in the Flinders Ranges—and within a few years the sheep stations were being broken up for wheat farms. Many of the new farmers clung blindly to the belief that rain would follow the plough. Inevitably, history repeated itself when the 1880–82 drought turned the wheat fields into dustbowls.

This century the Pound has served a number of other purposes, apart from that of wheat field. In 1921 it was gazetted a forest reserve and in 1945 it became a national pleasure resort, with a chalet just outside the entrance to house the eager young hikers. Finally, in 1972, it was combined with Oraparinna station (proclaimed a national park two years earlier) to form the Flinders Ranges National Park. As well as the Pound, this 78 426 hectare park encompasses much of the Heysen Range, named in honour of the great landscape artist whose paintings have done so much to spread the beauty of the Flinders Ranges beyond South Australia.

Although early theories about the Pound's creation suggested it was the result of a meteorite or comet impact, it is, in fact, the natural result of earth movements. The Pound quartzite forming all the major ridges in the Flinders Ranges, from the Gammon Ranges in the north to the Devils Peak near Quorn in the south, was laid down beneath a shallow sea in late Proterozoic times. Compressed and compacted into an exceedingly hard and dense rock, the sediments were ultimately uplifted thousands of metres during an extensive period of earth movement about 450 million years ago. Wilpena Pound, formed then, is actually a fine example of a synclinal basin formed by a downward-dipping fold pattern.

Between the Ordovician and the Tertiary periods, erosion reduced the high peaks to a fraction of their former might. During the Tertiary period this surface was uplifted again, with strong movement along the pre-existing fault lines. The hard, resistant quartzite has emerged as strong ridge lines while the softer sediments have been reduced to small rounded hills or cut by streams to form valleys. This is still a geologically unstable region, with comparatively frequent earth tremors. One, measuring 4.7 on the Richter scale, in 1972 dislodged boulders from the Pound walls which, crashing down, sparked a bushfire.

From the air, Wilpena Pound looks like a crater, but in fact was formed by natural folds in the rocks.

Other basins or pounds exist elsewhere in the Flinders Ranges, but none is comparable in size to Wilpena. At its north-eastern point rises St Marys Peak, at 1165 metres the highest point in the ranges. From its summit, occasionally sprinkled with snow in winter, the 54 square kilometre Pound is spread out like a vast football oval, the two red-gum-lined tributaries of Wilpena Creek snaking across the valley floor like opposing teams making their entrance, the grassy plain studded with sugar gums, wattles and straight-trunked native pines.

The Pound was the model for the Terrible Hollow of Rolf Boldrewood's classic novel, *Robbery Under Arms*, published in 1881. Boldrewood's 'big natural park, closed round on every side with sandstone rock-walls, as upright as if they were built' was ostensibly located in New South Wales, but the Peter Finch film of the book was shot largely in the Flinders Ranges.

Boldrewood changed his setting in one important detail: the inner walls of the Pound, far from being upright, are considerably gentler than the steep external slopes, which can be scaled only with difficulty in certain places. One of these is above Arkaroo Rock, a large boulder to the north-east of Rawnsley Bluff, the southernmost point of the Pound. An erosion cave in the boulder is covered with fine ochre paintings symbolising the Aboriginal legend of the creation of the Pound. In the Dreamtime, it is said that Yulu, the sacred kingfisher, flew south from the vicinity of Marree, lighting fires en route, the charcoal from which is today's coal deposit at Leigh Creek. Near Parachilna and Brachina gorges he noticed two large *arkaroo* (snakes) slithering towards the locality of the Pound, where the Adnjamathanha (hill people) were gathered for a circumcision ceremony.

Yulu arrived just as Wahla, the wild turkey, was about to circumcise the initiates with a firestick. Yulu intervened and demonstrated the advantages of using a sharp stick to perform the operation. As dawn approached, a large star to be west revealed itself to be the eye of the *arkaroo*. The snakes slid into the centre of the gathering and ate everyone except for two men, who became Arkaroo Rock and another large boulder nearby. The *arkaroo* joined together to form the walls of Wilpena Pound. To the Adnjamathanha this was a special place, where game was plentiful and water supplies reliable. It has remained so right up to the present day.

BELOW River red gums (*E. camaldulensis*) line the course of Wilpena Creek.
OPPOSITE, TOP Ants feed on nectar produced by a flowering grass-tree (*Xanthorrea* spp.).
OPPOSITE The towering cliffs of Rawnsley Bluff form the southern wall of the pound.

Arkaroola– Mount Painter

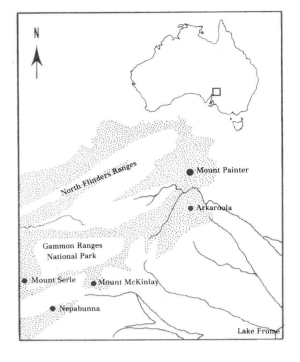

THE Flinders Ranges are not large, as mountain ranges go. Only 350 kilometres long from Crystal Brook to Mount Serle and up to 1100 metres high, they pale by comparison with the Rockies, the Himalayas, the Andes, or even our own Great Dividing Range. Yet once they rivalled the Andes for height: at least 6000 metres of rock have been eroded away over millions of years, and the remnants of this mighty mountain range are no less rugged for their diminutive size. In the remote north-eastern Flinders Ranges, around the Freeling Heights, there is scarcely a level piece of ground to be found. This is the Arkaroola–Mount Painter Sanctuary, one of the most spectacular landscapes in Australia.

The tumultuous upheavals that created the mountains seem to have had their genesis in this area. Ridge after ridge of stark, eroded hills, the relief accentuated by the arid climate, rise like a thorny devil's spines on every side. The minerals that first lured white men here in the late 1850s explode out of the hillsides, advertising their presence in a glittering array of colours as distinctive as neon signs.

The rocks here, the granites and metamorphic quartzites and schists, are among the oldest in the ranges, dating back 1600 million years. They are the basement rocks on which the mountains have been built. Overlying them throughout most of the rest of the ranges and in parts of Arkaroola are thick beds of sedimentary rock, laid down in stages beneath a shallow sea which lapped the shore of the then Western Australian continent some 500–1400 million years ago. Evidence of the sea remains as ripple rocks and marine fossils, including jellyfish, worms, algae and soft corals, some of which rank amongst the oldest fossil fauna yet discovered.

These rocks were uplifted thousands of metres as the earth buckled and folded during a period of mountain building known as the Delamerian Orogeny, 430–460 million years ago. At the same time, younger, lighter-coloured granites intruded through the base rock. Between Arkaroola and Umberatana homestead to the west is a group of volcanic plugs left behind after the surrounding tuff had been eroded away, and known locally by such evocative names as the Giants Head, the Needles and the Pinnacles. Intrusion of the magma metamorphosed the surrounding sediments, forming new minerals, including garnet, tremolite and albite feldspar.

Many interesting mineral deposits, most too small to be commercial, occur in the area, particularly copper and uranium ores. Mount Gee is virtually a mountain of quartz crystal, while there are thin seams of turquoise at East Painter. West of Mount Painter lies the thickest bed of glacial rocks in the world, 5000 metres of coarse boulder conglomerate deposited by mighty ice floes during a great Pre-Cambrian ice age. Other boulder beds at a higher level near Umberatana suggest there was also a second, later glacial phase.

What an amazing spot this is! Bubbling up through a major fault line known as Paralana Fault are the radioactive waters of Paralana Springs, the last vestige of volcanic activity in Australia. In 1926, a syndicate tried to establish a health spa here, but visitors seeking to take the waters were repelled by the primitive living conditions and the spa was soon closed. The uranium-bearing spring waters have been draining from the hills onto the flat, saltbush-covered Lake Frome plain for thousands of years, slowly building up a large body of uranium ore. This deposit, Beverley, is by no means the first radioactive ore body to be discovered in the area. As far back as 1910, Antarctic explorer Sir Douglas Mawson identified the uranium-bearing mineral torbernite from samples given to him by pioneer pastoralist and prospector W. B. Greenwood. The Radium Extraction Company of South Australia operated leases at Mount Painter and Radium Hill before and during World War I, and between 1923 and 1928 the Australian Radium Corporation camel-packed ore out of Mount Painter en route to Adelaide. World War II brought the stimulus of the Manhattan Project, and a new road was bulldozed into Mount Painter. Mining ceased here in the late 1940s and at Radium Hill in 1961.

Mines of other types, usually copper, stud the Arkaroola area, many of them are still marked by old buildings, boilers and smelters. Despite considerable investment, none of these ever paid: packing out the ore on camels to the nearest railhead was uneconomical. Perhaps the most unusual of all was the bat-guano mine in a cave near the entrance to the present-day sanctuary.

Arkaroola was, and still is, officially, a station, first taken up by W. B. Greenwood's son, Bentley, in 1937 from unwanted sections of surrounding leases. He named it after

Bararrana Gorge, on the way to Paralana Hot Springs. Camel teams packing uranium ore out from Mount Painter watered here.

Arkaroo, the giant serpent of Aboriginal legend. The Adnjamathanha people believed that the northern Flinders Ranges were formed by the serpent, who drank nearby Lake Frome dry, then dragged his bloated body back through the Arkaroola area, digging Arkaroo Gorge and leaving behind him waterholes where he stopped to relieve his overfull bladder. He ended his journey in the nearby Gammon Ranges, where a bilious condition causes his stomach to rumble (as earth tremors) until this day.

Bentley Greenwood sold up after ten or so years, but he made more of the all-slopes topography of his station than the pastoralists who had sold him his run had thought he would. The average rainfall here is less than 250 millimetres a year, and this is twice as much as on the surrounding plains. Consequently, many of the eucalyptus species found growing on the hillsides in the southern Flinders Ranges have been replaced by acacias, cassias and multi-stemmed mallees. Wild orange and tobacco trees and the red-flowering emu bush, with its bright green leaves, are prominent species. But the boulder-strewn creek lines are still shaded by graceful river red gums, and in the big gorges like 200 metre deep Barraranna permanent pools of water collect and the sun rarely penetrates. Amongst the spinifex sparsely coating the hillsides wind the trails of the sure-footed euro, well adapted to this difficult terrain.

Geologist Reg Sprigg and his wife Griselda bought the property in 1968 and have since converted it into a tourist resort with motel complex, swimming pool, and a fleet of four-wheel drives to carry wide-eyed tourists along the rutted mining tracks that criss-cross the ranges. It is a use that is far removed from the purpose to which the uranium ores of Mount Painter were once put.

Adjacent to Arkaroola is the 100 000 hectare Gammon Ranges National Park, formed in 1982 from the amalgamation of the much smaller existing park and Balcanoona station. The central feature of the park is a high plateau of Pound quartzite, rent by sheer-sided chasms and gorges, and covered with scrub that includes the Kangaroo Island melaleuca, broombush honey myrtle. First crossed in the late 1940s by Warren Bonython, the plateau remains an isolated and inaccessible place, visited only by a handful of experienced bushwalkers.

BELOW The all-slopes topography of the Northern Flinders Ranges. Mount Painter is in the foreground; Lake Frome, into which all the easterly-flowing streams flow, in the background.
OPPOSITE, TOP LEFT The Flinders Ranges are famous for their wildflowers. This is the pussy-tail or mulla mulla (*Ptilotus spp.*), which grows up to 60 centimetres high.
OPPOSITE, TOP RIGHT The rugged Gammon Ranges, first explored less than 40 years ago.
OPPOSITE, BELOW South Australia's floral emblem, Sturt's desert pea (*Clianthus formosus*).

The Great Salt Lakes

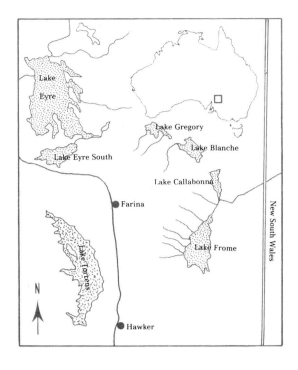

Every arid region in the world has its playas, vast open plains of deposition that occasionally fill with water to become huge, shallow lakes. But in no other continent do they occupy as much of the land mass as they do in Australia. From the ribbed sand ridges of the Great Sandy Desert in the north-west, south to the wheat country around Dumbleyung, east to the mallee country of north-eastern Victoria, and north through the New South Wales corner country into Queensland and the Northern Territory, it is the playa, the ephemeral lake that has deceived so many explorers, that is the norm.

Many of these playas are too insignificant to be marked on any but large-scale maps, claypans at most a few hundred metres across and surrounded by low sand ridges. Their surfaces range from a moist clay incapable of supporting even the weight of a man to a hard-packed cover that can be a highway, even a race-track, for motor vehicles.

It was on the gleaming white surface of Lake Eyre that Donald Campbell set a new land-speed record of 645 kilometres per hour in 1964, his great streamlined car, the *Bluebird*, flashing across a track smoothed out by lengths of railway track towed behind a Land-Rover. The attempt made world headlines, but it remains one of the few occasions on which a use has been found for the 9360 square kilometre salt lake.

The lake, which lies in the driest part of Australia, with an annual average rainfall of less than 125 millimetres and an evaporation rate of more than 2 metres, is a perfect desert, devoid of life save for the nondescript samphire bushes which in places grow up to 3 kilometres from shore, and a tiny gecko with pink eyes which apparently lives on errant flies and other insects.

This huge salt pan, at its lowest point 12 metres below sea level, is both the largest and most famous of the 'horseshoe' of lakes ringing the Flinders Ranges in South Australia. It is also one of the least attractive natural features in Australia, described by one writer as having only 'clear air and unlimited elbow room' and by J. W. Lewis, who explored the northern end of the lake and the course of Warburton Creek in 1974, as being 'useless in every respect'. He added, 'The very sight of it causes thirst in man and beast'.

Many of Australia's playas are caused by local runoff; they are drainage basins for the surrounding low hills and sand dunes and are composed of fine sediment washed down from the uplands and built up, sometimes to great depths, over the ages. But Lake Eyre is also the product of movements of the earth's crust. For more than 100 million years the Lake Eyre Basin has been geologically depressed. Through it flowed the ancestral Finke River, rising in the MacDonnell Ranges to the north, and the Diamantina, en route to the coast. A slight uplifting during the Tertiary period temporarily cut off the rivers' access to the sea. The result: a giant lake called Lake Dieri, 300 kilometres long and 160 kilometres north to south, formed behind the barrier before eventually breaking through and flowing along the old course of the Finke River to Spencer Gulf.

For 1 million years in the Pleistocene epoch this area was lush and green and teeming with life. Ten thousand years ago, well within the time frame of man's occupation of this continent, herds of rhinoceros-sized marsupials called diprotodons and mobs of giant short-faced kangaroos roamed the grassy flats. There were crocodiles, enormous turtles, flightless birds larger than emus, and big marsupial cats. The diprotodon, remains of which have been found at Lake Callabonna at the north-eastern corner of the horseshoe (and elsewhere in Australia) was the largest marsupial known to have lived. It became extinct perhaps 5000 years ago, possibly helped on its way by Aboriginal hunters.

About 8000 years ago the last Ice Age ended. Rainfall diminished and the lake began to shrink. Eventually, of the inland sea there remained just five smaller lakes—Eyre, Blanche, Gregory, Callabonna and Frome—and soon they too had dried up, leaving only playas, the string that had been formed by the drying Lake Eyre as well as an equally large group to the west of the Flinders Ranges, including two giants, Lake Gairdner (8781 square kilometres) and Lake Torrens (5760 square kilometres).

Lake Gairdner, the furthest west of the great salt lakes, was created by runoff from the red porphyry Gawler Ranges. The rocks form most of its southern and western shores and outcrop as islands as well. It is one of only two lakes in the group to have a crust largely composed of common salt; gypsum is more common and forms a principal component of the crust of Lake Torrens to the east. This 200 kilometre long,

OPPOSITE **An arm of Madigan Gulf, Lake Eyre, near Muloorina homestead, occasionally filled by Frome Creek (foreground).**

crescent-shaped salina was once thought to have joined to Spencer Gulf, but there is no hard evidence to support this hypothesis. In fact, the lake surface, now 30 metres above sea level, has been a drainage basin for the surrounding hills for more than 50 million years. Its soft brown gypsum silt blanket is smeared with white salt like a beach by tidal foam, and pockmarked by occasional artesian springs. Its eastern shore shifts constantly as the westerly winds play willy-willies with the dust and sand.

Cooper Creek, the Warburton, Macumba–Finke, Neales, and Frome rivers and others forming the Lake Eyre Basin, drain about one-sixth of the Australian land mass, an area of almost 1.3 million square kilometres. Most of this country is arid desert and semi-desert, but when the rivers 'come down' as much water descends on Lake Eyre as flows down the Nile in flood. In 1949–50 the myth that Lake Eyre would never fill was shattered. Two successive wet seasons brought down enough water to fill Lake Eyre North to an average depth of 2.1 metres, dissolving its 400 million tonnes of salt and becoming home to hundreds of thousands of fish, mainly bony bream and Lake Eyre hardyheads. But by 1951 the stench of dead fish was everywhere and 12 months later less than 8 per cent of the original body of water remained.

The lake bed dips slightly to the south, causing the waters entering the northern lake from Warburton Creek to carve out a channel known as the Warburton Groove. It was this channel which Bob Mossell and Denise Kuhne could not find when they sailed down the Warburton in an inflatable boat in 1977. The shrinking waters of Lake Eyre proved too shallow for their outboard motor and Mossell was forced to walk 150 kilometres across the sand dunes to the Alice Springs railway line.

The lake bed is now 4.5 metres higher than it was 20 000 years ago. The recent sediments are rich in gypsum which, blown northwards by the prevailing winds, gives the sands of the southern Simpson Desert a characteristic whitish hue. Most of the salt is deposited in Madigan Gulf and Belt Bay to the south, where it forms cakes like pack ice; elsewhere, islands grow around small objects left by the vanishing waters—a leaf, a blade of grass, a dead rabbit, the body of a bird—creeping ulcers up to 350 metres across. Low, clayey limestone and gypsum cliffs capped off with yellow-brown dunes line much of the shore.

Warburton minced no words when it came to Lake Eyre. He described it as 'terrible in its death-like stillness' and suggested that a weary traveller could die with equanimity in the surrounding dunes but to set foot on Lake Eyre 'would be like cutting himself off from the common lot of human beings'.

Despite this, Hunt Peninsula, Brooks Island, and parts of Jackboot Bay and Madigan Gulf have been declared a conservation park, named after the 'king' of Muloorina station, Elliott Price, who settled the lonely station on Frome Creek in 1941, gambling his savings on striking underground water. The park was established in 1967 and encompasses some of the most arid landforms in Australia. The Hunt Peninsula itself is a limestone mass partly covered in drifting sand and pockmarked by small saltpans. It has never been grazed. The vegetation, much of which dies off in times of drought and regerminates after rain, consists of bluebush, saltbush, Mitchell grass, nitre bush, some small cassias, grevilleas, wattles, mulga, and the odd native willow.

Galahs are not generally credited with having a great deal of commonsense, and certainly those which nest in the limestone cliffs of the Hunt Peninsula do nothing to counter this prejudice. Lake Eyre and the other great salinas remain among the most desolate places on earth—hardly the ideal environment in which to raise one's young.

BELOW Smaller ephemeral lakes fill briefly from local run-off.
OPPOSITE The parched surface of Lake Eyre South. (Trevern Dawes)

SOUTH AUSTRALIA

Sturts Stony Desert

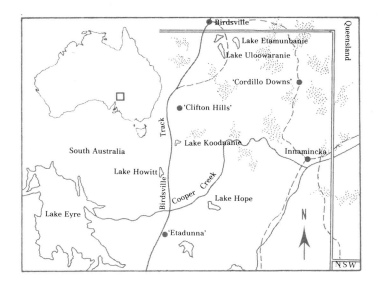

IT is an accident of history that a region of Australia has come to be known as 'Sturts Stony Desert'. For the desert to which explorer Charles Sturt referred in the journal of his 1844–45 journey into central Australia is in fact a mixture of landforms, of which the rock-strewn plains and plateaux are only one. And the stony pavement is not unique to this area in the far north-east of South Australia and far west of Queensland; it extends discontinuously, for example, from Port Augusta north as far as Tennant Creek.

But to Sturt, who first encountered the desert in August 1845, it was the ultimate horror of a nightmare journey. 'Herbless and treeless, it occupied more than one-half of the visible horizon,' he recorded, adding,

> our horses' hoofs were so brittle that pieces flew off them like splinters when they struck them against the stone ... It appeared as if McAdam had emptied every stone he ever broke to be strewed over this metalled region.

The stones range in size from tiny pebbles, scarcely larger than grains of sand, to boulders weighing 1 tonne or more. Although Sturt suggested that the stony pavement was unique to this continent, it is actually common to deserts everywhere. We call them gibber plains, but in the Sahara the plains of boulders are known as hamadas and those of pebbles, regs. In North America the rocky covering is described as desert armour.

Augustus Gregory, who travelled from the Barcoo River to Adelaide 13 years after Sturt, quickly found that this armour wore his horses' hoofs to the quick (he had removed their shoes for easier travel over the preceding mud plains).

Sturt's understandable inexperience with this type of country may well have been partially responsible for the problems he had with his horses, and for his abhorrence of it. The descendants of the pastoralists who, 30 years later, settled this land say that only horses bred in stony country will work it. Interestingly, many of them still prefer horses to motorbikes for mustering, while the stock like the grass that sprouts between the gibbers after rain better than any other feed.

Still, it is hard to disagree with the summary provided by later explorer John McKinlay: 'I never travelled through a more uninteresting country in all my life'. The featureless gibber plains excite the imagination only upon first sighting; after an hour or so, like Sturt 'lonely as a ship at sea', navigating by compass bearing only, with no landmarks to guide you, its sameness numbs the mind.

McKinlay and his men 'slept hard' on the rock-strewn surface, an experience everyone who has tried will not wish to repeat. The rocks are frequently more than surface deep, so that it is impossible to clear a spot smooth enough to sleep on or to drive in a tent-peg. Giant bindieyes and other burrs lie hidden among the stones, waiting to pierce the skin of the unwary.

It is a hostile country, this stony desert, an uncompromising landscape that gives new meaning to the term 'gibbering idiot'. In mid-summer it is so hot you can fry eggs on the gleaming stones, polished by wind-blown sand, lacquered over the millennia with a desert varnish of hydrous oxides of iron and manganese. Sand ridges straggle across the plains like giant red caterpillars, floating in the constant mirage. Horses and vehicles make little or no impression on the hard-packed surface, although erosion may be swift after a grader has scraped off the top layer of desert armour.

Yet this country has been settled for more than 100 years. Tiny Birdsville, the most outback town in Australia, services a string of cattle stations taken up in the 1880s. Beyond it, to the east, the great gibber desert stretches for more than 100 kilometres; to the west, the giant red waves of the Simpson Desert roll on almost to the centre of Australia. Threading a tenuous line south-east, down the flood plains of the Diamantina River and Warburton Creek is the notorious Birdsville Track, the 490 kilometre stock route to the railhead at Marree.

From time to time the tragic deaths of foolhardy travellers underlie the harshness of the Stony Desert, once classified with the adjacent Simpson as being the one, Arunta, desert. Yet, after rain the area is transformed, lush grasses sprouting between the adamantine gibbers. Cordillo Downs, a sprawling, 7896 square kilometre cattle station south-east of Birdsville, was once one of the largest sheep stations in the world, running up to 64 000 merinos on the gibbers and amongst the sand ridges. A succession of bad seasons and a slump in the price of wool drastically affected the station's profitability during the Depression years. Cordillo Downs was closed for six years, from 1930–36,

Gibbers are the detritus of ancient uplands, the "jump-ups" that sweep in a broad arc from Tibooburra through south-western Queensland into South Australia. Some are derived from Precambrian bedrock; others from the Tertiary duricrust capping of the jump-ups.

and was still not profitable after restocking. In 1941 its owners, the Beltana Pastoral Company, bowed to the inevitable and switched to cattle. The huge shearing shed, with its buttressed stone walls and rounded iron roof, was turned over to storage.

Jump-ups dominate the western half of the station, which is larger than several European countries. From them ephemeral streams flow to slice through the gibbers, their banks lined with coolibahs and the red-peeling trunks of minni ritchie trees. To the east, the red dunes predominate, the fine particles of sand stabilised by spinifex and canegrass. Despite an average annual rainfall of only 125–150 millimetres, there is usually surface water somewhere on the station, augmented for almost a century by artesian bores.

The presence of the stations and of oil crews probing beneath the earth creates only a veneer of civilisation in this country. Like the desert varnish coating the gibbers, if you scratch it away you will discover its true substance. Not even a major oil strike could break the implacable nature of this land. The Great Stony Desert of Sturt's diary will continue to brood, its shining stones sprouting green grass after rain, its sand ridges hovering menacingly in the constant mirage.

BELOW Sand dunes snake into the stony desert south of the Birdsville Track.
OPPOSITE So hard are the rocks of the desert armour it is said only horses bred in gibber country will work it.

SOUTH AUSTRALIA

The cliffs of the Nullarbor

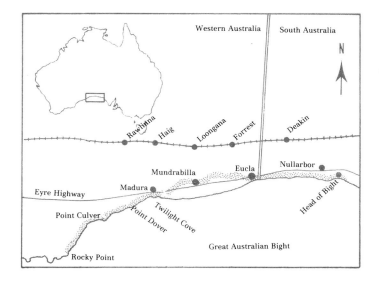

THE Nullarbor Plain is the largest continuous limestone area in the world; it boasts the longest underwater cave system; it is crossed by the longest straight stretch of railway line in the world (475 kilometres without a bend); it contains fewer trees than any other region of Australia; and it is bounded to the south by the longest unbroken cliff line in the world. Yet these superlative statements belie the dreadful monotony of the landscape: big it may be, but it is also harsh, unyielding and dreadfully uniform. It is as though the ocean has been suddenly metamorphosed by the Gorgons into stone, a solid chunk of limestone 200 000 square kilometres in area, stretching from the head of the Great Australian Bight to Point Culver and inland for up to 250 kilometres until the pitted, saltbush- and bluebush-covered rock is swallowed up by the sands of the Great Victoria Desert.

And in a sense the sea has been turned to stone, although the landscape was created long before the Gorgons passed into mythology. It was a sea or, more correctly, the bed of a sea, on which the skeletons and shells of countless billions of marine creatures were deposited after a large section of the land mass had subsided about 70 million years ago. These animal remains, rich in calcium, were compacted to form limestone. So numerous were they over the 60 million years of their accumulation that the rock is more than 275 metres thick.

When the sea bed rose again, probably near the end of the Tertiary period, about 2 million years ago, it did so uniformly, without tilting or folding, creating the apparently endless karst plateau that is the Nullarbor. The cliffs that form the southern edge of this plateau extend unbroken for 200 kilometres from Head of Bight to Eucla on the Western Australian border, then swing inland for a further 300 kilometres before rejoining the coast at Twilight Cove and marching south-west to Point Culver—a total distance of more than 650 kilometres. Nowhere else in the world can one find such impressive ramparts against the sea.

So bleak and uninviting is the aspect the cliffs present to the sea that Dutchmen François Thyssen and Pieter Nuyts, the first men to observe them from the seaward side, in 1627, decided there was no point in continuing to sail along the southern coast, and turned back only 300 kilometres short of Spencer Gulf. It was near the end of the next century before any other navigator sailed these waters and returned to tell the tale, and it was the beginning of the nineteenth century before anyone was bold enough to chart the entire coastline: Matthew Flinders, circumnavigator of a continent, aboard the sloop *Investigator*.

Flinders' charts, accurate in most details except when haze obscured his vision, described the cliffs from Head of Bight to Eucla as being 'from four to six hundred feet high, the upper part brown and the lower part white. Nothing is seen beyond them.' Flinders overestimated their height—they range from 40 to 90 metres (130–300 feet) above mean sea level—but not their impenetrability.

The strata upon which he commented are two layers of limestone, laid down over different periods. The bottom, thicker, layer is chalky and soft and contains fossil sponges. It is overlain by a harder, partly crystalline grey-brown limestone up to 30 metres thick. Erosion of the friable underlying layer by the giant swells spawned by Antarctic storms means that much of the cliff line has a precarious overhang which frequently can no longer be supported and goes crashing down into the booming surf. Large cracks appear in the rock, some many metres back from the cliff edge, making the coastline a treacherous place to visit. Below, where the thousand-tonne boulders have piled, salt-tolerant plant communities have established themselves, microcosms of the ground cover of the plain. The name Nullarbor, derived from Alfred Delisser's 1866 Latin title, *nullus arbor*, means no trees, much of the limestone plain does, in fact, carry a dense mallee and mulga scrub.

Despite the forbidding nature of the Nullarbor country, it was inhabited, albeit sparsely, by members of the Ngandatha tribe when Edward John Eyre made his historic crossing in 1841. They knew of rock holes where water collected after rain, and they covered them with rocks to protect them. Like Eyre, they dug water from the sandhills at the ends of the cliffs, and they mopped dew from the leaves of grass and bushes.

Eyre was at first unimpressed by the majestic cliff line, recording that it

> presented nothing very remarkable in appearance, being only the sudden termination of a perfectly level country, with its outer face washed, steep and precipitous, by the unceasing lash of the southern ocean.

BELOW No way down. The bases of the cliffs that gave explorer John Forrest vertigo remain unexplored.
RIGHT Sinkholes, many of them associated with long underground cave systems, pockmark the Nullarbor Plain.

176

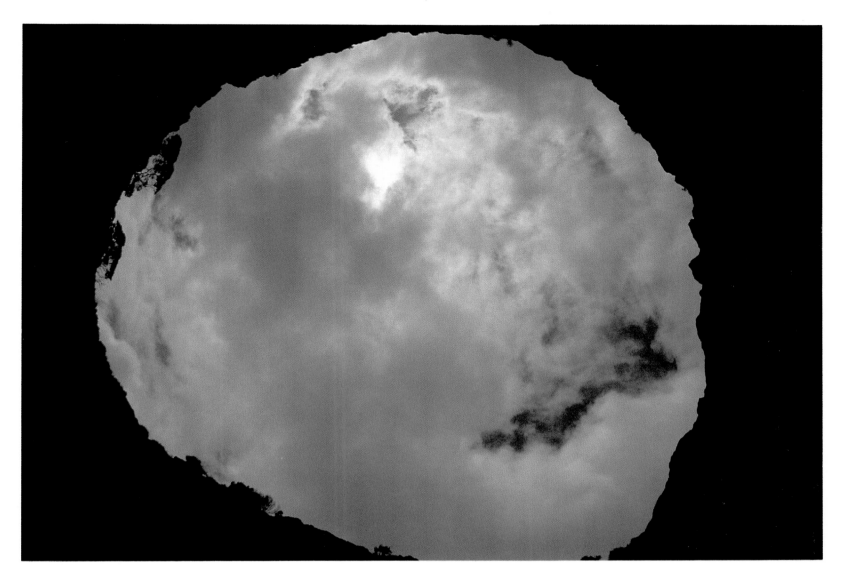

By the time he had followed the cliffs for 160 kilometres without at any point being able to descend to the sea, he was moved to remark, 'Alas! they still continued stretching as far as the eye could see to the westward . . .'. Later, after crossing the Roe Plain where the cliff line had been eroded inland by the higher sea level of the Pleistocene, he was forced to wrap the body of his murdered overseer, Baxter, in a blanket and leave it exposed because he was unable to excavate the crystalline limestone.

Eyre's initial indifference to the cliff line was not matched by later explorer John Forrest who, coming upon it in 1870, crept cautiously to its edge, gazed over, then 'ran back, quite terror-stricken by the dreadful view'. The base of the cliffs is almost totally unexplored, save where they briefly bevel off down to a shallow beach, near Eucla. Thousands of blowholes prick the surface of the plain, some inland as far as the railway, where a hut at one fettlers' siding has been deliberately built over one of the holes to take advantage of the cool breeze. In places rain leaching through the limestone has carved out huge underground caverns with roofs 30 metres or more high and filled with brackish water so clear and still it is possible even when carrying a light to step into it before realising it is there.

Daring scuba divers have explored many of the major cave systems and Aboriginal paintings and artefacts dating back more than 20 000 years have been found in Koonalda cave—although the modern Ngandatha believed that a monstrous snake named Ganba lived in the darkness, and stayed clear of the cave and its associated sinkhole. Bodies of animals which have stumbled into the blowholes and sinkholes over the millennia have become mummified. They include a Tasmanian tiger—extinct everywhere except in Tasmania when Europeans first settled Australia—which died 4200–4900 years ago.

It is this bleak plain which, coupled with the Indian Ocean to the west, makes Perth the most isolated major city in the world, Australia became a nation, unified, not on 1 January 1901, but on 8 December 1877, the day the first message was transmitted between Adelaide and Perth over the laboriously constructed Overland Telegraph

Line. It was this enterprise, a massive undertaking for its day, as was the later Transcontinental Railway to the north, that brought European civilisation to the Nullarbor. The largest township that has ever existed between Penong and Norseman, a distance of over 1000 kilometres, is Eucla, on the Western Australian border; at its peak, in the 1890s, its population numbered fifty.

Eucla was a repeater station on the telegraph line, its existence made necessary by the primitive equipment and the vast distances. Until 1909 the messages were copied out by hand, then re-transmitted to the next repeater station. With up to 600 messages a day passing through it, Eucla became the busiest non-capital-city communications centre in the country. Microwave towers alongside the road have made redundant the wires, which were relocated alongside the railway line for ease of access in 1920.

Eucla was built from local sandstone, the streets neatly paved with asphalt, and the town supplied by sea, using a jetty that was never quite long enough to allow the ships to tie up alongside. Water was brought in a lashed-up water cart from a sandhill soak 1 kilometre away. A rabbit plague which struck in 1898 decimated the thin covering of vegetation binding together the sand dunes, and drifting sand became a constant problem. Today, most of the buildings, those that have not been disassembled to help build the new motel complex on top of Eucla Pass, have all but vanished beneath the golden tide.

Lonely sheep stations, among the largest and most isolated in Australia, have given their names to the string of modern motels-cum-garages that appear at staggered intervals on the Eyre Highway. The new road, which only partly follows the route of the potholed monstrosity put in by army and civil engineers during World War II to replace the rutted track alongside the Overland Telegraph Line, detours close by the cliffs in several places, making it easy for travellers to share Forrest's vertigo.

The indomitable spirits of men like Eyre and Forrest seem to rise with the sun, to vanish, perhaps, in the searing heat of midday. Temperatures frequently reach 50°C on the plain and, when they do, life pauses for a time. It is a salutary reminder of the Nullarbor's power.

Nowhere is the unending flatness of the plain better illustrated than at the cliff edge. The cliffs run for more than 650 kilometres, including an inland deviation.

SOUTH AUSTRALIA

The Cobbler Desert

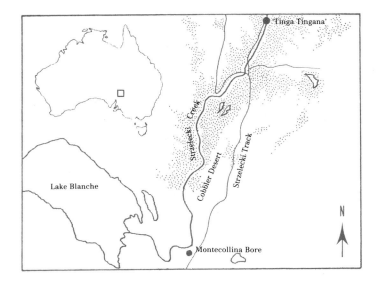

IN July 1845, Charles Sturt and his two companions, Browne and Stuart, struck out on a bearing of 255° from their base, Fort Grey, on a lake in the extreme north-west of New South Wales, near the present junction of that state with Queensland and South Australia. They crossed sand ridge after sand ridge, at one point surprising a group of Aborigines hunting on the dunes for hopping mice, until they came to country

> of a salsolaceous character, like a low, barren sea coast. The sand hills were lower and broader than they had been, and their sides were cut by deep fissures made by heavy torrents.

Sturt was crossing what was later to become known as the Cobbler Desert, named after the last sheep to be shorn, usually the biggest and toughest in the mob. To the men who later were to drove stock and lead camel trains laden with wool down the Strzelecki Track and across this desert—actually one giant white sand dune, 65 kilometres wide, sprawling between Lakes Blanche and Callabonna—this was the last, and worst, obstacle to overcome before the track wound out onto the plains surrounding the Flinders Ranges.

The track slices arrow-straight across the undulating surface of the treeless dune, along the broad, coolibah-studded bed of the Strzelecki Creek to Cooper Creek and the tiny hamlet of Innamincka. Water only flows down the Strzelecki and into Lake Blanche when the Cooper is 2 metres deep over the causeway at Innamincka, so that flooding is spasmodic and unpredictable, although the creek will run occasionally after local rains. It is the white sand which has been swept down the Strzelecki during floods that has created the Cobbler. Dry as the surrounding country is, in 1974, the wettest year in outback history, the water surrounded Merty Merty homestead, built on a hillock in the creek bed, for months, and the owners were evacuated by helicopter.

The first white man to take this desert route from Queensland to South Australia was Augustus Gregory who, acting on a rumour that the lost explorer Ludwig Leichhardt was being held captive by escaped convicts in the centre of Australia, journeyed with a party of eight from the Barcoo River, a tributary of the Cooper, along the Cooper and then down the Strzelecki in the winter of 1858. At the end of June he passed between 'the eastern point of Lake Torrens' (Lake Blanche) and an 'independent lake', describing the space between—part of the Cobbler—as 'level sandy ground, covered with salcomia'.

The Cobbler apparently held no fears for Gregory, who called the Strzelecki 'far the best line of route into the interior which has yet been discovered' and suggested, prophetically, that water could be obtained by sinking 'wells of moderate depth'. Gregory smashed the myth of Lake Torrens, that the great string of salinas around the Flinders Ranges formed a continous horseshoe, a fallacy created by Edward John Eyre in 1840 and perpetuated by Sturt. Having crossed the Cobbler, Sturt fetched up against the south-eastern shore of Lake Blanche which, because of Eyre's mistake, he incorrectly assumed was part of Lake Torrens. He and Browne ventured onto the lake's surface but 8 kilometres out found it too soft and were forced to turn back.

Soon afterwards, Sturt, Browne and three others made another foray from Fort Grey, this time north-west towards the centre of the continent. They reached Strzelecki Creek and explored along it without apparently recognising that it was the same watercourse they had met with on the earlier journey. Sturt named it after the conqueror of Mount Kosciusko, Paul Edmund de Strzelecki.

Three years after Gregory's successful expedition, in 1861, Burke and Wills died on Cooper Creek, following an abortive thrust down the Strzelecki towards Mount Hopeless, named by a despairing Eyre 21 years earlier. The route was not one for a demoralised and debilitated party. But it was not impossible, as Gregory had proved.

Armed with this information and more gall than the Scarlet Pimpernel, in 1870 a cattle duffer named Harry Redford and two accomplices stole 1000 head of cattle from Bowen Downs station in Queensland and drove them more than 1000 kilometres through the desert to Blanchewater station, north of the Flinders, where he sold the mob for 5000 pounds. A white bull, which he disposed of at nearby Artacoona station, almost proved to be his undoing; it was readily identifiable and landed Redford in court. However, to the fury of the presiding judge, the partisan jury in Redford's home town of Roma acquitted him of the charge.

Metre-high roly-poly plants (Salsola kali) cover vast tracts of the Cobbler. The dried-out skeletons of the plants blow about as tumbleweed, dispersing their seeds.

Other, more legitimate, overlanders followed in Redford's footsteps and waterholes were dug along the 267 kilometre stretch from Cooper Creek to Mount Hopeless, as suggested by Gregory. Early this century, a bore was sunk at Montecollina in the Cobbler; more recently the outflow was enlarged by a Highways Department crew to form a swimming hole.

Settlers followed, taking up properties at Nappacoongie and Tinga Tingana on the track. A small township grew up at Innamincka. Stage coaches crossed the Cobbler, carrying passengers and mail north to Innamincka and south to Blanchewater. Camel trains transported the wool clip from mighty Cordillo Downs, north-east of Innamincka, to the railhead at Farina. Some hardy shearers rode bicycles up the track to Cordillo. For all of them, the Cobbler proved to be the worst stretch of the run, and many chose the alternative and easier Birdsville Track to the north.

Tinga Tingana and Nappacoongie are now abandoned; the hotel and hospital at Innamincka closed in 1952, to be superseded by a new, prefab hotel-motel and general store in 1974. The Strzelecki now is the access road to the great oil and gas fields at Moomba in South Australia's far north, and the cattle, like the unlaid pipelines, travel in lumbering road trains. But Moomba has brought no more than a modicum of civilisation to this most arid part of the Australian outback. Survey parties that break the rules may still meet with tragedy. In the searing heat of summer, when the thermometer tops 50°C, a day without water in the featureless white dune known as the Cobbler Desert may be 24 hours too long.

Metre-high roly-poly plants (*Salsola kali*) cover vast tracts of the Cobbler. The dried-out skeletons of the plants blow about as tumbleweed, dispersing their seeds.

The Ballroom Forest, on the shores of Lake Dove, below Cradle Mountain

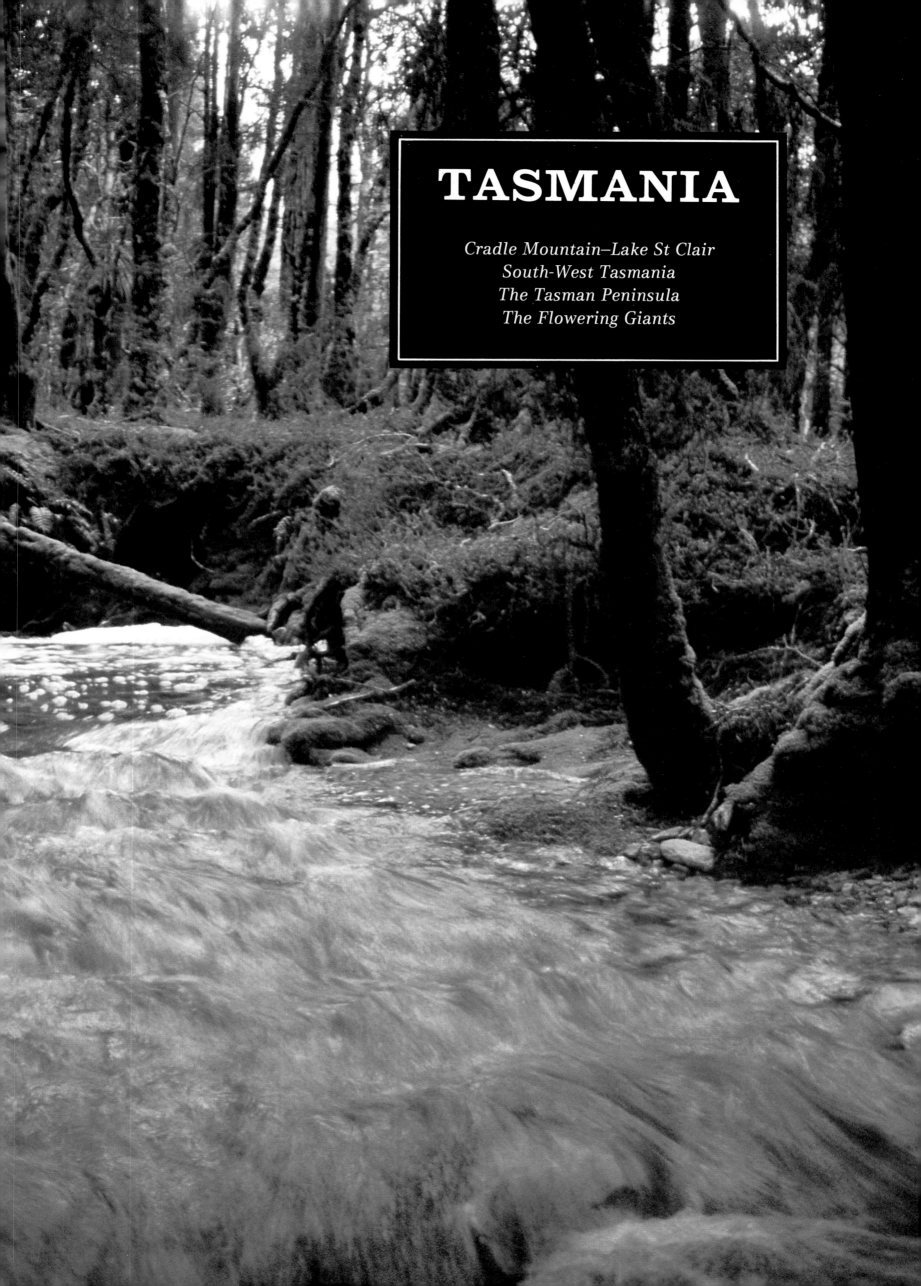

TASMANIA

Cradle Mountain–Lake St Clair
South-West Tasmania
The Tasman Peninsula
The Flowering Giants

Cradle Mountain–Lake St Clair

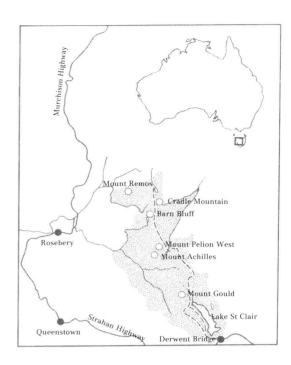

EACH year more than 3000 people, many of them overseas visitors lured by the promise of the unspoilt grandeur of the dolerite peaks, walk the 80 kilometre Overland Track which threads its way across plateaux and through valleys from Cradle Mountain south to Lake St Clair. The magnificence of the region, included on the World Heritage List in December 1982, is famous and, with its endemic flora and fauna and chill Roaring Forties winds, unique in Australia.

At the Cradle Mountain end of the 131 915 hectare park the average annual rainfall is almost 3 metres, dropping away to about half that amount at Cynthia Bay on the southern shore of Lake St Clair. But even on days when no rain falls the skies may be overcast and the mountains shrouded in a cold, clammy mist: this country receives less sunshine than any other part of Australia, and is subject to sudden and unpredictable changes of weather that may cause temperatures to plunge 20 degrees or more within an hour.

Snow and hail may fall at any time of the year, so even day walkers need to carry warm, waterproof clothing. For those on the Overland Track, tents are mandatory, despite the ten huts strategically located along the route: not only are the huts often full to capacity, but poor weather conditions may make pushing on even a few extra kilometres extremely hazardous. Most walker fatalities, and there have been many, are caused through over-exertion which has led to hypothermia.

In winter, a mantle of snow covers all the peaks in the park and about 25 kilometres of the tough northern end of the Overland Track. The snow at this end of the park is soft and wet, and most langlaufers prefer the crisper cover on Mount Rufus (1416 metres), south-west of Cynthia Bay, where three ski huts have been erected. Several mountains in the park are more than 1500 metres high, including Tasmania's highest, Mount Ossa (1617 metres), from the small summit plateau of which it is possible to glimpse the glacier-etched white peak of the Frenchmans Cap thrusting above the ranges to the south like a sail bobbing in a stormy sea.

This is a fascinating country, its high peaks born in fire in Jurassic times, 165 million years ago, when vast sheets of dolerite were intruded into the Permo-Triassic sedimentary rocks overlying much older Pre-Cambrian metamorphics, and brought to prominence by the subsequent erosion of the softer sediments. Later, the landscape was carved and moulded by the slow-moving glaciers of the Pleistocene Ice Age. All the major peaks in the park are capped with grey dolerite, the rock characteristically

A rainbow forms in the cold, moist air over Lake Dove, beneath snow-covered Cradle Mountain.

formed into long, rectangular columns during solidification. So perfectly symmetrical are the columns atop the appropriately named Acropolis, in the Du Cane Range north of Lake St Clair, that it seems inconceivable they should have been made by natural forces.

The Acropolis is but one of the many features in the park to have names taken from Ancient Greece. Nearby are the triple peaks of Mount Geryon (in Greek mythology, Geryon was a three-headed monster); there is a Parthenon; Narcissus Bay; Mounts Achilles, Thetis, Pelion and Nereus; and, guarding the dark depths of Lake St Clair, the looming bulk of 1463 metre Mount Olympus, home of the gods.

Cradle Mountain was named, it is believed, for a far more prosaic reason—its fancied resemblance to a miner's cradle—by surveyor Joseph Fossey, who visited the area in 1826. But it was not until 1831 that a party led by Henry Hellyer succeeded in finding a way through the surrounding thick scrub and rainforest into Cradle Valley and onto the summit of the mountain. Hellyer wrote in forceful terms of the difficulties they encountered.

> Dead logs and branches impeded us at every step and we were continually meeting with large tracts of dense thickets from 30 to 40 feet high, so closely woven and made together as to be impenetrable below ... We were often obliged to be walking upon those never dry slippery branches covered with moss, as much as 20 feet off the ground ...

Even where tracks have been cut, it is still difficult to walk through the temperate rainforest that is the dominant forest type below 1000 metres. The roots of the aged and gnarled trees stretch out, seeming to wish to trip the unwary. Water drips from every leaf and branch and trickles into muddy pools where leeches wait to latch onto passers by. Unlike tropical rainforest, the number of different species of plant that grows here is small, but those which do are well adapted to the rigorous climate. They include King Billy pines 1000 years old; Tasmanian myrtles; celery-top pines; and Tasmania's only deciduous native tree, the fagus or tanglefoot, a smaller and more contorted version of the myrtle, with similarly shaped but corrugated leaves which turn golden-brown before they fall in autumn.

No sun filters through the dense rainforest canopy to nurture a luxuriant under-storey of flowering plants. Their place is taken by a profusion of ferns, mosses and liverworts, and lichens that are brilliantly, almost luminescently, green.

The pencil pine, a smaller relative of the King Billy pine, is found bordering the tarns, lakes and streams of the high moors; above the treeline, herbs, the hard mounds of cushion plants and the paper-like petals of everlasting daisies await the winter snows. But none of these plants is as strange as the 5–10 metre high palm-like pandani, a giant heath endemic to Tasmania, which guards the edge of the rainforest and shakes its shaggy locks across the buttongrass plains.

BELOW The dolerite peak of the Little Horn, part of the Cradle Mountain complex.
OPPOSITE The strange giant heath, the pandani (*Richea pandanifolia*) grows up to 10 metres in height.

This is the country that Austrian-born Gustav Weindorfer first visited in 1909, 55 years after James Sprent had placed a cairn on top of Cradle Mountain. Weindorfer was captivated: the ice-sculptured ramparts of Cradle Mountain reflected in the kidney-shaped Lake Dove at its base, the dank and gloomy forests, the smaller lakes and tarns glistening among the maze of ridges and valleys. Standing on top of Cradle Mountain the following year, he stretched his arms wide and proclaimed to his companion, R. E. Smith, 'This must be a national park for the people for all time.'

To help realise his dream, Weindorfer managed to extract a small sum from the Tasmanian Government. He used it to build a bridge over Pencil Pine River and took up land in Cradle Valley. He and his wife, Kate, used King Billy pine to build a chalet, which he called Waldheim, and by Christmas 1912 they were ready to receive their first guests. The rates were not cheap but many people were prepared to pay a high price and face the 12 kilometre walk or horseback ride from the end of the nearest road to the chalet in exchange for the solitude of the mountains. Weindorfer continued to explore the area, pinpointing and naming many of the natural features. After the death of his wife, in 1916, he moved to live permanently in the high mountain valley.

After World War I the Government built a road to within 5 kilometres of Waldheim and, in 1922, following vigorous representation from Weindorfer and others, the Cradle Mountain area was declared a scenic reserve. Lake St Clair, Tasmania's largest and deepest lake (17.5 kilometres long and more than 200 metres deep) was gazetted a scenic reserve in the same year. It fills a basin gouged by a great glacier which extended down the valley from the north 15 000 years ago.

Until his death in 1932, Weindorfer continued to press for the extension of the northern road as far as Waldheim, but it was the Overland Track to the south that was completed first, blazed by Bert Nichols in 1930–31 along the route of several pre-existing paths.

Access to the southern section of the park improved greatly in 1932, when the winding and tortuous Lyell Highway to Queenstown was opened. An all-weather road to Cynthia Bay followed in 1934. A tourist camp was established on the lake in the mid-thirties, with a view ranging across the boulders and driftwood on the narrow beach and the mirror-like surface of the lake to the pointed peak of Mount Ida and the flat grey cap of Mount Olympus. This view was permanently altered in 1937, when the Hydro-Electric Commission built a small dam across the Derwent River, which flows out of the south-eastern corner of the lake, raising the level of the lake by 3 metres. A pumping station was added subsequently, and the introduction of brown and rainbow trout (quickly displacing the smaller native trout which is endemic to other lakes and streams in the park) lured fishermen from all over Australia. A boat service to Narcissus Bay, the northernmost reach of the lake, has operated since the mid-thirties.

Weindorfer's dream was realised posthumously, when the road to Waldheim was completed in 1941 and the reserve was declared a national park in 1946. In 1978 the chalet, which had deteriorated badly, was faithfully rebuilt from hand-hewn King Billy pine and it is still used for accommodation.

Five major rivers take their rise within the park's boundaries: the Derwent, Forth, Mersey, Murchison and Mackintosh. The headwaters of the Mackintosh and Murchison flow beyond the well-trodden route of the Overland Track, through a labyrinth of deep ravines and gorges seldom visited by man. A dam soon to be built on the Murchison completes the damming of all five rivers.

Exploitation of other nearby resources has also been considerable. A wolfram mine and its associated processing plant operated until late 1982 in the Oakleigh Conservation Area, within 5 kilometres of the central section of the Overland Track. Pulpwood concessions border much of the park, and it is planned to log the Oakleigh Creek catchment area. Hemmed in by development on all sides, the Cradle Mountain–Lake St Clair National Park should nevertheless remain inviolate for the foreseeable future. The task facing Tasmanians is to minimise the impact of civilisation on what is arguably the most significant park in Tasmania.

BELOW, LEFT **Leaves of the fagus (***Nothofagus gunnii***), Tasmania's only deciduous tree, carpet the forest floor.**
BELOW, RIGHT **A rare albino Bennett's wallaby (***Macropus rufogriseus***), photographed at Lake St Clair.**
OPPOSITE **The pointed peak of Mount Ida lies directly north of Cynthia Bay, across Lake St Clair. (Michael Richardson)**

South-West Tasmania

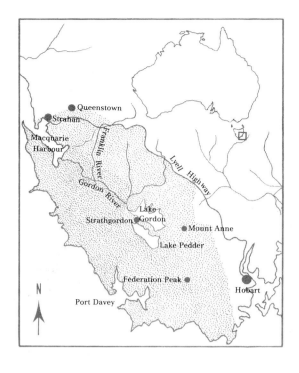

Tasmania's 'empty quarter' is incomparably, hauntingly beautiful, and so unlike the rest of Australia as to rank as one of our greatest natural treasures. Small wonder the plan to flood the last major wild river in Tasmania, the 125 kilometre Franklin, aroused opposition strong enough to topple governments and to cause a landmark decision to be handed down in the High Court.

Yet, despite that decision to preserve the Franklin, much of the south-west remains under threat. A great slab of land (405 000 hectares) is reserved for logging; other chunks of land are zoned as conservation areas, nominally under the control of the National Parks and Wildlife Service but in fact able to be mined and logged. Much of the south-west is set aside as national park—the sprawling 440 240 hectare South-West National Park (which grew from the much smaller Lake Pedder National Park of 1955) and the 181 075 hectare Franklin–Lower Gordon Wild Rivers National Park (proclaimed in late 1983 and incorporating Frenchmans Cap National Park)—but a 14 125 hectare strip along the lower Franklin, Olga and Gordon Rivers has been revoked from the latter park and is still under the control of the Hydro-Electric Commission. Together with the adjoining Cradle Mountain–Lake St Clair National Park, this is Tasmania's World Heritage Area, accepted for listing by UNESCO in 1982.

The most obvious natural features of the south-west are its very high rainfall, up to 3500 millimetres in the Wilmot Range near Lake Pedder, and its mountains. Mere molehills compared to the Himalayas or the Andes—the highest peak in the south-west is Frenchmans Cap, 1443 metres—these are mountains nevertheless, grey walls rising from the buttongrass plains like whales bursting from the sea, snow-capped for much of the year, aloof, majestic, indomitable. It is ranges such as the Frankland, the Arthur, the King William, and the Gordon that catch the racing, rain-laden clouds of the Roaring Forties and shake the water loose from them, giving rise to hundreds of rivers and making the region the most valuable in Australia for hydro-electricity generation.

Tasmania lies 10 degrees closer to the equator than the British Isles, but the climate in the south-west is often as rigorous, sometimes more so. It is directly exposed to the chill Antarctic winds and there is no benign Gulf Stream to exercise a moderating force. Extremes are commonplace, and massive weather changes the norm: temperatures of nearly 40°C one day; a 30 degree drop the next.

The mountains of the south-west are of two types: distinctive quartzite peaks like Frenchmans Cap and the Arthurs, and the less common dolerite-capped peaks in the east of the region, such as Mount Anne, Mount Eliza, Wylds Craig and Precipitous Bluff. The high peaks were extensively affected by glaciation during the Pleistocene ice ages. From any vantage point, the ranges run in unbroken succession to the horizon, like waves in a gale. The contrast with the arid plains of the outback is absolute: the salt pans replaced by scores of lakes and rock-rimmed tarns, the spinifex and mulga by some of the most impenetrable rainforest in Australia.

The high rate of precipitation gives rise to a unique forest, a place of gloom and moss and moisture. The number of plant species growing in this cool temperate rainforest —one of the last surviving examples of such a forest in the world—is limited, but the number of individuals of each species is not. The most common tree is the Antarctic beech, or Tasmanian myrtle, which can grow up to 40 metres and has a dense foliage of small, serrated leaves. Alongside it may grow the smaller native laurel, the sassafras, the King Billy pine, the celery-top pine and the fragrant leatherwood, the flowers of which produce some of the finest honey in the world.

This region is also the home of the vine-like bauera and the notorious horizontal scrub, slender trees which are more responsible than any others for the difficulty associated with traversing these forests. They grow vertically to 5–10 metres then, finding their own weight too much to support, they bend over at right angles, sending out new shoots which intermingle with those of other trees until an impenetrable maze is formed. Rather than hack his way through this scrub, a man may walk atop it, 3 metres or so above the ground. There is a constant risk of injury because it is impossible to tell the rotten branches from the sound ones.

Specimens of the famous Huon pine, the honey-coloured timber which was much prized for boat-building last century, are occasionally found alongside rivers; they were once common from Macquarie Harbour to Port Davey, but are now comparatively rare. They are extremely slow-growing trees: one specimen floated out of the Gordon River impoundment in 1975 was more than 200 years old when Christ was born, making it

High mountains surround the lower Gordon River, protecting it from the strong winds of the Roaring Forties.

the oldest tree ever recorded in Australia. Many Huon pines are regenerating naturally along the lower Gordon River, but it will take centuries for them to reach maturity.

No lush undergrowth flourishes in this forest, save the delicate fronds of ferns and the ubiquitous mosses, lichens and liverworts. Strange, colourful mushrooms, some as big as saucers, others little larger than pinheads, dot the forest floor and live on the mouldering carcasses of trees.

But rainforest is not the only plant community of the south-west. Much of the region, particularly around its eastern and north-eastern fringes, is covered with tall eucalypt forests, exploited for their timber. Elsewhere, there are open plains of buttongrass, apparently easy to walk across but in fact underlain by soggy peat into which a walker's boots can sink past the ankles. The buttongrass (named for its long-stalked, mace-shaped seed heads) grows in tussocks and mounds, like spinifex, and the plains support many other plant species, including tea tree and silver banksia.

Fire is a major factor in promoting the ascendancy of eucalypts and buttongrass over rainforest. It stimulates the growth of eucalypt forest but destroys the fire-susceptible rainforest species. So, after a fire eucalypts will be the first trees to germinate, followed by rainforest species as soon as a tree canopy has formed. Eventually, if no further fires follow, the eucalypts will die, resulting in a pure rainforest. Buttongrass, too, will burn, and surprisingly soon after rain. The peat underlying it can also be ignited by walkers' cooking fires and may subsequently flare up spontaneously, creating a bad wildfire. Peat set on fire in this way has been known to smoulder for more than 18 months.

Buttongrass sedgeland also often covers the slopes of south-west peaks, only to be supplanted around their caps by a thick scrub which may include the Tasmanian snow gum. The varnished gum is frequently found in the high quartzite areas: Australia's smallest eucalypt, it grows no more than 1 metre high.

Above the tree line, on the exposed open mountain plateaux, ground-hugging plants brave the chill winds and snow drifts. They include the cushion plants—tightly packed colonies like brain coral which form bright green mounds often decorated in late summer with tiny blooms only a few millimetres in diameter—and various alpine herbs and stunted shrubs. Sphagnum moss, which soaks up water like a giant sponge and releases it into the streams after the snow melts, is also common. The high plateaux are frequently even soggier than the buttongrass country, with chains of shallow pools glinting amongst the vegetation.

The chirps and cries of more than 50 types of land birds penetrate the stillness of the forest. Species include the brown scrubwren, the grey fantail, the crescent honeyeater and the yellow-tailed black cockatoo. The south-west coast is the breeding ground for the endangered orange-bellied parrot, of which at most 75 breeding pairs

The isolated dolerite peak of Precipitous Bluff (1200 m) is a notable landmark for walkers on the South Coast Track from Cockle Creek to Port Davey.

are thought to remain. The green ground parrot, now rare on the mainland, also inhabits the area.

Two species of wallaby, Bennett's wallaby and the rufous wallaby, or pademelon, are also common and will hop into campsites to beg for food. Wombats, brush-tailed possums, spotted native cats, Tasmanian devils, platypuses and echidnas are frequently seen, and there is a possibility that the Tasmanian tiger, or thylacine, may inhabit remote sclerophyll forests in the region.

The Aborigines, it is believed, inhabited only the fringes of this harsh and difficult country. The south-west tribe numbered perhaps 200–350 people, divided into 4–6 bands, who travelled along well-defined paths around the coast. Unusually for Aboriginal people, they built semi-permanent dwellings, dome-shaped huts thatched with grass and lined with paperbark, and they also used bark-hulled catamarans to cross rivers and harbours. Their primary insulation against the cold of winter was a thick layer of animal fat and charcoal smeared over their bodies. Food included shellfish, crayfish, seals, wombats, wallabies and bird eggs; fish with scales were, for some reason, taboo. In the north of the wilderness, other tribes inhabited the Franklin River valley and the Florentine Valley. Artefacts found at sites in these areas have been dated at 20 000 years BP and 12 500 years BP respectively. These people probably pre-dated the south-west tribe, being the most southerly people on earth during the last Ice Age.

In 1798 George Bass and Matthew Flinders circumnavigated Tasmania in the 25-tonne sloop *Norfolk*, proving that it was an island. Captain James Kelly used a four-oared open whaleboat to effect his circumnavigation in 1815, and his explorations led to the settlement of the only two harbours along more than 250 kilometres of western coastline: Macquarie Harbour and Port Davey. Over the next few years, lonely gangs of men worked the great stands of Huon Pine at these settlements.

Then Lieutenant-Governor Sorell decided that Macquarie Harbour would make a splendid site for a penal stronghold. The first unlucky convicts sailed into the 285 square kilometre harbour in January 1822. The place had been chosen for its isolation and for the pines which grew along the banks of the King and Gordon Rivers. The men felled the trees, often standing for hours, waist-deep in the near freezing water, then the logs were floated downstream into the harbour.

Between 250 and 350 convicts lived on Sarah Island, near the mouth of the Gordon River. Administration at the settlement was deliberately brutal: of 182 prisoners confined there in 1822, 169 received an average of 40 lashes each. Those who were still defiant were banished to nearby Grummet Island, a mere rock on which a two-roomed building stood, frequently accommodating 30 or 40 men.

Food was often in short supply at the station and scurvy was rife. Small wonder that

The Franklin River, in tranquil mood, before it plunges into the deep ravines.

many men attempted to escape, despite the forbidding and almost impassable nature of the surrounding countryside: tall hills covered with rainforest rose sheer out of the water on every side. Subsequent explorers reported travelling as little as a kilometre or so a day over this terrain, and it was more than 120 kilometres to the settled areas in the east. Of 112 convicts who escaped in the first 11 years of the settlement, 62 perished in the bush and nine were murdered and eaten by their starving companions.

The most depraved of the white cannibals was Alexander Pierce, known to his fellows convicts as 'The Pieman', who fled the settlement in September 1822 with seven other men. Faced with starvation, three of them returned to Macquarie Harbour, one dying en route. A more sinister fate awaited those who remained. Four of the men set upon and killed the fifth and weakest of their number and ate his body, then three killed another, and so on, until finally only Pierce was left. He managed to reach pastoral country to the east, but was recaptured and returned to Macquarie Harbour. He escaped again, this time with a single companion who was destined to become several meals. When apprehended, Pierce broke down and confessed his sins, and was hanged in Hobart.

The most successful escapees were those who, like bushranger Matthew Brady, left by water. The moist and melancholy bush was no place for ill-equipped 'bolters'.

Yet the very qualities that made it such an ideal location for a penal settlement caused the abandonment of Macquarie Harbour in January 1834. It was too distant to service properly, and the 80 metre wide entrance to the harbour (known as Hells Gates) was treacherous in the extreme. Besides, the station had already been recognised as a blot on the British record. In 1852, less than 20 years after its closure, historian John West wrote of Macquarie Harbour,

> [Its] name is associated exclusively with remembrance of inexpressible depravity, degradation, and woe. Sacred to the genius of torture, nature concurred with the objects of its separation from the rest of the world; to exhibit some notion of a perfect misery. There, man lost the aspect, and the heart of man!

Later travellers, unfettered by chains and fear of the lash, viewed the area differently. David Burn, who accompanied Lieutenant-Governor Sir John Franklin and his wife, Jane, on an epic journey through the south-west in 1842, wrote of the country near Frenchmans Cap (which towers over Macquarie Harbour),

> It transcends the power of the most gifted pen . . . Its magnificent grandeur—its boundless extent—its infinite variety—its romantic loveliness—its pictorial wildness—the enchanting graces of its innumerable panoramic beauties, astound and delight, fresh subjects of admiration wooing the eye at every turn.

The phenomenon which led to the voluntary arrival of large numbers of men in this inhospitable region was the lure of minerals, especially gold. In 1881, a prospector named Cornelius Lynch struck paydirt on a creek running into the Queen River, 8 kilometres south-west of Mount Lyell. By then, the massive Zeehan silver–lead deposit and various goldfields along tributaries of the Pieman River to the north were being worked, and the 1871 discovery of a 'mountain of tin' (Mount Bischoff) had led to the establishment of the village of Strahan as a supply depot.

The famous 'Iron Blow', an iron outcrop 8 metres high in the Linda Valley, was discovered in November 1883. It was worked as a gold mine for many years, then exploited for its copper content, following the development of the first commercial pyritic copper smelters in the world by American Robert Sticht. Pyritic smelting ended in 1922, but by then sulphurous fumes, combined with bushfires, indiscriminate tree felling and soil erosion, had stripped every last leaf from the surrounding hillsides, especially Mount Lyell and Mount Owen. The result is a surrealistic *mélange* of pinks and browns and oranges and a lesson to all of the value of conservation.

The destructive tentacles of the mines at Mount Lyell reached out through the surrounding countryside. The King River, which rises beyond Mount Lyell, has been polluted beyond salvation: it was once possible to sail a 200 tonne vessel 16 kilometres upstream, but siltation from the denuded hills around the mines has blocked the river mouth. Pollutants washed down the river have also killed many of the fish in Macquarie Harbour which, because of its narrow entrance, is poorly flushed by the sea.

BELOW The new Lake Pedder, seen from beyond the rugged Arthur Ranges to the south.
PAGE 197, TOP A rugged promontory forms the southern headland of Port Davey, centre for Huon pine logging in the 1870s.
PAGE 197, BOTTOM The notorious horizontal scrub (*Anodopetalum biglandulosum*) impedes access to much of the south-west wilderness.

Queenstown, where Sticht's smelters belched fire and smoke, became the major township for the Mount Lyell Mines in the early years of this century. With a population of 4300, it is the biggest town in the west of Tasmania. The Lyell Highway, from Derwent Bridge to Queenstown, was completed in 1932. Strahan, which in 1969 ceased to function as a sea port for the mines, is now a sleepy fishing village and tourist centre.

The activity around Mount Lyell did, however, provide improved access for exploration of the south-west, particularly in the Frenchmans Cap region. The distinctive white quartzite mountain, which dominates the northern section of the wilderness, was named by Captain George Vancouver in 1791 because of its resemblance to the French revolutionary Phrygian caps. Glaciation has carved a sheer, 300 metre high rock face from its eastern flank and excavated numerous tarns and lakes from the slopes nearby. The mountain is bounded on three sides by the Franklin River, which rises in the Cheyne Range near Lake St Clair and was first crossed by escaped convict Alexander Pierce in 1822. In 1859 Charles Gould's party ascended 70 falls and rapids on the river, including those of the Great Ravine, where the cliffs tower up to 500 metres above the fury of four fierce rapids: The Churn, Coroscades, Thunderush and Cauldron. Thomas Moore forded the Franklin twice when he made the first conquest of 'The Frenchman' in the 1880s.

Attempts to find routes for a road or a railway to Macquarie Harbour and Port Davey were foiled by the country. Adolphus Ibsen, an assistant to Gould, cut a track from Goulds Landing on the lower Gordon River, through the Wilmot Range to the Gordon Bend and on to the town of Hamilton, but it was never more than a track. It was for many years, though, the only overland access to Macquarie Harbour. Francis McPartlan, ex-convict turned postman, travelled this way once a month. In 1881 McPartlan blazed a trail from Mount Field to the buttongrass plains near Lake Pedder. The highest point on this road, at 651 metres, is the pass between Tim O'Shea and The Needles, overlooking the Florentine Valley, the floor of which is formed of limestone and contains some of the deepest and longest caves in Australia. Near the end of the road lies the town of Strathgordon, an ugly, prefabricated construction village, 160 kilometres from Hobart, nestling under the looming bulk of the Twelvetrees Range. A few kilometres beyond it, the 140 metre concrete arch wall of the Gordon dam, finished in November 1974, stems the flow of the Gordon River only 16 kilometres upstream from the second of the famous Gordon River Splits.

First explored in 1928, the two gorges called the Splits are so deep and narrow that for many years it was thought the river ran underground. Floodmarks in the gloomy canyons indicate that the river may rise 30 metres above the summer low point: the 170 kilometre river carries more water than any other in Tasmania and is navigable by tourist boats for 42 kilometres upstream from its mouth. The proposed Gordon-below-Franklin dam would have flooded both Splits, as well as the Olga River and most of the lower Franklin and Denison rivers.

One of the primary goals for long-distance bushwalkers is Port Davey, at the south-western tip of the island. In the 1870s this flooded river valley supplied most of the Huon pine cut in Tasmania. About 50 people used the lonely settlement there as a base, many of them working 25 kilometres or more up the rivers and sleeping in bark-covered huts known as 'badger-boxes'. In the 1850s Port Davey also supported a short-lived whaling industry, but now the only industry is tin mining. The metal has been mined at Melaleuca Inlet on Bathurst Harbour, a broad reach of Port Davey, since the 1930s. Today two men—Denny King and Peter Wilson—hold adjoining leases, scraping a living from the minor ore body.

For walkers, the Mecca of the south-west is 1203 metre Federation Peak in the Western Arthurs, first glimpsed in 1901, the year of Federation. For rafters and canoeists, Mecca is the Franklin River: they put in at the Collingwood River Bridge, on the Lyell Highway and take an average of 14 days to roll, tumble and paddle downstream to the navigable reaches of the Gordon River.

It was the Gordon down which Lithuanian-born Olegas Truchanas paddled a collapsible kayak in February 1958, portaging around the most difficult stretches. Truchanas had flown into Lake Pedder, then followed the Serpentine River to its junction with the Gordon. His solo journey remains one of the epics of south-west exploration. He was a tireless worker for the preservation of the region and his bushwalking exploits, among them the first solo climb of Federation Peak, are legendary.

But the wilderness was shrinking. In 1963 Truchanas was dismayed by the Government's announcement that the Gordon River would be dammed, and even more so when it became clear in 1967 that the scheme would also flood Lake Pedder, the centrepiece of the Lake Pedder National Park. In the same year devastating bushfires burnt down his house and destroyed his precious slide collection. Undaunted, Truchanas set out to replace what he had lost, retracing his steps through the south-west. He could not stop the destruction of Lake Pedder, but he might be able to halt the the second stage of the scheme, the Gordon-below-Franklin dam.

In early 1972 Truchanas determined to make another journey down the Gordon, to re-photograph the incomparable gorges with their waterfalls and seething rapids. A short way downstream from his launching point, Truchanas slipped into the water and drowned, watched by a helpless friend. His body was recovered three days later.

Yet the spirit of Olegas Truchanas lives on in a reserve that bears his name, a unique forest of Huon pine trees on the Denison River, and in the success of the fight to protect the Franklin River from the fate that befell Lake Pedder. The south-west is still there; sullied, it is true, but still magnificently remote and wild.

The Tasman Peninsula

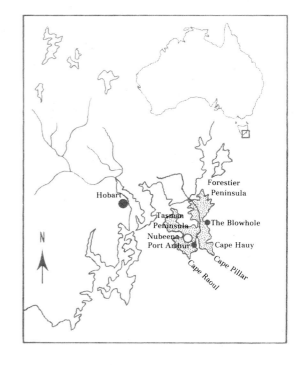

TWO hours after stepping off the plane at Hobart airport it is possible to be contemplating the orange sandstone walls of the vast penitentiary at Port Arthur, having previously glimpsed a 50 metre high natural rock arch, the delicate symmetry of a 250 million year old sandstone pavement, and the surging fury of an ocean blowhole. Across the bay from the convict ruins virgin hardwood forests clothe Cape Pillar in a coat of olive green, a scene unchanged since the first prisoners stepped ashore at Port Arthur in 1830. The cape ends, as do its nearby brothers Cape Hauy and Cape Raoul, in massive dolerite cliffs, among the highest in Australia and against which the Southern Ocean swells expend their might. A few kilometres away, on the sheltered northern coast of the peninsula, yachts lie peacefully at anchor, the only sounds the slap of water against their hulls and the cries of wheeling gulls.

All this is packed into a land area only 32.5 kilometres from east to west and just over 30 kilometres from north to south. Tasmania is renowned for its compactness: one of the most mountainous islands in the world, it is a state of contrasts, and nowhere are they more marked than on Tasman Peninsula.

The base rock of the peninsula is Triassic and Permian sandstone, laid down beneath the sea during a period of marine incursion which covered more than half of Australia 200–300 million years ago. One hundred and sixty-five million years ago, violent volcanic activity uplifted these sediments, simultaneously intruding tongues of igneous dolerite into the strata. As the dolerite cooled it solidified into long, dark columns, more resistant than the surrounding rock, which has gradually been worn away, leaving the dolerite pillars standing as bastions against the angry sea.

It was the topography of the area that first attracted Lieutenant-Governor Colonel George Arthur to consider it as the site for a prison, soon to become one of the British Empire's major penal settlements. The narrow isthmus of Eaglehawk Neck, a 400 metre wide strip of beach and sand dunes, is the peninsula's only link with the Forestier Peninsula to the north, which in turn is joined to the main island by an equally slender land bridge known as East Bay Neck.

Arthur reasoned that the two necks would be easy to guard and that escape, therefore, would be virtually impossible. He wanted somewhere to keep the colony's most recalcitrant convicts, then incarcerated at Macquarie Harbour on the isolated west coast. Port Arthur, within easy sailing distance of Hobart, seemed an ideal choice.

So enthused was Arthur by the peninsula's natural attributes that he attempted to use it as a trap for Aborigines flushed out by the infamous 'Black Line'. Two thousand men, on a 192 kilometre front, started a sweep of the island on 7 October 1830, with the intention of driving the Aborigines across Eaglehawk Neck onto the peninsula, whence they could be taken to selected reserves. But the conditions in the thick bush were too tough for the sweepers, many of whom soon became tired and dispirited. After 17 days, the Europeans had succeeded in rounding up only two Tasmanians, and in shooting two others. None reached the Tasman Peninsula, save perhaps the Pyedarererme, whose home was there.

The unfortunate British convicts arrived in Port Arthur in September 1830 and were set to work erecting wooden accommodation huts, a military barracks and a store. Flogging was still a common form of punishment in the new gaol, while for unrepentant miscreants the coal mines at Plunkett Point on the north-west coast of the peninsula awaited and, later, the refined torture of the Model Prison. It was said to be no accident that the lunatic asylum, built in 1864–68, was erected next to this latter institution: the regime of total segregation, except in chapel, is said to have broken the spirit of even the hardest men.

The most notorious and longest serving commandant of Port Arthur was Captain Charles O'Hara Booth, who served from 1833 to 1844. It was Booth who initiated the chain of semaphore stations that made escape doubly difficult: they stretched across the Tasman and Forestier peninsulas and across Frederick Henry Bay to Hobart. News of a 'bolter' could be relayed to Hobart and Eaglehawk Neck within minutes. There was a guard room on Eaglehawk Neck manned by two sentries in the day and four at night, and across the isthmus fierce dogs were chained centimetres apart at full reach. To discourage swimmers, rumours were fostered that the waters of Eaglehawk Bay were shark infested. Nevertheless, some prisoners did manage to escape, including bushranger Martin Cash, who outflanked the guards by clinging to a branch in the water.

Tasman Arch, one of the spectacular landforms on Eaglehawk Neck.

From 1834–45, a juvenile establishment at Point Puer, across Carnarvon Bay from Port Arthur, housed up to 730 boys at a time, some of them as young as eight years of age. They had been sentenced for a variety of offences, the most common of which was stealing. It was intended that the boys should be reformed and taught useful trades, but the authorities later conceded that some of the worst criminals of all had been institutionalised at Point Puer. By 1845 the buildings had deteriorated to such an extent that the station was moved to nearby Safety Cove, and in 1850 the boys were transferred to Hobart.

Some 12 700 prisoners passed through Port Arthur during the 47 years of its existence as a penal settlement. Death secured the release of 1769 of them and they are buried in unmarked graves on a lonely island known as Ile des Morts (isle of the dead). The 180 free settlers and soldiers who were also interred there were accorded the status of headstones. Port Arthur was abandoned in 1877, 24 years after transportation to Tasmania had ceased. By then the number of ageing convicts left in the prison had dwindled to only seventy.

One imagines that few of the prisoners appreciated the natural beauty of their peninsular home. Escape meant a battle with scrub that must have seemed almost impenetrable, a nightmare swim across Eaglehawk Neck, then more scrub before facing the second cordon at East Bay Neck. Some escapees built crude boats, captured specimens of which Commandant Booth lined up like trophies on the verandah of his house. Some never made it off the peninsula; the skeleton of one man, who had died of starvation, was found at the signalman's hut atop 462 metre Mount Raoul, years after the signal station had closed.

Novelist Marcus Clarke skilfully managed to weave the natural features of the peninsula into his classic *For the Term of His Natural Life*. The hero 'John Rex' makes his escape from the settlement, only to be pursued onto the narrow isthmus of Eaglehawk Neck by men and dogs. It was a filthy night, 'the wind ravaging the hollow heaven', and

every now and then dull but immense shocks, as of a mighty bird flapping the cliff with monstrous wings, reverberated around him, and shook the ground where he stood. He looked towards the ocean, and a tall misty form—against the all pervading blackness—beckoned and booed to him. He saw it distinctly for an instant, and then, with an awful shriek, as if of wrathful despair, it sank and vanished. Maddened with a terror he could not define, the hunted man turned to meet the material peril that was close at hand . . .

The wraith was, in fact, the spout of the Blowhole, which in the story claimed the life of the dog chasing Rex. This phenomenon, located just south of Pirates Bay and Eaglehawk Neck, has been created by wave pressure acting along a fault line in the sandstone. Even in relatively light seas it pulses and spits, the waves rushing to and fro with the precision of a steam engine. In a big sea the sight of the water being thrown tens of metres into the air is awe inspiring. It is possible to walk along the cliff top above the entrance to the Blowhole cave and watch the sea surging into the opening beneath. A sign warns of freak waves on this coast: in 1956 two honeymooners were swept away from the side of a rugged channel the sea has cut through the headland alongside the Blowhole.

Nearby, another tunnel through the cliffs has been greatly enlarged by the sea, so that it now forms a giant arch more than 50 metres high. Alongside it, a similar arch has collapsed, carving a 60 metre deep chasm in the cliff line. This is the Devils Kitchen.

North of Eaglehawk Neck, the sandy beach of Pirates Bay gives way to a low rock platform, sliced into blocks as perfect as any made by the stonemasons of Port Arthur. This tesselated pavement was created by earth movements which fractured the rock in three directions, two of which have produced the tiled appearance. Erosion by waves carrying sand and gravel, and by chemical action caused by salt water, has worn the surface of the rock flat.

The tesselated pavement at Pirates Bay.

English novelist Anthony Trollope, who visited Port Arthur in 1872, described Tasman Arch as 'certainly the grandest piece of rock construction I ever saw', but predicted that no one would ever see it once Port Arthur was closed. Trollope's books have withstood the passage of time better than his predictions.

South again of the Devils Kitchen the dolerite headlands begin. The most northerly of them is Cape Hauy, visible from Tasman Arch, a stubby, scrub-capped finger of rock poking out into the Tasman Sea. Here the land is gradually losing its tussle with the ocean, and several columns of dolerite, the Candlestick, the Needle and the Lanterns, have become detached from the headland and now face the breakers alone.

The next headland down the coast is Cape Pillar, whose cliffs tower even higher than those of Cape Hauy, their dolerite columns facing the battering southern swells like tightly bound palisades. A white lighthouse shines bravely out to sea from nearby sheer-sided Tasman Island. This was a sight (lighthouse excepted) that must have greeted thousands of convicts sent to Port Arthur before the Norfolk Bay tramway was built; as they sailed up Maignon Bay towards Port Arthur, other dolerite columns would have appeared through the sea mist, grim grey pillars as unyielding as prison bars. Before their ship vanished behind West Arthur Head they might have glimpsed the sinister-looking spines of Cape Raoul, most southerly on the peninsula, its dolerite columns perforating the skyline like the jagged ruins of a ransacked city. The cape took its name from the pilot of the French survey ship *La Recherche*, one of two vessels which visited Tasmania under Admiral Bruni D'Entrecasteaux in 1792.

Between Cape Raoul and West Arthur Head, the tides race in and out of a square-walled sea cave that bores right through the cliffs, like Tasman Arch, to a pit in the ground. Remarkable Cave is unique in presenting two entrances to the sea, both cut along faults in the dolerite–sandstone contact zone.

Beyond the salt-stunted vegetation of the coast, the dense eucalypt forests that provided income for the settlement for almost 50 years cover the hillsides. Free settlers had taken up farms on the peninsula even before Port Arthur was closed, but the forest still dominates the neat, cleared farmlands and the quiet, sheltered bays. More than a century has passed since the last convict left the peninsula, but it is said that the odd figure clad in grey prison garb is still seen flitting among the sandstone ruins.

BELOW The jagged dolerite columns of Cape Raoul tower up to 180 metres above the ocean.
OPPOSITE, TOP Waves smooth pebbles cast up on a beach in Blackman's Bay, between Forestier Peninsula and the mainland. It was near here that a boat from Abel Tasman's ships, the *Zeehaen* and *Heemskirk*, landed on December 2nd, 1642.
OPPOSITE The sea surges into the twin portals of Remarkable Cave, on Maignon Bay.

TASMANIA

The Flowering Giants

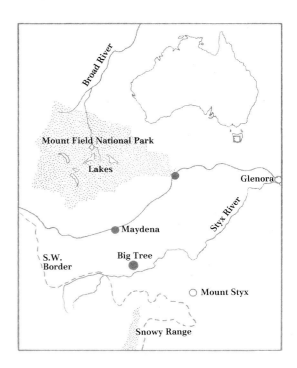

SOMEHOW, tall trees seem alien to the Australian landscape: wide, brown plains and creeks lined with squat coolibahs are more in keeping with the popular image of this country. Yet dense forests grow on the well-watered hills of south-western Australia, along the Great Divide, and throughout much of Tasmania; forests which contain some of the mightiest trees in the world, including the world's tallest flowering plant, the mountain ash or swamp gum, *Eucalyptus regnans*.

These giants of the plant kingdom are endemic to Victoria and Tasmania. The Victorian mountain ash grows in the high country in the eastern half of the state, and there is a small outcrop in the Otway Ranges; the Tasmanian swamp gum is common in the Huon and Derwent valleys, and in the north-west of the state. Because of the generally cooler climate in Tasmania, *E. regnans* rarely grows there at altitudes greater than 600 metres, but in Victoria it is found above 900 metres and never below 150 metres.

These trees are fast growing and long lived. Half of the mature height of a tree is achieved within the first 35 years of growth, when the plant may be 30 metres tall and about 1 metre in diameter. However, exceptional specimens may reach 90 metres or more after 250–300 years, if they are not killed by wildfire. Unlike many eucalypt species, *E. regnans* is not fire-resistant, although its seeds germinate best on burnt ground.

Indiscriminate logging and wildfires (particularly the devastating Victorian fires of 1939) have decimated the stock of really tall trees but the hope remains that a giant tree may be found growing unobtrusively in some unexplored mountain gully. It may be not only the world's tallest hardwood, but also the world's tallest tree. At present the record is held by a conifer in California's Humboldt State Park, a coast redwood which, when last measured, soared 111.6 metres above the ground.

BELOW Dead swamp gums, killed by a wildfire, poke gaunt fingers above the regrowth near Maydena, Tasmania.
OPPOSITE Beautiful Russell Falls lie in the heart of Tasmania's tall timber country.

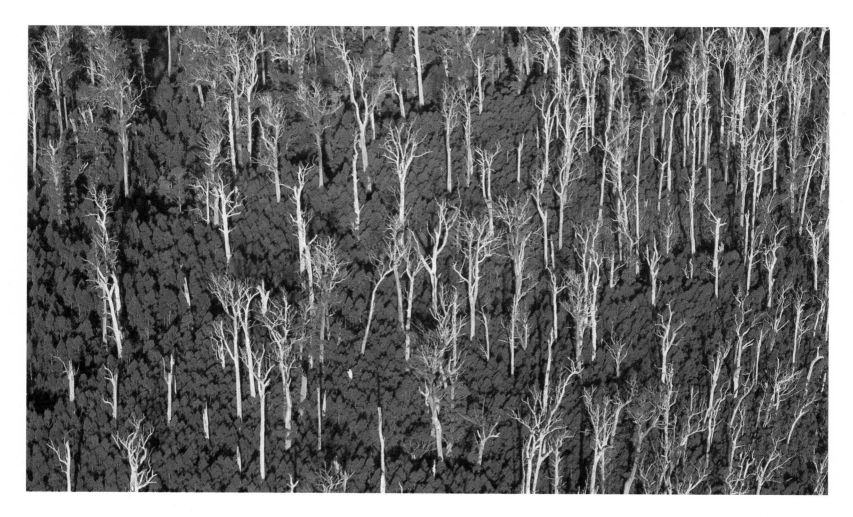

Victorian mountain ashes as tall as this were felled last century. One, measured by surveyor George Cornthwaite in 1888, was 114.3 metres tall; another, recorded and photographed by an official party in the La Trobe Valley, reached 99.4 metres. Gerraty's tree, which was destroyed by storm and fire in January 1939, grew in the same valley and was estimated to be 106 metres tall. The tallest *E. regnans* that has ever lived may have reached 120 metres, but none known today exceed 100 metres.

The search for the big ones has now switched to Tasmania, where swamp gums have been the mainstay of the newsprint industry for more than 40 years. One 400-year-old tree felled on Nichols Spur, near Maydena, in 1942 may well have been the largest, if not the tallest, swamp gum recorded in modern times. It measured 78 metres when cut down, but had lost 16 metres out of its crown in a storm. What was remarkable about it, though, was its bulk: 4.6 metres above the ground its girth was 13.9 metres.

Today's biggest known swamp gum grows in the valley of the Styx River, a tributary of the Derwent, on the 160 000 hectare Australian Newsprint Mills forest concession. This specimen soars to more than 90 metres from the thick understorey of man ferns and other rainforest species. It was once 95 metres tall but a recent storm snapped off part of the crown—ancient trees like this are vulnerable to crown damage, particularly if they stand out above the rest of the forest. Its maximum girth is 13 metres and the height to the first limb is 61 metres.

On a nearby ridge grows a reserve of trees known as the Andromeda Stand. Slimmer and younger than the Big Tree, some of these magnificent specimens may nevertheless

exceed 90 metres. Some sources suggest that one tree in the valley is 98.75 metres tall, although Australian Newsprint Mills' management at the nearby town of Maydena is unaware of it.

Wherever it grows, *E. regnans* is a most distinctive tree. It favours moist, deep, rich, well-drained soil with a rainfall of 750–1500 millimetres a year. It has a long, straight trunk, often buttressed, with a tiny, open crown, making it look rather like a child's drawing of an elongated tree. The first 14 metres or so of the trunk are covered with rough, sub-fibrous bark which higher up is shed in long ribbons, leaving a smooth, white or grey surface. It is impossible to mistake this majestic tree for anything else, even though in Tasmania it usually grows in association with other big eucalypts, such as alpine ash and stringy-bark, both commercial species.

The timber is used for everything from veneer to firewood, but most of the swamp gum cut on Australian Newsprint Mills' concession is pulped for newsprint production at the company's Boyer mill. Commissioned in 1941, this mill produces more than 40 per cent of Australia's newsprint requirements.

The company town of Maydena, where the logging depot is located, was once the terminus for the Port Davey track, built in 1898 as an escape route for shipwrecked sailors, and the jumping-off point for exploration of the south-west. All traffic to Strathgordon and Lake Pedder passes through the town, which is 8 kilometres west of the entrance to Mount Field National Park.

Mount Field became Tasmania's first national park in 1916, although Russell Falls,

The Styx River flows through the Australian Newsprint Mills forest concession.

a feature of the park, was proclaimed a reserve in 1885, having been discovered by a settler named Browning 29 years before. The beautiful, 45 metre high falls trickle silver fingers over a series of mudstone ledges among a forest of man ferns. The creek below the falls flows through a mixed forest surmounted by swamp gums and gum-top stringy-bark, with an understorey of musk, dogwood and blackwood, green with moss and lichens. Further up the slopes, typical rainforest species, including sassafras, Tasmanian myrtle, native laurel and celery-top pine, predominate. Higher still, these species give way to hardy yellow gums and, eventually, to snow gums, fagus, King Billy pine and pencil pine in the high country surrounding a cluster of glacial lakes, one of which, Lake Fenton, was dammed in 1939 to provide water for the people of Hobart.

Mount Mawson, above Lake Dobson, is one of Tasmania's two downhill ski resorts, its derelict-looking visitors' centre and creaking T-bar lifts bursting into life when the pineapple grass and cushion plants of the high moors are buried in snow. Red ski poles mark the cross-country route across the dolerite-capped plateau to the park's highest peak, Mount Field West (1439 metres), overlooking the heavily logged Florentine Valley and, beyond, Adamsfield, in 1925 the scene of an 'osmiridium rush'.

The whine of the chain saws echoes harshly across the valley, but forestry is an integral part of the state's economy and the cessation of operations here is unthinkable to most Tasmanians. Careful management and monitoring are, however, essential to the conservation of the wet sclerophyll forests that may yet be proven to conceal the world's tallest tree.

BELOW Brightly coloured fungi decorate the forest floor.
BOTTOM Man-ferns (*Dicksonia antarctica*) frame the swiftly flowing Horseshoe Falls, above Russell Falls in Mount Field National Park.
OPPOSITE The tallest known flowering plant is this 90-metre high swamp gum in the Styx River valley. (Michael Richardson)

Glossary of technical terms

The use of some technical terms has been unavoidable in this book. Their meaning is given below.

adamellite: light-coloured medium- to coarse-grained acid plutonic rock composed of quartz, feldspar, and some hornblende and/or biotite.
all-slopes topography: area in which there are no significant expanses of flat or gently sloping land.
angiosperm: a plant in which the seed is in an ovary.
anticline: upfold or arched structure.
aquifer: natural underground reservoir of water, usually between rock strata.
asthenosphere: the partially molten zone immediately beneath the Earth's crust or lithosphere.
astrobleme: literally, "star-wound"; an impact crater caused by a meteorite or other extra-terrestrial object.
arkose: type of sandstone containing more than 25 per cent feldspar.
basalt: a fine-grained volcanic igneous rock, usually black in colour, composed of plagioclase feldspar and pyroxene.
bolide: fireball associated with meteorite (Greek for javelin), generally with a distinct fiery tail and a sharply defined head which frequently splits into several parts before vanishing.
calcrete: duricrust rich in calcium carbonate.
chalcedony: silica mineral formed of tiny crystals or fibres, usually grey, cream or milky in colour. Usually translucent; often turbid and sometimes opaque.
chert: sedimentary rock composed of microcrystalline quartz and fibrous chalcedony.
conglomerate: sedimentary rock composed of pebbles and rocks "cemented" together.
country rock: rocks invaded by an igneous intrusion or mineral veins.
cuesta: a markedly asymmetrical ridge, the gentle dip slope contrasting sharply with the scarp slope.
diorite: medium- to coarse-grained, medium-coloured intermediate plutonic rock, composed mainly of feldspar and hornblende (a plutonic rock is one formed by solidification of magma underground).
dolerite: dark-coloured medium- to fine-grained basic igneous rock composed mainly of feldspar and pyroxene minerals.

duricrust: a tough capping to the land surface, usually laterite, silcrete or calcrete.
dyke: a mass of igneous rock intruded through a crack or fissure in the Earth's crust.
Epeirogenesis: gentle Earth movement, likened to a "breathing" of the Earth's surface.
exfoliation: the progressive weathering of layers of rock.
fault: break or fracture in the rocks, along which there has been a displacement of one side relative to the other.
feldspar: one of the most widespread important groups of rock-forming minerals—silicates of aluminium, calcium, potassium, sodium and (rarely) barium.
geosyncline: linear trough that has subsided over a long time, and that has been filled with a thick succession of rocks.
gibber: the stony carapace or veneer found in desert regions; individual rock making up such a carapace.
gneiss: coarsely crystalline metamorphic rock.
granite: medium- to coarse-grained acid plutonic rock, composed mainly of quartz, feldspar and some biotite or hornblende (see adamellite).
greywacke: type of sandstone, usually dark-coloured and tough, containing at least 33 per cent ferromagnesian minerals.
gypsum: chemical sedimentary rock formed by the evaporation of water from small seas and lakes.
helictite: small, irregularly shaped dripstone formation.
igneous rocks: rocks formed by the action of heat.
karst: terrain with distinctive characteristics of relief and drainage arising primarily from a high degree of rock solubility in natural waters.
laterite: red, porous, iron-rich duricrust. Also known as ferricrete.
lava: molten rock or magma emitted from fissures and vents onto the Earth's surface.
limestone: sedimentary rock containing more than 50 per cent calcium carbonate, formed from accumulated marine fossils and shells or organic material.
lithosphere: the solid outer 100–150 kilometres of the Earth's surface. According to the theory of plate tectonics, it is divided into 10 main and a number of smaller interlocking plates on which the continents rest.
magma: molten material beneath the Earth's crust.
mallee: eucalypt found in poor soils or areas of low rainfall which has several slender stems growing from a central rootstock.
matrix: the mother or host rock of a mineral.

metamorphic rocks: rocks altered by heat and pressure.
monocline: fold that dips in the one direction.
mudstone: sedimentary rock composed of particles less than 0.06 mm in diameter.
orogeny: episode of mountain-building, especially by folding and thrusting of the Earth's crust.
peneplain: surface of subdued rolling or undulating relief left by long, continued erosion operating on a stable land mass.
playa: basin of deposition in arid area.
plug: mass of solidified rock which once blocked a volcanic vent.
porphyry: igneous rock composed of large crystals set in a fine-grained matrix and created by differential cooling first at depth, then on the surface.
quartzite: divided into two types: sedimentary or otho-quartzite which are sandstones cemented with silica; and metamorphic (meta-) quartzites, which have a granular texture.
sandstone: sedimentary rock in which the particles range from 0.06 mm to 2 mm in diameter.
schist: medium- to coarse-grained metamorphic rock composed primarily of micaceous minerals.
sclerophyll: plant with hard, stiff foliage, usually (in Australia) *eucalyptus* spp.
scoria: rough, clinker-like masses formed by the cooling of molten lava and honeycombed with air pockets.
sedimentary rocks: rocks laid down in layers, usually underwater.
shale: mudstone able to be split into thin sheets.
shield: extensive continental area, composed primarily of Precambrian rocks, which has remained relatively stable over a long period of time.
silcrete: type of duricrust rich in silica.
siltstone: type of relatively coarse-grained mudstone.
slate: fine-grained grey regional metamorphic rock.
stalactite: dripstone formation growing downwards from the roof of a cave. It may ultimately unite with a stalagmite or reach the floor of the cave, forming a column or pillar.
stalagmite: cylindrical or conical dripstone formation growing upwards from the floor of a cave.
syncline: downfold or trough in bedded rocks.
tillite: consolidated sediments deposited by moving ice.
tor: rocky hill or peak; boulder.
trachyte: light-coloured igneous rock.
tuff: rock formed by volcanic dust and fragments thrown from a volcano, settling in sedimentary layers.
xerophyte: drought-resistant plant.

Index

Text only indexed. Entries in bold type indicate major sections.

Acknowledgements

Many people in all parts of Australia have contributed to the compilation of this book, but special thanks are due to the following: Mike Freeman and Dennis O'Byrne of the Northern Territory Department of Minerals and Energy; Terry Bartlett, John de Koning, Iain Marshall, Geoff Saler and Peter Egan of the Northern Territory Conservation Commission; C. P. Haynes, Project Coordinator, Kakadu National Park; Dr Luise Hercus of the Australian National University, whose knowledge of the Aboriginal tribes of the Simpson Desert is unrivalled; Berkeley Wiles of the New South Wales National Parks and Wildlife

Service; E. S. Elphick of the New England Resources Centre; Bruce Browning and Ron Edgar of Wollomombi; Dr Reg Sprigg of Arkaroola; A. Prescott of the South Australian National Parks and Wildlife Service; Gordon Heard of Derrinallum; J. M. Cransie of the Victorian Department of Minerals and Energy; Richard Crow of the Forests Commission of Victoria; Graeme Kelleher, Chairman of the Great Barrier Reef Marine Park Authority; Richard May of the National Parks Authority of Western Australia; Kym Creak of Australian Newsprint Mills Ltd; Ray Barnes, Peter Bosworth, Chris Rathbone and Peter Mooney of the National Parks and Wildlife Service, Tasmania; and the staff of the Mitchell Library in Sydney.

The publishers wish to express their thanks to the Griffin Press, especially Joy Willis, for their co-operation in the production of this book.

Robbi Newman's photographs were taken on 35mm format cameras. Leica were used exclusively except for the panoramas where a Widelux wide view camera was used.
Sakura film was used exclusively with the panorama camera. Film stock used on the other cameras was a mixture of Kodachrome, Ektachrome or Fuji depending on the look I wished to obtain, whether it be mood or total realism. I wish to thank Konica (Aust) for their assistance with Sakura film and Leica cameras for their constant attention and assistance.

The author acknowledges with thanks, the photographs by Trevern Dawes, Carol Carter and Michael Hill, their work is credited within the book.

First published 1984 by Golden Press Pty Ltd
Incorporated in New South Wales
2–12 Tennyson Road, Gladesville, NSW 2111, Australia

© Golden Press 1984

National Library of Australia cataloguing-in-publication data.

Richardson, Michael (1949–   )
    Australia's natural wonders.

    ISBN 0 85558 914 0.

    1. Landforms — Australia — Pictorial works.
    2. Natural history — Australia — Pictorial works.
    I. Newman, Robbi. II. Title.

551.4′0994

Typeset 10/11 pt Media and Printed at Griffin Press Limited, Marion Road, Netley, South Australia.